CONTENTS

SETTING

The play takes place in three large, ground-floor rooms of "Linden" at 26 Acland Street,   St. Kilda. The mansion was built by the Michaelis family during the economic boom that overtook "Marvellous" Melbourne in the late 1880s. Moritz Michaelis had made his fortune selling leather goods to the Victorian gold rush. Later the building was to become a boarding house and eventually an art gallery after it was acquired by St. Kilda Council in 1985.

On arriving at the front door the audience are divided into three groups (red, blue, grey). Each group then views the three acts of the play in different orders, rotating through each of the rooms and their three time periods (Drawing Room 1900, Boarding House 1975, Art Gallery 1988) before coming together for a final Act in the Hallway at the end.

Each Act is started by CHIMES announcing "8 o'clock"

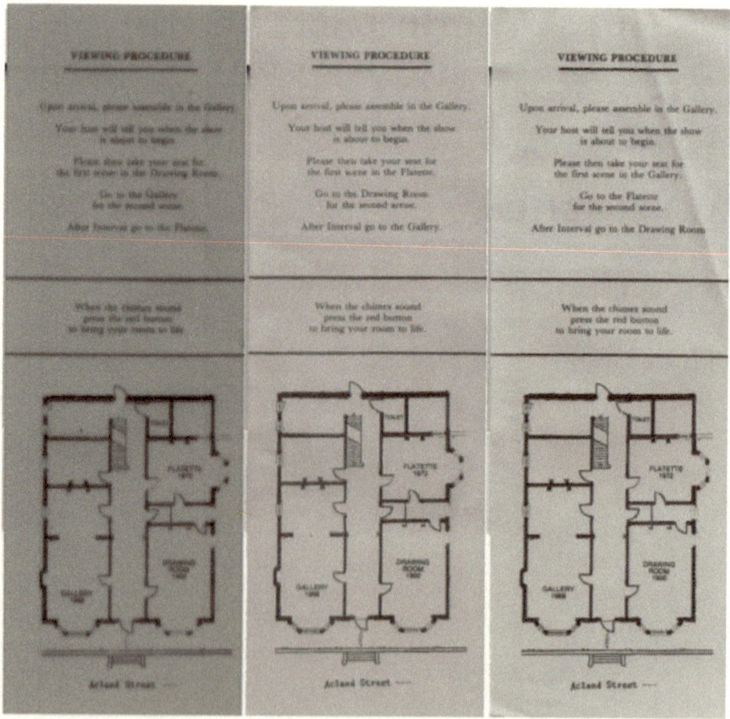

CAST

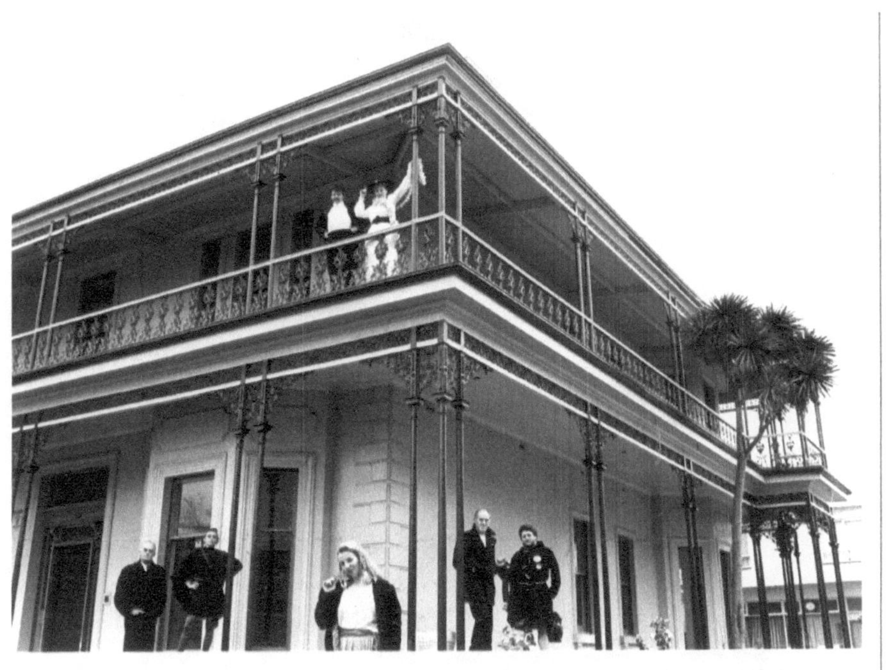

TOP: KEVIN COTTER (DEEGAN), ROSIE TONKIN (ESTELLE)
BOTTOM (L-R): PETER SOMMERFELD (LEON) , CAZ
HOWARD (MONIKA), LEONIE HURRY (MARTHA/MIRIM),
CLIFF ELLEN (BEAUMGARDINER/CHILLA), PAUL DAVIES
(PAUL BUGDEN)

LIVING ROOMS

SCENES IN A FAMILY MANSION

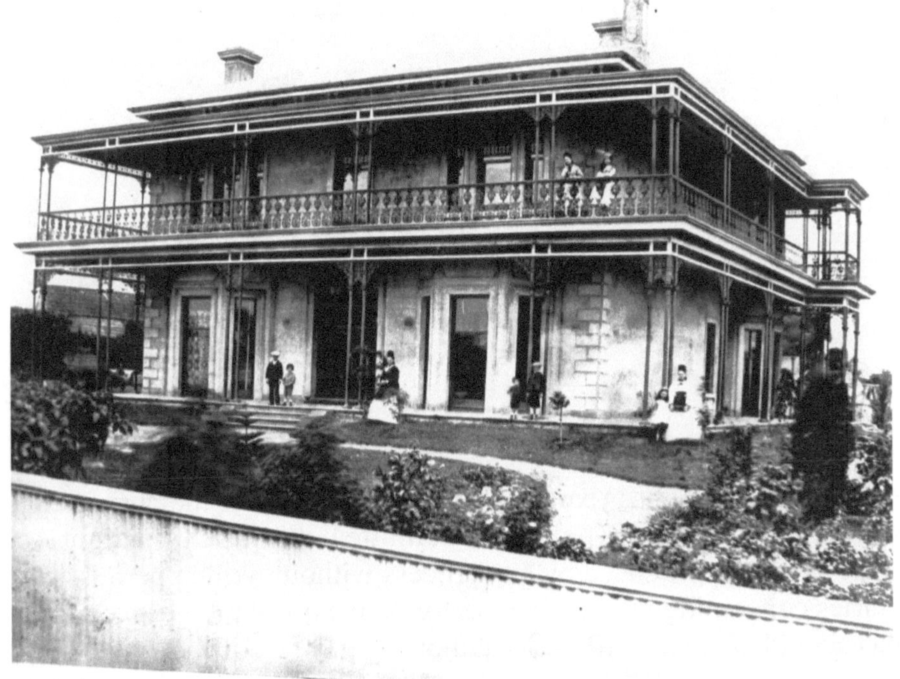

TEXT: PAUL DAVIES
PHOTOS: RUTH MADDISON
DIRECTION: CAZ HOWARD, PETER SOMMERFELD,
PAUL DAVIES, ANDREA LEMON
PRODUCTION: THEATREWORKS
DESIGN: PETER ALAND
PROPS & COSTUMES: SUSAN WEISS

FIRST PERFORMED AT "LINDEN" 26 ACLAND STREET, ST. KILDA
JULY-AUGUST 1986

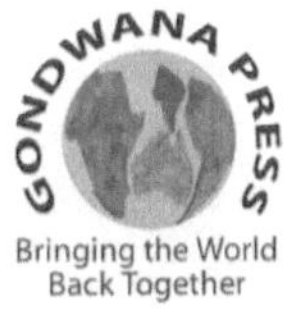

A Picture Play

Volume 5 "*Living Rooms*"
1st Edition Published by Gondwana Press
October 2019
Suffolk Park NSW 2481 Australia

This book is copyright. Apart from any fair dealing for the purpose of private study, research or review, as permitted under the Copyright Act, no part may be reproduced by any process without written permission. Inquiries concerning publication, performance translation or recording rights should be addressed to the author.

Any performance or public reading of *Living Rooms* requires a licence from the author. The purchase of this book in no way gives the purchaser the right to perform the play in public, whether by means of a staged production or a reading.

© The moral right of the author has been asserted.

Act 1
The Drawing Room(1900)

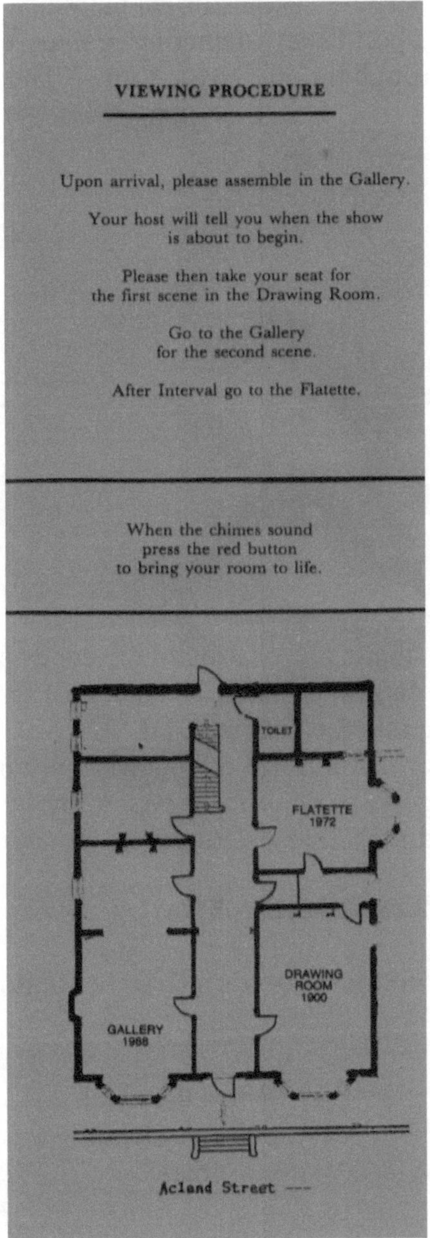

The Drawing Room is a splendid example of late Victorian decoration - solid wooden furniture blending in with potted palms, imported rugs, bookshelves, a piano, and a chaise longue set in front of the ornate marble fireplace.

Various aristocratic portraits and historical paintings line the walls - including a classic Rupert Bunny depicting scantily clothed men riding wild white horses through the surf in St. Kilda ("The Forerunners" 1895):

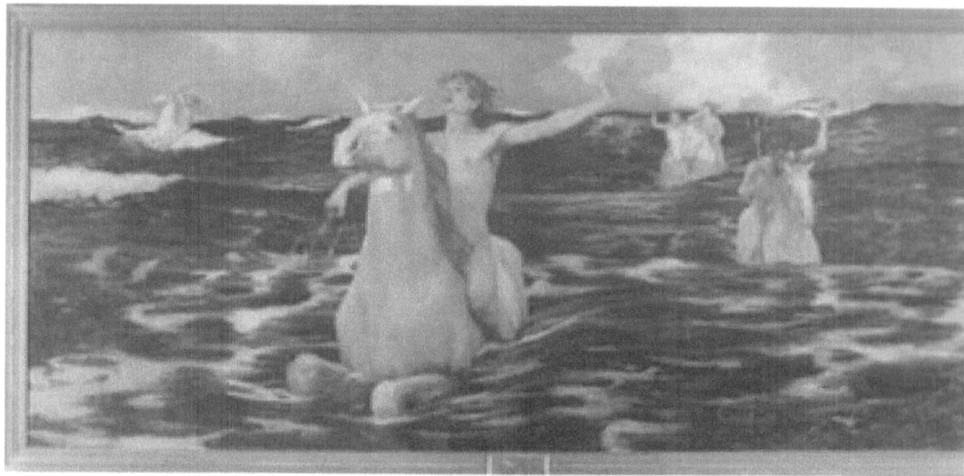

As people settle into chairs placed around the edges of the room they might notice the still figure of Lt. MICHAEL DEEGAN nursing a glass of sherry, and staring into the fireplace. DEEGAN is in his late thirties, dressed in the blue formal uniform of Victoria's Second Contingent to the Boer War, and strangely, he does not appear to move. In fact he appears to remain rock still, almost like a statue.

Somewhere off a clock CHIMES 8pm.

On the wall near the doorway there's a large red button with a sign above it reading:

> "When the clock
> chimes, please
> press."

Somebody does so. There's a dull BUZZING sound.

DEEGAN immediately comes to life, just as the door bursts open and ESTELLE LAWSON sweeps in, extricating herself with a polite laugh from some tiresome yarn out in the Hallway. There's obviously some grand social event going on throughout the house.

DEEGAN looks up sharply.

     ESTELLE. Oh- sorry.

She's about to leave again.

     DEEGAN. What ?

ESTELLE hesitates in the still half-open doorway.

     ESTELLE. I startled you.

     DEEGAN. You can't frighten an artilleryman that easily. We're supposed to have nerves of steel.

They share a brief smile.

     ESTELLE. I'm glad to hear it.

MICHAEL looks back into the fireplace, a bit shy and unsure of his ground.

     ESTELLE. (shrugs about to leave again) Oh well…

He looks back up quickly.

     DEEGAN. But that's not what you meant is it ?

She frowns at him.

     DEEGAN. It's you who was startled.

     ESTELLE. I... I really must go. . .

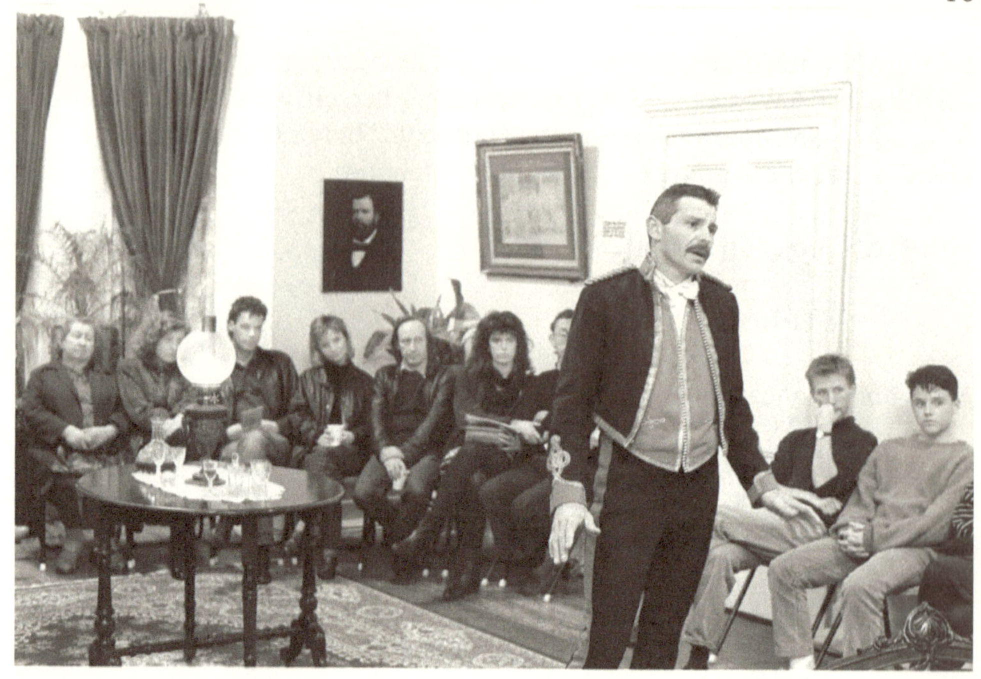

DEEGAN. You don't have to apologise for being in the
same room as me.

ESTELLE. Michael, he's only just out in the Hallway.
You know what he's like.

DEEGAN. We never discuss what we really feel, do we
?

She closes the door behind her, but doesn't come forward. Perhaps she
owes him this much.

ESTELLE. Is that a question, or a manifesto ?

DEEGAN. We always seem to skirt around it, avoiding
it. Afraid of it.

ESTELLE. Oh god Michael, I can't go into all that. Not
now.
Not in the middle of one of his parties.

DEEGAN. You know we sail in two days?

She takes a deep breath, her patience wearing thin.

DEEGAN. I may not see you again.

ESTELLE. Will you stop feeling so goddamn *sorry* for yourself!

But she immediately regrets her outburst.

ESTELLE. I'm sure the Boers aren't that good a shot.

It doesn't exactly lighten the mood.

DEEGAN. I have to know…

ESTELLE. And I'm not free to discuss it.

DEEGAN. Not free ? Or not willing ?

She turns to go.

ESTELLE. I don't have to listen to this.

But DEEGAN physically restrains her. He feels a sense of time running out.
He's impatient with the party and disenchanted with its host.

DEEGAN. He doesn't *own* you, does he? As well as the house ?

ESTELLE ignores the insult.

ESTELLE. You know he's decided to divorce his wife and move in here permanently.

That is a bit of a shock, but DEEGAN buries his reaction.

DEEGAN. I want to know how to begin to talk to you.

ESTELLE. It's really very simple, Michael, you just
open your mouth and let the words come out.

DEEGAN chooses to ignore the sarcasm.

DEEGAN. What am I doing wrong ? I've got a right to
know, haven't I?

ESTELLE. Maybe I'm fed up with the gap between
what you profess to believe in and what you actually *do*,
Michael.

DEEGAN. You'd better explain what you mean by that.

ESTELLE. I don't care much anymore. I'm 34, my life
is going nowhere.

DEEGAN. I can't help being attracted to you.

ESTELLE rounds on him, finally angry.

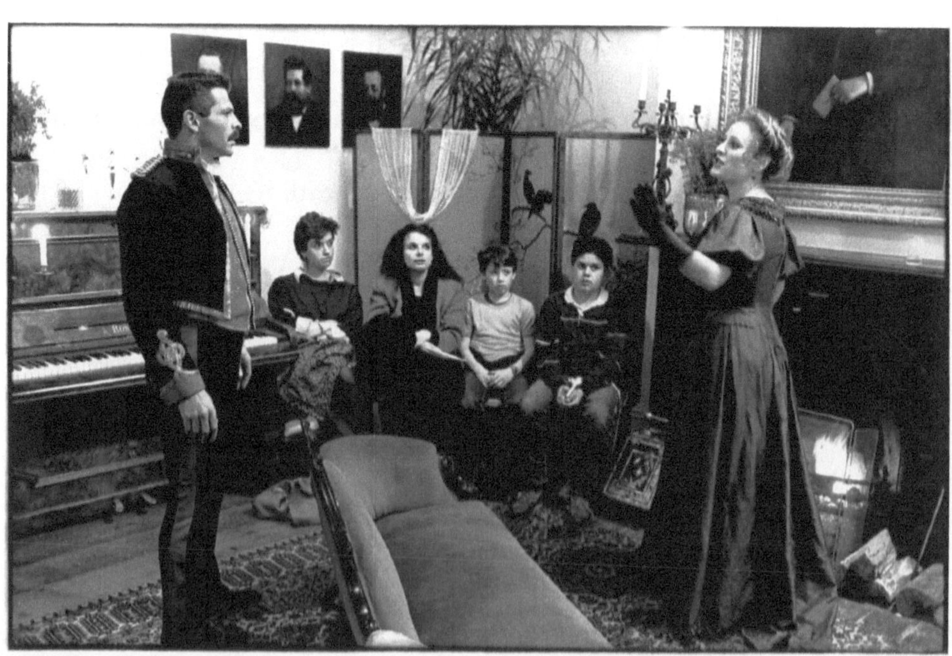

ESTELLE. Then why go off to your boy scout war!

He flinches, weathering the blast.

ESTELLE. I mean, look at you! All dolled up to make sure the sun never sets on the British Empire.

DEEGAN. I wouldn't say that's all there is to it.

ESTELLE. It's a funny thing an Australian Republican should fight for.

DEEGAN. I enlisted because the colony needs men who can ride horses and shoot straight. I grew up on a station. I know about horses.

ESTELLE. And kill ? Do you know how to kill, Michael ?

DEEGAN.(quietly) If it means an end to slavery for the native African.

ESTELLE. And you think there's no slavery in the British Empire?

DEEGAN. There's no law that sets one race above another.

ESTELLE is astounded at his naivety.

ESTELLE. No law ? When has the law ever had anything to do with stopping discrimination?

DEEGAN. In Johannesburg the native people aren't even allowed to walk on the footpath. The president of Transvaal himself has said they have no more soul than a monkey.

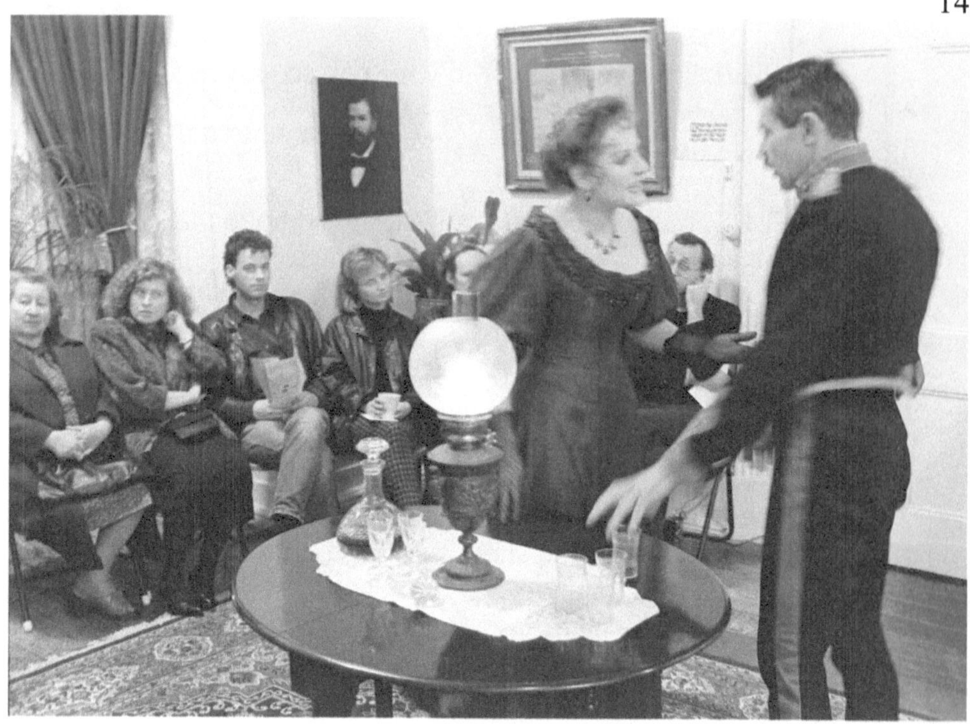

ESTELLE. And to change the Boer you feel you've got to pound him into submission - on a battlefield?

DEEGAN. Forgodsake they're besieging three major towns 100 miles inside British territory.

ESTELLE. And in less than a year we've suffered 10,000 casualties.

DEEGAN. Kitchener's army is mostly on foot and totally bogged down. The Boer cavalry has run rings around them. That's why they need jackeroos like me over there. Who else is going to rescue the poor Tommy bastards ?

ESTELLE. After a century of thrashing natives with spears I daresay the British Army is a trifle unused to Dutchmen wielding German rifles.

DEEGAN. I didn't really come here to talk about the British Army.

ESTELLE. You may be backing a losing side, Michael.

DEEGAN. That's never worried an ex-Queenslander.

Again, they share a smile. The heat seems to go out of their argument.

ESTELLE. Still - look at you, an expert horseman and they put you in the artillery.

DEEGAN. The whole point of big guns is to cause a funk amongst the enemy. They rarely do any real damage.

ESTELLE. So you'll just scare them into surrendering.

DEEGAN. I hope so. I'd rather have British justice than Calvinist oppression any day.

ESTELLE. British gold or Boer diamonds is more like it. All war is about power Michael. Financial or military, it's the same thing.

DEEGAN. Were we to just let them roll through Natal and the Cape with their armed commandos ?

ESTELLE. And yet at the height of the diplomatic crisis that lead to hostilities the British Governor of Cape Colony went off cycling with his mistress through the English countryside.

DEEGAN. I'm not denying the British didn't want the war, but now that it's started there are no … easy options.

ESTELLE. And I'm sure there are people saying exactly that on the other side. Until we alter that kind of logic nothing will ever change.

DEEGAN. Obviously the problem lies with men who
have mistresses.

ESTELLE doesn't really care to go into all that, certainly not now. The
conversation peters out for a few moments.

ESTELLE. Despite what you think Michael, I owe
Cuthbert a lot. He's been very good to me.

DEEGAN decides to come straight out with it, it's been preying on his
mind to tell her.

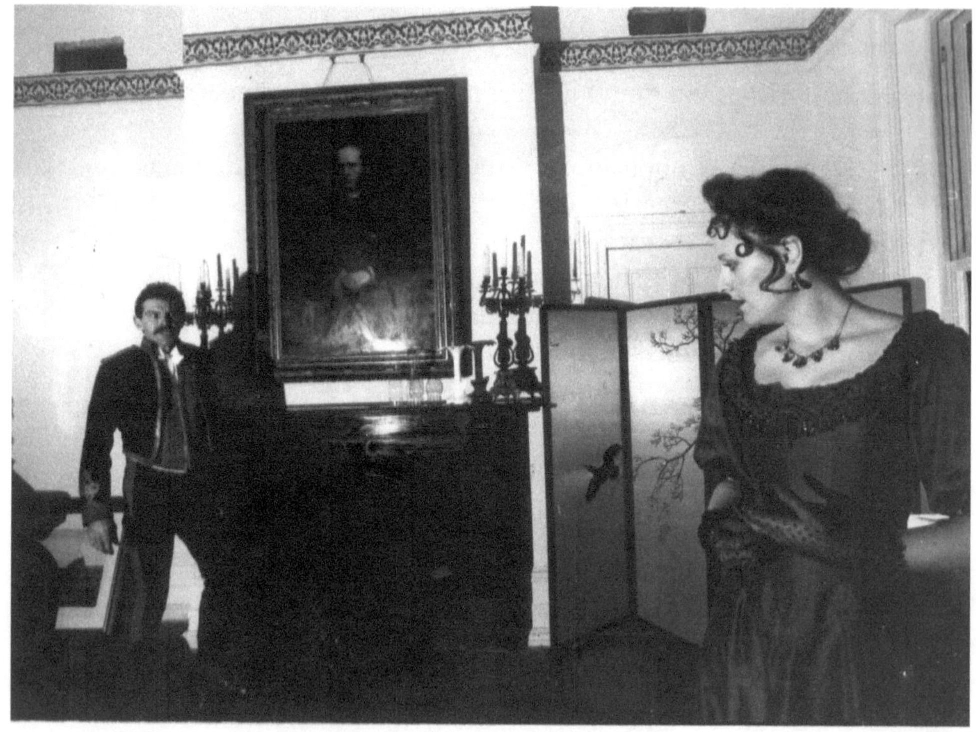

DEEGAN. You know he's got other women.

ESTELLE. (sharply) Is there anything else you wanted
to say before you leave ?

DEEGAN. There's someone he takes from Richmond to a hotel in Ivanhoe. He collects her in a hansom cab.

ESTELLE suddenly feels very cold.

ESTELLE. So you're going from the bored whore to the Boer War are you ?

DEEGAN. That's not what I meant.

ESTELLE. You don't want me, Michael, you want some image of yourself in a relationship - a fantasy you can take on board with all your other baggage.

DEEGAN. I just want you to know what you're letting yourself in for.

ESTELLE. And I just want a man who'll stay here and fight at home - not against enemies, but against prejudices.

DEEGAN. Prejudices are held by people. In South Africa they're held by people with guns.

ESTELLE takes a deep breath.

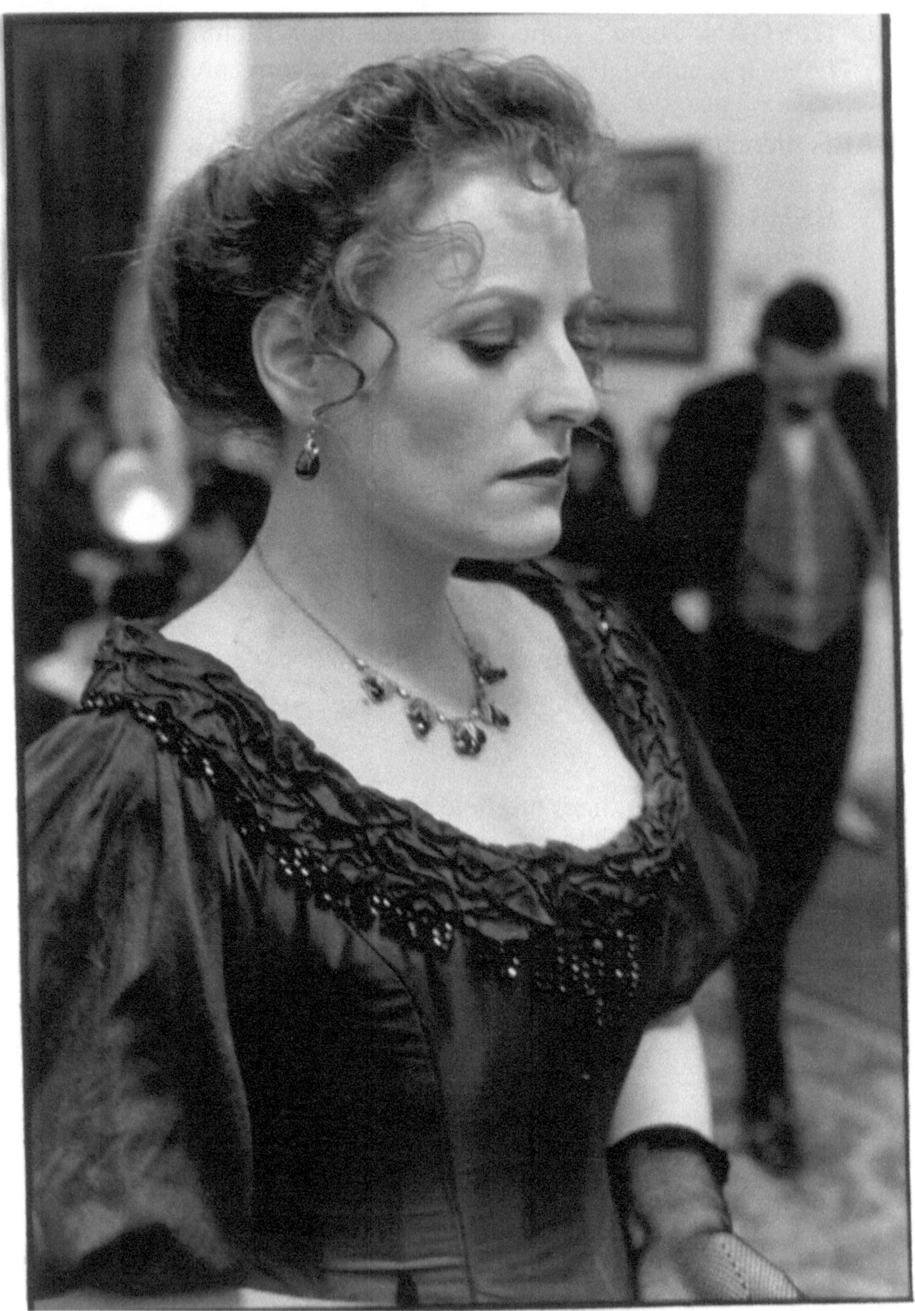

ESTELLE. We're just going round in circles.

DEEGAN. Men are sensitive creatures too, you know - especially when it comes to having their reasons.

ESTELLE. I never said we had a monopoly on feelings.

DEEGAN. Look, ten years ago shearers near our property in Barcaldine took up arms against the machine guns and bayonets sent by squatters and out of that the Labour Movement was born. And now we've seen the first socialist government in the world ! In Queensland!

ESTELLE. It only lasted a week.

DEEGAN. It gave us a chance to look through the files. We'll be better prepared next time.

ESTELLE. You're so convinced aren't you, of your great new Australian civilization?

DEEGAN.I believe we have an opportunity to be different - to be free from Europe and all its appalling class structure. And yes, alright, we have to change the British as much as the Boer.

ESTELLE. I'd like to see you convince someone like Cuthbert of that.

DEEGAN. Cuthbert's class is finished.

ESTELLE. I think you might find that people are stronger than war, Michael - and Cuthbert's class surprisingly resilient. They're never going to let the working class take control. Besides, the affection people feel for each other can be far stronger than feats of arms or bloody revolution.

She moves over to the bay window, glancing down at the patch of front garden illuminated by the lights from the Drawing Room.

ESTELLE. I'd prefer to build my civilisation on that, and whatever it is that pumps life into the rosebush out there.

Now it's DEEGAN'S turn to be sarcastic.

DEEGAN. You're talking about a blind, natural force every bit as violent and self serving as the law of the jungle !

ESTELLE. Then there's nothing more to discuss is there?

For the first time DEEGAN himself wants to go. He's finally got the message, he drains his glass, gathers his hat, ready.

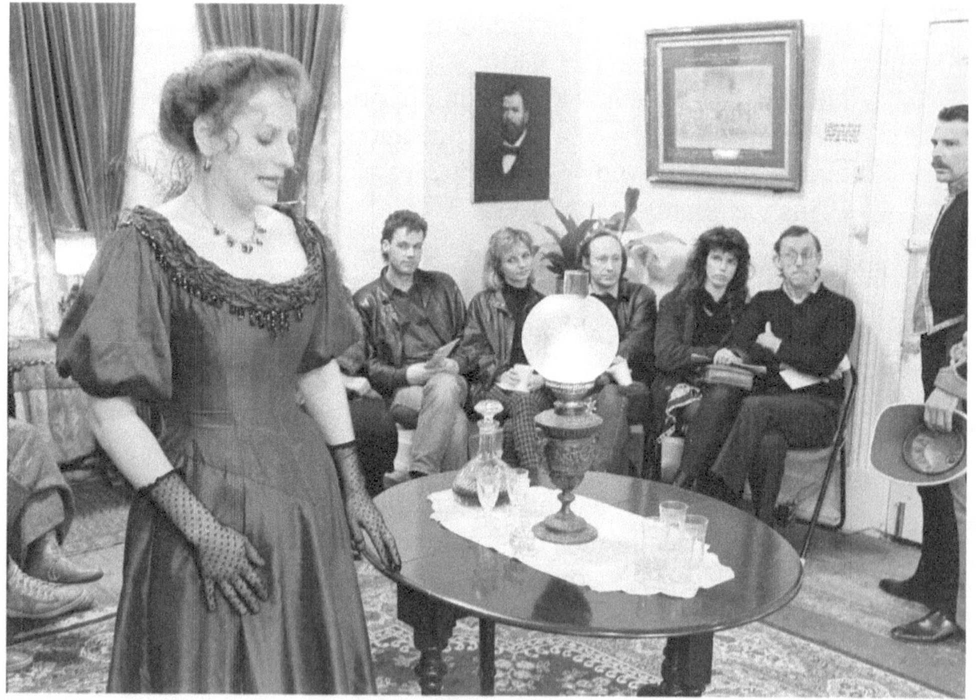

DEEGAN. What have we lost - You and me?

ESTELLE. What did we ever have ?

DEEGAN. You tell me.

ESTELLE. You're the one asking.

He puts his glass down.

DEEGAN. Funny thing about war - it turns so many people into travelers.

ESTELLE. Or refugees.

DEEGAN. Well … I suppose this is it, then.

ESTELLE. You can't slink away now - he wants to make a fuss over you.

DEEGAN. I couldn't bear it, I'm sorry. I never could stand long speeches.

ESTELLE. Well, I'm sorry I can't come with you. I'm not really the Florence Nightingale type.

He smirks.

DEEGAN. That's what I like about you.

She offers her hand, he takes it, holding it.

DEEGAN. Am I imagining things? The way we've felt for each other - ever since I came back to St.Kilda?

ESTELLE. (sidestepping it- withdrawing her hand) He's very fond of you, Michael, you can't blame Cuthbert for everything that's gone wrong.

DEEGAN. He only wants me around to facilitate his other flirtations.

ESTELLE. Despite what you think he doesn't own me and I make no claims on him.

DEEGAN. And how often will he be home at night, when he finally does move in here?

ESTELLE. He's a veterinary surgeon, he's called out at all hours. Do you know how many cab horses there are in Melbourne?

DEEGAN. I know there are quite a few young women who enjoy being ferried around in them - to all sorts of seedy destinations.

ESTELLE glances around the room.

ESTELLE. Funny how you tend to think of a place as your own, just because you occupy it. I was happy to keep his secret and be the mistress of his "Bachelor Hall". I never thought it would end in us living together, as a couple.

DEEGAN seizes his chance.

DEEGAN. I can't bear to see him treat you like this. It's not just because I feel the way I do about you, it's the principal of the damned thing. I'm amazed that you even put up with it.

He goes to pour himself another sherry, but knocks the glass, shattering it. Then furious with his own ineptitude he flings the broken bits into the fire place, cutting a finger in the process and compounding his own self loathing. ESTELLE has seen him do this many times before. It's almost a DEEGAN family trait.

ESTELLE. Oh, Michael, you're so clumsy aren't you. How are you ever going to survive over there ? On a battlefield ?

DEEGAN. I can't believe you're actually feeling sorry for me.

ESTELLE. I'm only pointing out the obvious.

She takes his hand and gently dabs at the blood on his finger. His whole
soul goes out to her.

DEEGAN. If you leave him, I'll support you.

ESTELLE. On junior officer's pay ?

He takes the handkerchief to do it himself, but somehow manages to hold
on to her hand. She doesn't resist.
DEEGAN. I keep forgetting how beautiful your hands
are.

ESTELLE. They're really very ordinary.

DEEGAN. I knew you'd say that.

He grins at her.

ESTELLE. I just want to lead a simple, uncomplicated
life.

DEEGAN. And I want to share it with you.

He kisses her hand

DEEGAN. I love you, Stella.

ESTELLE. Don't say that, it won t work if you say that.

DEEGAN. What am I supposed to say ?

ESTELLE. That we can be friends

DEEGAN. I'm going to miss you.

He takes her hand and presses it to his cheek just as MARTHA, the
parlour maid, bursts in. There's an audible gasp she takes in the scene.
ESTELLE immediately detaches herself. MARTHA backtracks.

ESTELLE. What is it, Martha?

MARTHA. Begging your pardon, ma'am, but I'll be off to the concert now.

ESTELLE frowns.

ESTELLE. Off to where? What are you talking about ?

MARTHA. The Grand Patriotic Concert, ma'am, to farewell the troops. In the Melbourne Town Hall.

ESTELLE. You never asked permission for this.

MARTHA. But it promises to be so exciting, ma'am. There's to be living pictures of the war and everything ... I think it's called a "Biograph" and- I didn't ask because I was afraid you might say no.

ESTELLE. I am saying no.

MARTHA. (pleading) But ma'am…

DEEGAN. Oh let her go, Estelle, it's all to raise money for the cause surely.

ESTELLE. But she can't just walk out now. In the middle of a smoke night ! What will Dr. Beaumgardiner say ? You'll be lucky he doesn't sack you on the spot.

MARTHA. If you'll excuse me, ma'am, I wanted to give my notice anyhow.

ESTELLE. What ? Throw away a perfectly good job ?

MARTHA. I've got a position in a shoe factory in Collingwood, ma'am.

ESTELLE. You'd leave us for a boot factory, Martha ?

MARTHA. Only you see, the pay is better and the hours much shorter than any domestic appointment.

ESTELLE is outmaneuvered.

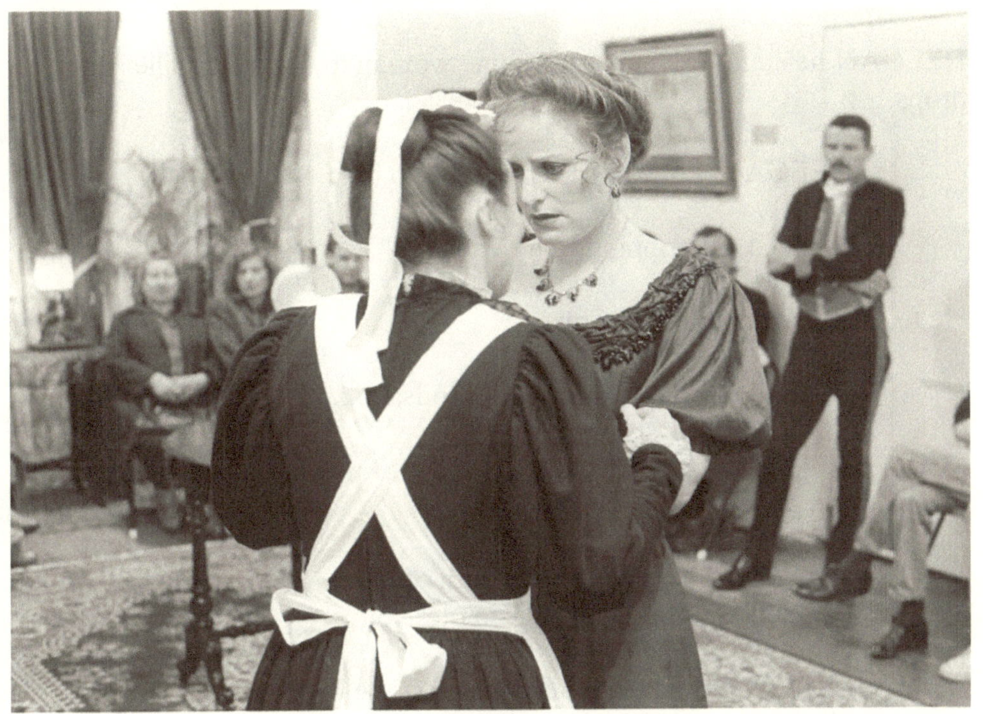

ESTELLE. You can't do this to me Martha. I won't let you.

DEEGAN. Why shouldn't she get better employment if she can ? That's freedom too, isn't it ?

ESTELLE. (Rounding on him) Don't you buy into this.

DEEGAN. (somewhat sarcastically) Surely you can do without a servant for one evening, Estelle.

ESTELLE. Martha isn't just a servant

The women share a look. There seems to be a subtext to all this that DEEGAN doesn't understand.

DEEGAN. (heading for the door) Perhaps…you'd both like to talk this through in private.

ESTELLE. (threatening) Don't you walk out on me too You're the one who started all this.

DEEGAN hesitates, glancing from one woman to the other. The penny drops.

DEEGAN. I'm sorry I really had no idea.

ESTELLE.(stopping him) Michael !

He feels embarrassed, out of place.

MARTHA. Oh, let him go forgodsake...

MARTHA'S objection seems to rear up out of nowhere. ESTELLE is taken aback.

MARTHA. You can't have both of them. You can't tear yourself apart like this. I won't let you.

ESTELLE. Martha, don't try and force the issue - please. It's complicated enough as it is.

MARTHA comes forward, puts an arm around ESTELLE, hugs her affectionately.

MARTHA. Don't you see. That's why I had to go like this. I couldn't have given you any notice. If I'd warned you, you never would have let me escape.

ESTELLE. I hardly thought of it as a prison, Martha. You had a good wage, all your meals provided for.

MARTHA. You know what I mean. I can't bear to see you hurt like this.

ESTELLE. I'm hurt because you're leaving me.

DEEGAN. She's only moving across the river.

ESTELLE ignores him.

> ESTELLE.(to Martha) Just don't expect me to forgive
> you that's all.
> Martha accepts that. and reads it correctly as Estelle's
> recognition of a *fait accompli.*

> ESTELLE. And apart from all that I don't know how
> we're going to cope without you (meaning
> domestically).

Strangely, MARTHA seems to revert to a menial position again.

> MARTHA. I'm sure you'll get another girl, ma'am.

> ESTELLE.(coldly, almost distantly, admitting the fact)
> Not on the wages we can offer I'm afraid.

DEEGAN starts pouring them all a drink.

> DEEGAN. Well, you'd better let your hair down with
> us, then, Martha. We're all workers here, you know.

> MARTHA.(taking her glass) Oh- if you 'say so, sir.

MARTHA feels slightly awkward, not quite accepting that ESTELLE
could be considered a "worker"

> DEEGAN raises his glass.

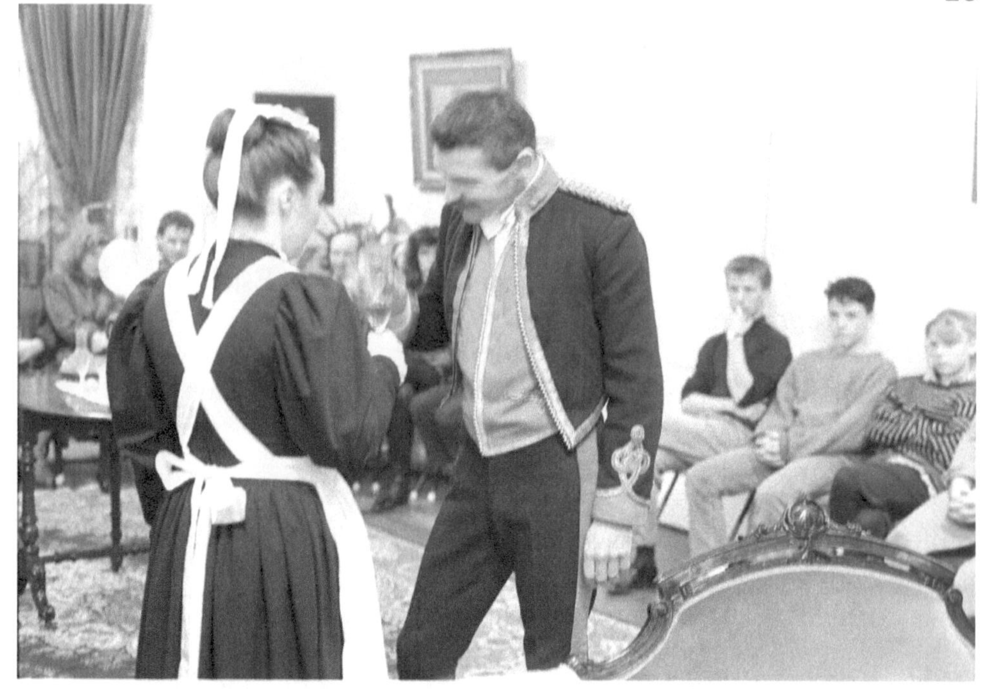

DEEGAN. To your future, Martha, and your very good health.

MARTHA. And to you, too, sir. May good luck go with you.

They all touch glasses and drink. But Martha finds she can't face the alcohol. She puts he glass down.

MARTHA. I'd better go now - don't want to miss the biograph.

Without looking at ESTELLE she heads quickly out the door, almost on the point of tears.
ESTELLE is confused by the abruptness of it all.

ESTELLE. Martha! (sighs) It's as if the whole colony's gone mad with the damn war. They'll be queuing in their thousands to see you off on Saturday

DEEGAN shrugs. That's the last thing on his mind. ESTELLE turns back to the fire place.
For a moment nobody speaks. Then:

ESTELLE. When I was young we thought we could see into the future in a fire.

She thinks about it; almost annoyed with him.

ESTELLE. How could we have any future, you and I ? You always seem to be traipsing off somewhere.

She continues to gaze into the fire and he regards her fondly, almost standing back from the moment.

DEEGAN. I'd love to take a photograph of you.

She looks up at him.

DEEGAN. I think it would almost keep me alive to have some memory.

ESTELLE. I can write letters, you know. And as for staying alive I simply hope you've got enough common sense to keep your head down.

He grins.

ESTELLE. And in no circumstance are you to do anything even remotely heroic.

DEEGAN. (crossing his heart) I promise, absolutely.

ESTELLE. You're no great match, you know, a lieutenant in your late thirties, you should at least be a captain by now.

DEEGAN. I'm only ambitious in love, you see. In fact I've decided it's the only career worth having.

She smiles at him.

ESTELLE. How very Oscar Wilde of you.

But the smile fades, her head is suddenly spinning. She feels quite dizzy.

DEEGAN. Besides I only joined for the duration as
they say. I hardly want to be a soldier forever.

He trails off as she sinks into a chaise longue, he's concerned at how pale
she looks.

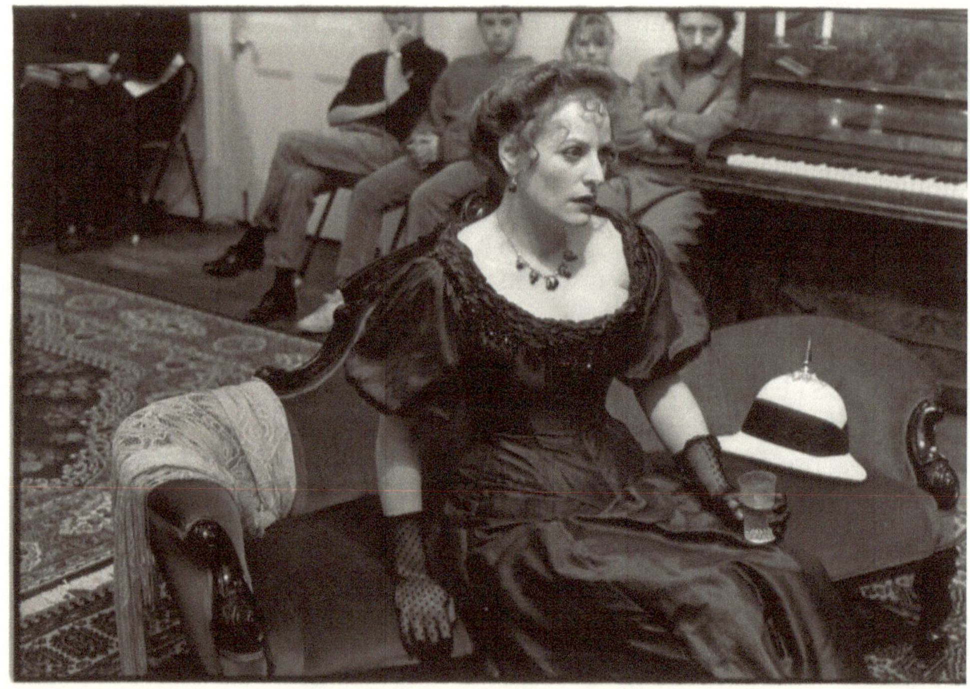

DEEGAN. What is it ?

ESTELLE. I'm alright.

DEEGAN. You don't look alright.

ESTELLE. It will soon pass.

DEEGAN. Shall I call Dr. Beaumgardiner?

ESTELLE. I'm afraid Cuthbert's only a vet.

DEEGAN. Yes, and more in love with his bay mare
than he is with you.

DEEGAN immediately regrets that. ESTELLE winces in pain. DEEGAN
stands there at a total loss.

ESTELLE.I can't go with you Michael. I can't leave this
place.

DEEGAN. Forgodsake why ! ?

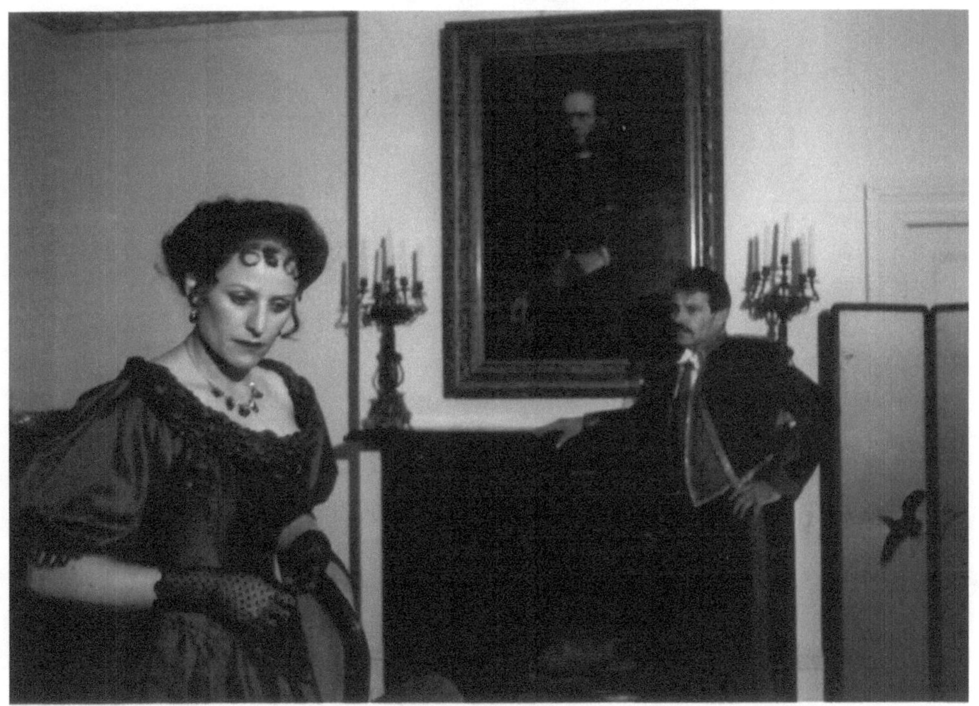

ESTELLE. I'm carrying his child.

There's a long pause. He just stares at her as it slowly sinks in.

DEEGAN. Oh. . .

ESTELLE. So you see, Michael, you and me, it's not possible.

DEEGAN. Have you told him ?

ESTELLE. Good lord no ! He'll want to have it. He hasn't got a son and heir yet.

On second thoughts. . .

ESTELLE. Or at least not one he wants to lay claim to.

ESTELLE looks around.

ESTELLE. I have to lie down.

DEEGAN. Let me help you.

ESTELLE. No, Michael, I'm fine.

DEEGAN. You look terrible, you should go to bed at once.

Without a second thought he scoops her up in his arms and carries her towards the door just as it opens and DR. CUTHBERT BEAUMGARDINER sweeps in. He pulls up short at the sight of ESTELLE in another man's arms. There's a shocked pause. CUTHBERT'S jealous mind is racing to all sorts of non-innocuous conclusions. He might be almost about to throttle DEEGAN.

CUTHBERT.(forced casualness) I thought I heard voices in here. You're missing the party.

He smiles thinly, eyes blazing.

DEEGAN. Estelle was feeling a trifle indisposed.

CUTHBERT looks from the prostrate body of his mistress to the physically past-it but still faintly good-looking officer holding her. On balance DEEGAN is probably stronger than CUTHBERT (with his gout, his liver damage and decades of the high Victorian lifestyle).

ESTELLE drops to her feet, out of DEEGAN'S arms.

    ESTELLE. I'm alright now.

    CUTHBERT.(from one to the other, intensely suspicious) What's going on ?

    ESTELLE. Just a dizzy spell, I suspect the sherry may not have agreed with me.

CUTHBERT touches her forehead to feel her temperature and takes her pulse with the other hand; soon satisfied that there's nothing seriously wrong.

    CUTHBERT. Bloody Portuguese rubbish!

Turning to DEEGAN as if only another man could understand. .

    CUTHBERT. I told her to present only the South Australian stuff. I mean this may look like just another booze up but it's a loyal send-off to you, too, my boy. (embracing DEEGAN, almost phyiscally trying to contain him). Let's keep it all in the Empire I say.

He glares at ESTELLE, almost choking on the word.

    CUTHBERT. Portugal !

    DEEGAN. I was just taking her up to bed.

CUTHBERT'S eyes pop, his arm drops from DEEGAN's back and he stabs a look of pure venom at them both,

    ESTELLE. Cuthbert, isn't it time you proposed the toast to Lt. Deegan?

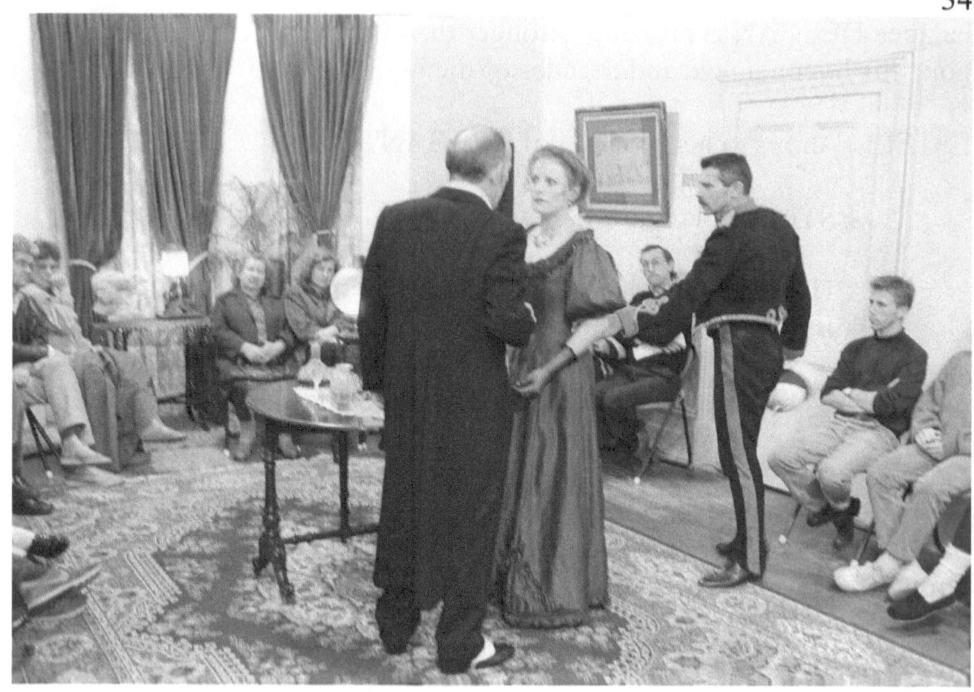

CUTHBERT. (vaguely) Toast ?

ESTELLE. That's the whole point of this evening isn't it ?

CUTHBERT. Why yes. Yes, I suppose it is. Is everybody here … ?

He glances round the room. ESTELLE'S dizziness seems to pass.

ESTELLE. Just about.

CUTHBERT. Call them in, Estelle, bring the rest of them in from the Hallway.

As she drifts out he notices:

CUTHBERT. Oh no! Their glasses are empty! Where the hell is Martha ? We can't have a toast without drinks. And get rid of that awful plonk she's been serving.

DEEGAN covers for the fact that MARTHA is gone.

>DEEGAN. I'll see to it.

>CUTHBERT. Eh ?

CUTHBERT is distracted, DEEGAN already has a decanter ready.

>DEEGAN. How do you like your scotch, Dr.
>Beaumgardiner ?

>CUTHBERT. Oh.(smiling, anticipating his own joke)
>Strong and often thank you, Lieutenant.

CUTHBERT laughs, holding out his glass for the top up and immediately adopts the traditional, toastmaster pose, fiddling with his gold watch chain.

>CUTHBERT. (warming to his theme) Michael, it's
>fallen to my happy lot…

CUTHBERT looks around, distracted, suddenly really annoyed.

>CUTHBERT. Where is that damned girl!(indicating a
>guest) Digby's tumbler's as dry as an old sows arse.

This time ESTELLE comes back in with a decanter, still covering for the fact that MARTHA has gone. CUTHBERT immediately resumes his "mine host" role.

>CUTHBERT. Michael…(again the warn formal tone)
>Lt. Deegan, 15 years ago it was my special privilege' to
>be present in Sydney when our own New South Wales
>Imperial Lancers went off to avenge General Gordon in
>the Sudan.

DEEGAN is becoming restive and uncomfortable.

CUTHBERT (continues, oblivious) I believed then, as now, that our tainted convict past would be washed away by the waters of the Nile…

DEEGAN. (unable to contain himself) Look, Dr. Beaumgardiner, I'm sorry-I've heard it all in school a 100 times before. It's not that I don't appreciate it, it's just that I don't think I'm doing anything special.

CUTHBERT. Nonsense, my boy.

He puts an arm through DEEGAN'S - paternally, almost proprietorially.

CUTHBERT. People want to cheer their heroes and bask in the warm sunshine of their glory. What you're doing as a true son of the British Empire is a fine example to the whole Australian branch of the race. All over Melbourne tonight people are celebrating you and your comrades' noble sacrifice.

ESTELLE. We certainly don't intend to let him be sacrificed, Cuthbert.

CUTHBERT. (taken aback) Eh ?

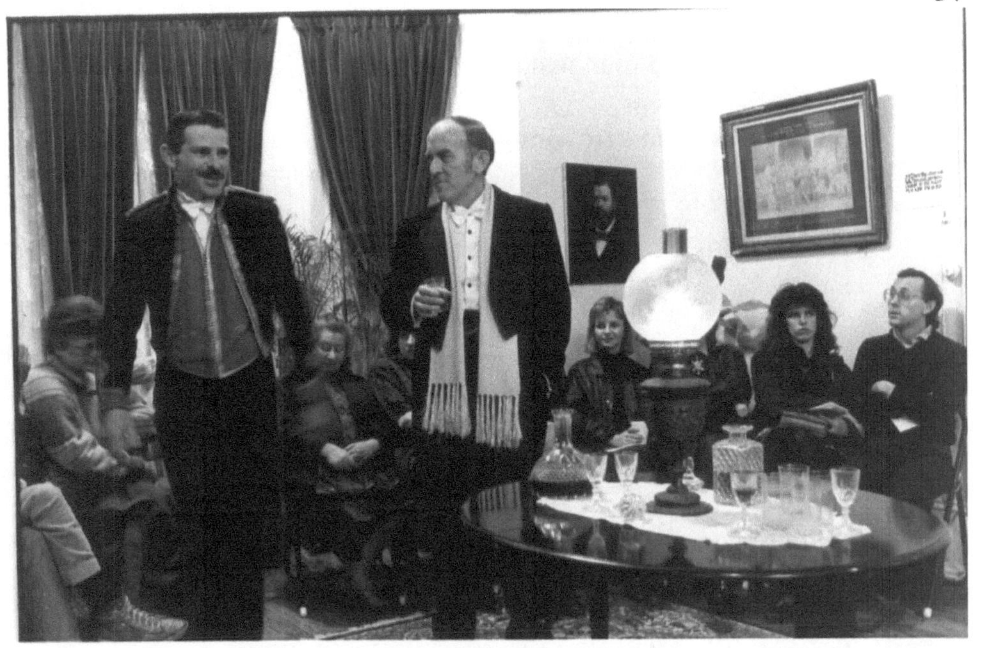

DEEGAN. (amused) Estelle's got this funny notion that I'm more use to Queen and Empire in a living, breathing condition.

CUTHBERT. (looks from one to the other) Well, I speak metaphorically of course.

DEEGAN (cutting in again) Actually, doctor, there's a tremendous shortage of veterinary surgeons amongst the cavalry units on the veld. Men with your qualifications are needed more than any of us.

CUTHBERT thinks that's a huge joke.

CUTHBERT. You've as much chance of getting an old fox like me into uniform as you have of teaching a cab pony to do the waltz.

He laughs out loud.

CUTHBERT. No. War's a young man's game. (thankfully)

ESTELLE. Old men just start them.

CUTHBERT stares at her, frowning.

> CUTHBERT. You're in a peculiar mood tonight, Estelle. Has all your patriotism vanished with the dago sherry ?

> ESTELLE. I'm sorry, but I completely fail to see how a rabble of irregular farmers thousands of miles away constitutes any real threat to all of us here in Australia Felix.

CUTHBERT is astounded at her attitude.

> CUTHBERT. Are you serious? With the world situation the way it is ? America at war with Spain, Russia threatening Afghanistan, and the Kaiser himself sneaking German sailors into the Boer camp. The world's a veritable powder keg ! What we need in South Africa now, is an unambiguous demonstration of the overwhelming might of British arms.

> ESTELLE. Then the whole thing really is a farce. British arms have been thoroughly out-gunned and out-manoeuvred by the Boers.

> CUTHBERT. You don't throw in the towel after the first round, my dear. (holding it up, waving it triumphantly about) Haven't you read the "Argus" today, Lord Roberts and Lord Kitchener are just arrived in Capetown with a huge new army. The war, in all probability, be over by the time Lt. Deegan gets there!

> ESTELLE. That's what you prophesied before the first contingent left.

But CUTHBERT is too wound up, he ignores ESTELLE 'S cynicism and slams the paper down. Point made, he gathers up his glass again.

CUTHBERT. So, Michael, it falls to my happy lot…

DEEGAN. (cutting in again) I'm sorry, doctor, I only really accepted your invitation here tonight (looking directly at ESTELLE) as one last chance to say good-bye. I know you've fallen oh hard times lately, and you shouldn't really be going to all this expense on my account.

CUTHBERT. (explodes) Hard times!?

ESTELLE. Well you have had to sell your Parkville terraces Cuthbert, and people are starting to wonder about the subdivisions in Abbotsford that have left many tenants with houses barely wider than that bay window. (indicating the window facing Acland Street)

DEEGAN. (interrupting both of them) Look, all I'm trying to say is - you've gone to a lot of trouble and expense for nothing.

But CUTHBERT is astounded that anyone could think him indigent.

CUTHBERT. Me? Broke ? That's a laugh ! With South African wool production slashed by the war, my farm in Bacchus Marsh is going to be worth a fortune. I'm celebrating (raises his glass). So here's to all those poor bloody Boer framers, long may their pastures burn and their mines remain flooded.

ESTELLE. I thought this was supposed to be a toast to Michael.

CUTHBERT.(offhandedly, slightly embarrassed now) Oh, yes, we ah, bought this briar pipe for you, as er … a token of our regard, Michael. (almost shoving it at DEEGAN) Now drink up everybody, there's plenty of grog where that came from. Going broke indeed ! (snorting into his glass)

DEEGAN regards the pipe with little enthusiasm.

> DEEGAN. Half my battery's been given these ... things.
> Either that or tobacco pouches and leather bound
> diaries. I mean I don't even smoke. Meanwhile, the
> saddles we've been issued with are falling apart, many
> of the recruits can't tell left from right, and we're buying
> munitions with pennies donated by children in primary
> school. That's the sort of army the Victorian branch of
> the empire is sending forth to battle (handing pipe
> back). So thank you but…

However CUTHBERT is hardly even listening. He's still smarting from
the perception that he's going under.

> CUTHBERT. How could I be going broke when I can
> turn this masterpiece of classic Georgian architecture
> (indicating the house around him) into a 26 room
> boarding house any time I like ! We'll rip up all that
> vegetation out the front and put in a carriageway for
> cabs.

> ESTELLE. (protesting) That "vegetation" was laid out
> by the same artist who designed the Botanical Gardens.

But CUTHBERT is now too wound up to listen.

> CUTHBERT. When I arrived out here on the diggings,
> 30 years ago, I didn't have two shillings to jingle
> together in my pocket. And now look at me.

ESTELLE too, grows impatient, she's heard it so many times before.

> CUTHBERT. Proud owner of a grand mansion with a
> magnificent view of the sea.

> ESTELLE. Which you'll readily destroy if you think
> there's a pound in it.

CUTHBERT. Destroy ? Just because I choose to make the
thing productive! I'll wager you, my dear, in a 100 years
time when the rest of Acland Street is all pulled down
this house will still be standing. Not because some
"Botanical Artist" planted the front lawn, but because I,
Cuthbert Beaumgardiner Esquire, turned it into an
honest living for someone.

ESTELLE. If, in 100 years time, there are no houses left
in Acland Street, Cuthbert, it will be because you and
your profit obsessed mates pulled them all down. No
thing of beauty, no elegance of Nature is safe from you.

CUTHBERT. Safe ?! What would you know about
safety ? When I first came here, it wasn't safe to ride a
pony from Kilda to Melbourne.

ESTELLE. (groans). Oh not this story again.

CUTHBERT. In one afternoon no less than 19 people
were tied to trees on the St. Kilda road and robbed by a
gang of convicts who then went to lay siege to the
Royal Hotel.

ESTELLE. You're boring everyone to tears, Cuthbert.
CUTHBERT. (ignoring her) Now, the biggest danger
out there is being run down by some infernal cable car
bringing hoardes of riff raff from Fitzroy or Richmond
to our lovely bayside suburb. That's your "progress " for
you.

ESTELLE. Interesting that your thoughts should turn to
the riff raff from Richmond, Cuthbert, I understand
there's at least someone there who doesn't need the
cable car because she always gets ferried back and forth
in a hansom cab.

This brings CUTHBERT up short. He looks anxiously from DEEGAN to
ESTELLE.

CUTHBERT. So, there is something going on between you two !

Their lack of response convinces him. CUTHBERT rounds on DEEGAN, clearly pretty inebriated by now

CUTHBERT. I've half a mind to bloody your nose!

DEEGAN is thoroughly fed up.

DEEGAN. Half a mind is all you ever had, Beaumgardiner.

DEEGAN is just a little too physically intimidating. CUTHBERT finds it safer to turn his attention back to ESTELLE.

CUTHBERT. Have you no affection for me - after 5 years of caring for you?

Now CUTHBERT is being truly pathetic.

ESTELLE. I simply feel I can't be … the kind of woman you expect, Cuthbert.

CUTHBERT. I put a roof over your head.

ESTELLE. Where there is no affection there can be no affection.

CUTHBERT. Then get out ! Get out of my house!

DEEGAN. We're leaving anyway.

That brings CUTHBERT up short. He didn't mean them to take it quite so literally. So quickly.

ESTELLE puts her arm through DEEGAN'S.

ESTELLE. Michael and I are hopping over to the Mounted Infantry Ball at "Oberwyl" in Bennett Street.

CUTHBERT. You can't possibly go out with the
wretch. He's off to war on Saturday.

DEEGAN. I'm taking Estelle to my cousin's house and
if she'll wait for me there, we might one day settle on
some patch of scrub outback where you can see the
stars at night and actually believe there's some purpose
to it all ... (turning to ESTELLE) if she'll have me.

ESTELLE. I'm prepared to think about it.

CUTHBERT. You've deceived me, the both of you !
Under my own roof.

Even now ESTELLE almost pities him.

ESTELLE. Don't you see what a chance we have,
Cuthbert - even you with your money and race horses,
you too can be part of this truly new nation, on the brink
of a new century, where the only things that really
matter can't be bought and where (turning to DEEGAN)
maybe, through loving one person fully, we earn the
capacity to love all people, everywhere.

CUTHBERT. You' re more deluded than I thought.

DEEGAN. Not deluded, liberated.

CUTHBERT. You're both going to regret this, in the
morning when you wake up in the gutter!

ESTELLE. On the contrary, Cuthbert, I'm quite looking
forward to tomorrow, it promises to be the first day of
the rest of my life.

CUTHBERT. Then get out before I throw you out!

He tugs manically at a long sash dangling from the ceiling. Somewhere
off a servant's BELL can be heard ringing.

CUTHBERT. Where the devil is the girl!?

DEEGAN. Thanks for the swell send off, Cuthbert. It's one I'll always treasure.

ESTELLE and DEEGAN go happily off arm in arm. CUTHBERT is frantic.

CUTHBERT. Martha ! (continuing to tug at the sash with no result) Where are you ? Martha, you trollop, come here when I call you.

He's heading for the door, but at the last moment stops, remembering his guests.

CUTHBERT (to audience) Go on, get out, the lot of you ! You've seen enough to keep you gossiping for months !

He starts herding them towards the door.

CUTHBERT. Get out, get out of my house.

He's taking the glasses off them as they go.

CUTHBERT. And don't think you can walk out with the crystal either. He puts the glasses down and roughly shoulders his way through the audience out into the Hallway.

CUTHBERT. Martha ! MAR-THA !!

But halfway out a sudden, sharp pain hits him in the chest. He doubles over in pain.

CUTHBERT. My chest…

Gasping for air, he staggers off and disappears into the "Green Room".

MUSIC fades up as people exit the Drawing Room and make their way into Hallway where they enter the second room designated for their particular group.

Act Two
The Flatette (1972)

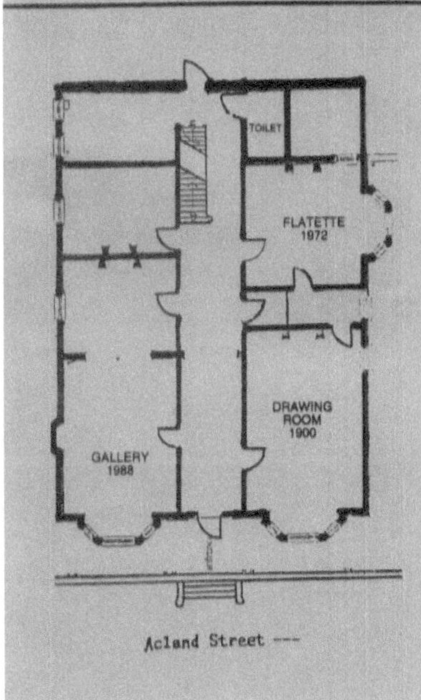

The place is crammed with more beds than will reasonably fit into it. Two grey, tin lockers act as a kind of wardrobe. On a bare, wooden table a frying pan is plugged into the overhead light socket and against one wall there's a broken bathroom sink with rusted taps. On its side on the floor is a battered black and white TV set with a coat hanger for a aerial (squeezed into a rough outline of Australia)

On the wall above the fireplace are some posters, one advertising a meeting in the St. Kilda town hall with Gough Whitlam and Bob Hawke, part of Labour's 1972 election campaign. On a ledge above the fireplace lie a couple of rat-sized "mice" caught in large traps. The once grand old marble fire place is boarded up with mildewed masonite and in place of a fire there's an ancient bar heater.

The heater is sitting on cracked lino and connected to some very dodgy power points. There's rising damp, cobwebs thick as mist, and shattered windows taped up with plastic bags overlooking another block of featureless brick matchboxes built too close next door.

As audience members enter they pass what appears to be a frozen character standing in the doorway clad only in a "Homicide" t-shirt and y-front undies. PAUL BORDER is wrapped in a towel and holding an old airline bag.

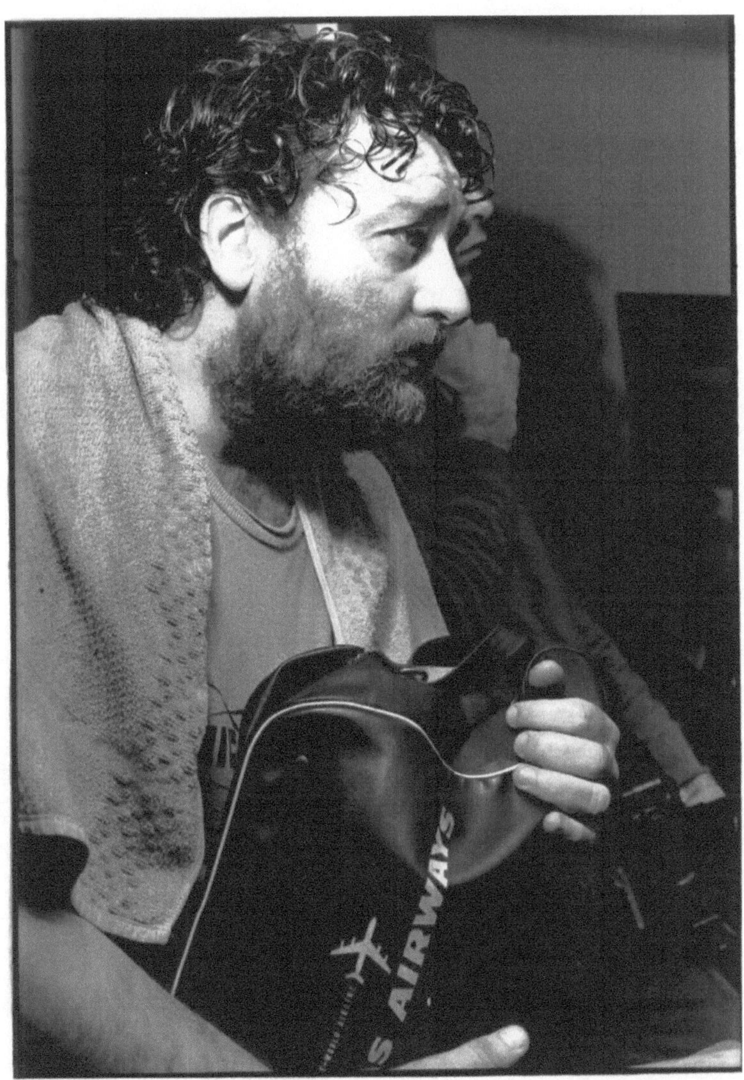

Somewhere off a clock CHIMES 8 o'clock.

On the wall near the doorway there's a large red button with a sign above
it reading:

"When the clock
chimes please press"

Somebody from the AUDIENCE does so. There's a dull BUZZING sound.

Immediately PAUL BORDER comes to life and enters fully into the room which he surveys with a deep sigh. It's a place stuffed full of poverty and dilapidation.

The sight of it all sends a shiver up.

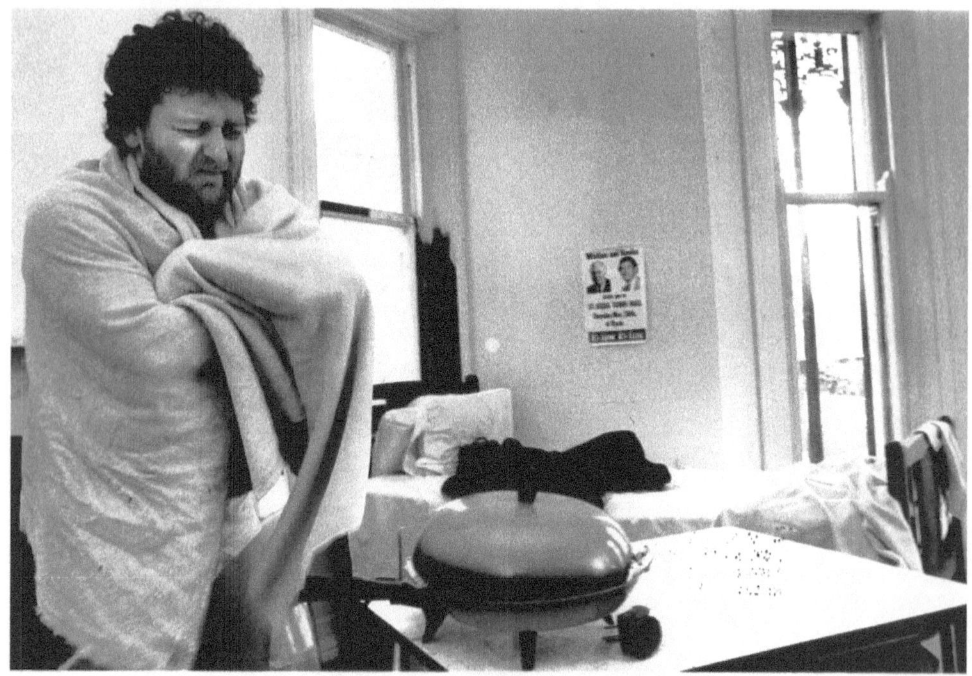

PAUL. Gee-zus! It's cold! Early December and still bloody freezing !

His hair is wet from a shower he's just had in a bathroom down the hall. He switches on a heater in the fire place.

PAUL. No wonder people who live here are the most dissatisfied bunch in the country.

He catches sight of himself in an old cracked mirror.

PAUL. But then, what can you do with a place that was actually founded by a Batman !

He CHUCKLES.

PAUL. Batman and Fawkner. "An excellent site for a village". (dubious) Yeah. That's what they said before they stole the Yarra Valley from the Wurundjeri nation.

PAUL. (quizzically) Am I talking to myself again? Out loud ? I must be mad…

He checks his hair in the mirror, tizzing it up a bit.

PAUL. Or practicing ... (smiles at himself) ... practicing the dialogue.

He becomes aware that the heater isn't working.

PAUL. Come on-

He kicks at it, switches on the frypan and presses his hands into the plate to warm them. But suddenly the plate is too hot.

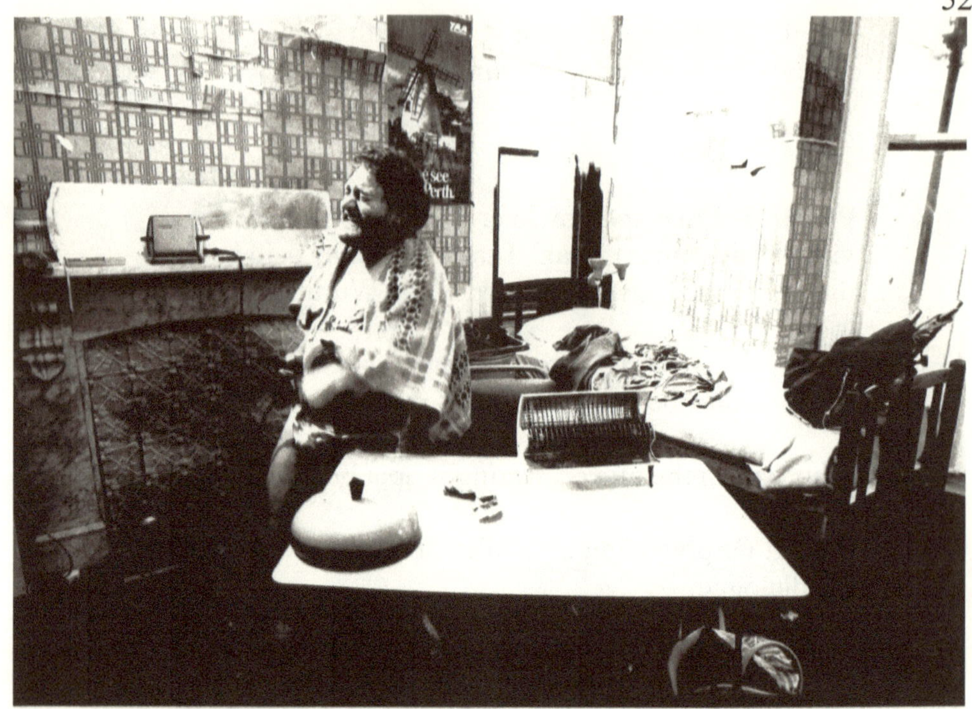

PAUL. Ow !

He blows on his hands, grabbing for his shirt, but it's a summery light cotton thing and it's freezing. So hitting on bright idea, he bundles his clothes up, stuffs them in the frypan with his thongs and whips the lid back on.

As he waits something catches his nose. He sniffs his towel.

PAUL. Ah - the glorious perfume of briquettes! That's the smell of Melbourne.

He turns his clothes over a little, letting them get done evenly on all sides.

PAUL. 'Like to travel light.

He dumps the contents of an old backpack/duffle bag onto one of the stretcher beds. Odd rags, books, posters, notebooks, bits of fruit, cans of food, an iron and other plastic bags fall out.

PAUL. And use a lot of bags - it distributes the weight.

Suddenly he notices a "cigarette" on the floor.

PAUL. Oh, shit ! Who threw that away? (scooping it up) Excuse me. Didn't realise I was taking over a flat from the hoi polloi who can afford to chuck away half smoked ciggies.

He holds the "cigarette" and regards it quizzically. It looks more like a joint!

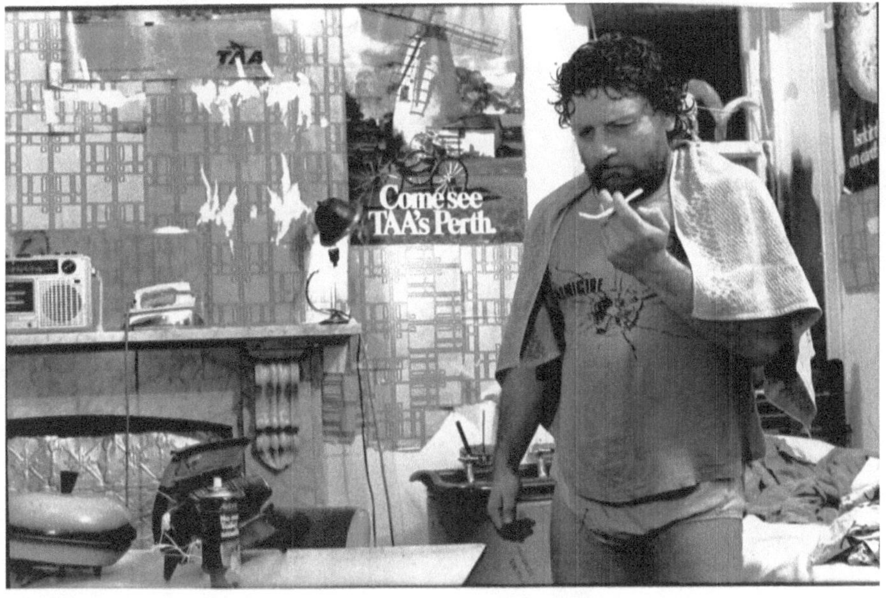

He shrugs, takes a old tin out of his bag and secretes the joint away. Then turns back to the frying pan and considers his clothes "done".

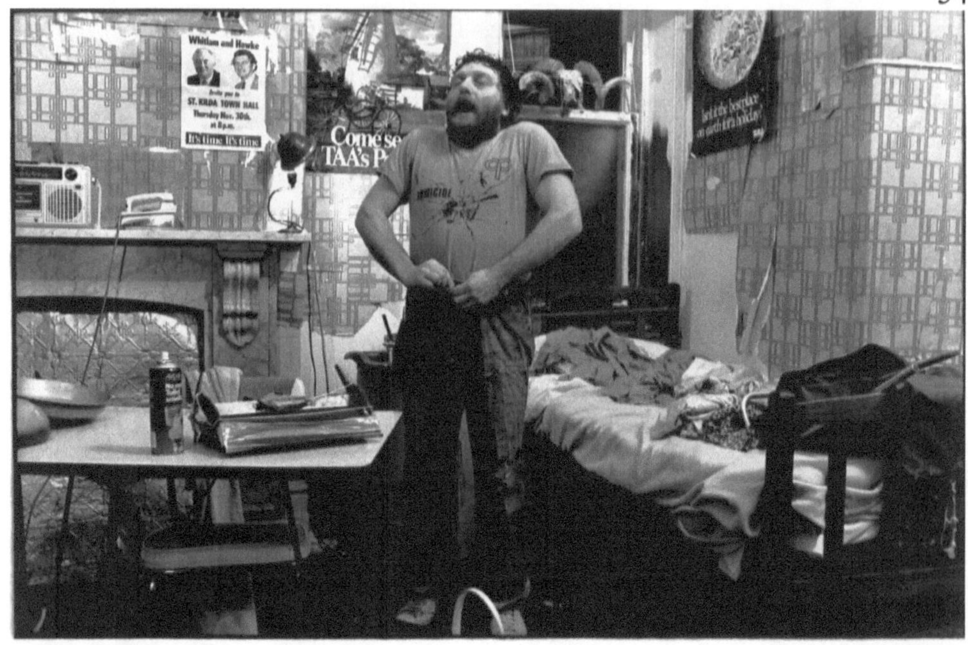

So he slips on his grubby old jeans

Then he sits on one of the beds, leans back on his elbows and with a sudden shock realises he's resting on top of somebody. He springs to his feet.

> PAUL. Jesuschrist! Where did you spring from? (surprised and annoyed) I didn't think I was going to have to share ! $8 a night for a "furnished Flatette" and they cram two of us in here ?

PAUL tries to shake the "body" awake.

> PAUL. Hey… mate ? Hey -

There's no response, the MAN is virtually lifeless. Or catatonic.

> PAUL. (giving up) Oh, yeah, so you just want to lie there and sleep. Alright. I'll respect *your* privacy.

PAUL is laying down the rules, expecting at least the same in return. He goes back to sorting out his junk on the other bed.

PAUL. Shit $8! What a bloody rip-off.

He extracts an poster from his stuff and sticks it up on the wall. It's an ad for a meeting at the St. Kilda town hall this very evening. His hero, Gough Whitlam beams down at him. Along with Bob Hawke

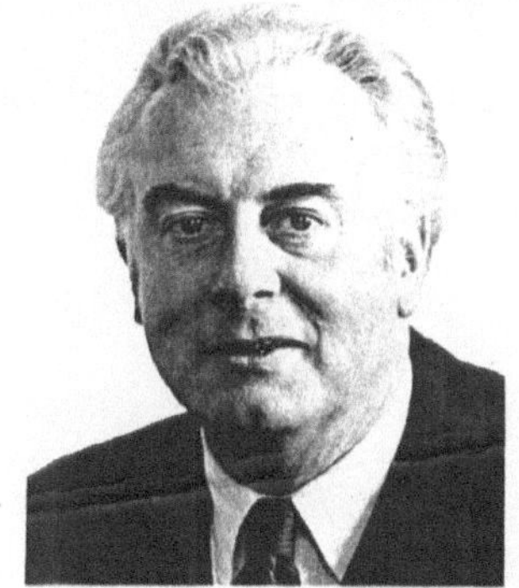
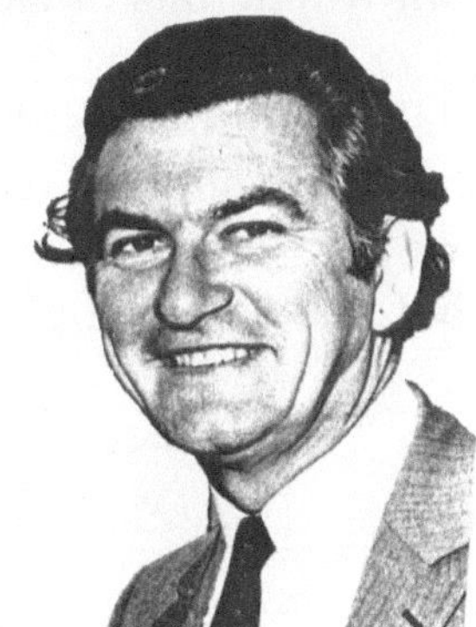

State Library of Victoria
1972

PAUL. But all that'll change, eh Gougho? Soon as the greatest living Australian becomes Prime Minister - two nights from now, about 9 pm. The trend's always clear pretty early when there's a big swing on. Oh, yes.

Things are going to be different around here soon. There'll be
no more over-crowding in boarding hi uses for a start.
(to "THE BODY") Eh, mate ? We'll stop tearing down
all these old derelict places ... (glancing round the
room) and … start doing them up for a change. Let's
build on what we've already got, I say. No more
bulldozer mentality. Oh yeah. The quality of life in the
Republic of Australia is going to rise immeasurably.

He starts to throw odd bits of clothing into one of the lockers.

PAUL. Eight dollars! For no privacy, a shower bloody
miles away, and you can't even go to the loo without
some jerk staring through the gap where the door used
to be. And no heating!

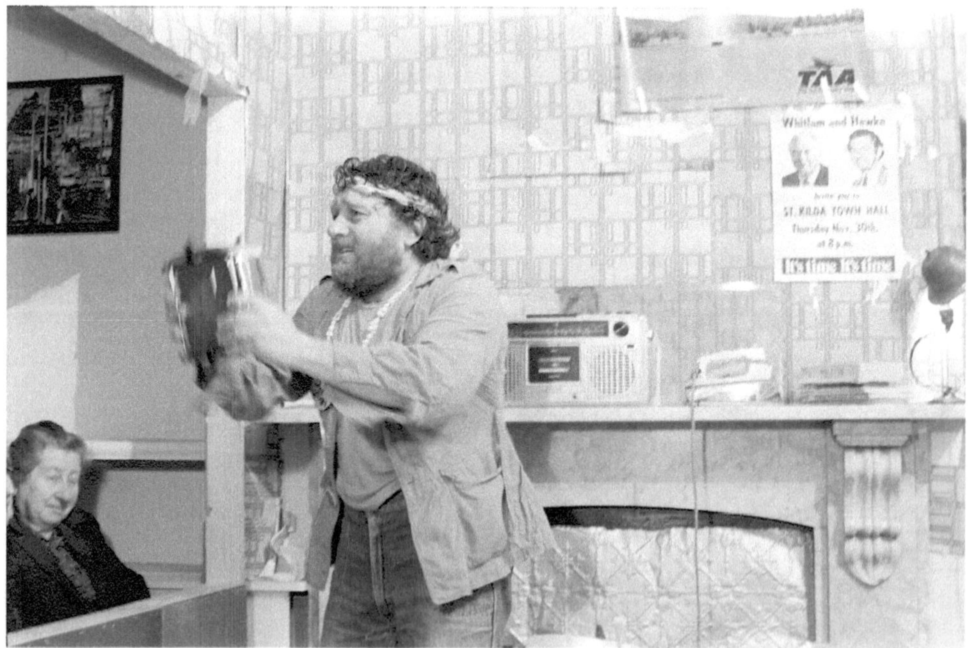

He rattles the heater violently.

PAUL. Oh come on!

And turns instead to the toaster, switching it on, waving his hands above
it.

PAUL. (to "THE BODY") I've seen a lot of bad
landlords, I tell you what, but for sheer miserliness this
guy is the grand champion.

He shakes out an old army great coat from the mess on the bed.

PAUL. Yeah, I've seen a lot … since I started travelling
… (he's coy about it, half expecting to be sprung by
some hidden surveillance) … when I turned 19 … a
coupla … years ago…

The great coat is covered in moratorium badges, peace symbols and "It's
Time" stickers. From the way he holds it, it's a treasured item. But
something's wrong. He sniffs it cautiously, reels back.

PAUL. Gawd, what a pong !

He quickly hits it all over with a blast of air freshener from a pressure-
pack can.

PAUL. (anticipating a cynical reaction from "THE
BODY") Well, it's cheaper than dry cleaning isn't it ?

Satisfied with the new odour he puts the old army greatcoat on. Then he
tacks an electoral map of Australia to the wall above his bed: Liberal/
Country Party seats in blue, Labour in red.

PAUL. (regarding the map) We've only got to win in
western Sydney and Melbourne, then everyone will be
able to afford dry cleaning.

Sick of unpacking, he throws the rest of his junk straight into the locker.

PAUL. Behold ! A port-full of broken dreams !

He extracts a few books, setting them on the top ledge of the locker.

PAUL. Dylan Thomas, Albert Camus, Judith Wright,
and...

Pulling it out last, regarding it ambiguously.

> PAUL. The Archbishop Duhig Memorial Baton for
> outstanding cadet under-officer, 1966.

He adopts a military stance, coming to attention and saluting an imaginary general, as if receiving the baton again, on the school parade ground.

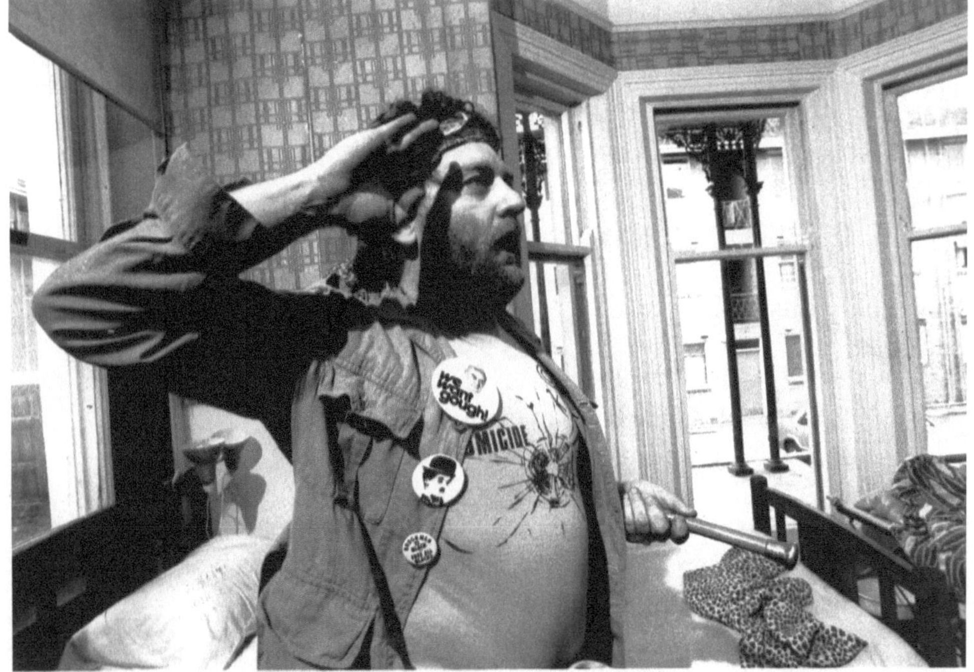

Looking down at the baton. Feeling its weight.

> PAUL. That's my inheritance.

He considers it all for a moment.

> PAUL. A bit contradictory, but still…

He slams the embossed silver knob of the baton into the palm of his hand.

> PAUL (cheekily) Bloody handy though - for walloping
> neo-Nazis at anti-Springbok demos.

He throws the baton back down with the mess on the floor of the locker.

> PAUL. (to "THE BODY") Sorry mate, did I say "port-
> full" of broken dreams just then ? Sorry. "Port's" a
> Queensland term. You say "suitcase" down here don't
> you? Almost a different language, really. (considers a
> moment) Certainly a different state of mind. I find you
> lot are more "flat—minded" down here. 'Cause of the
> sorta place it is, right? Especially after Brisbane and
> Sydney. You've got these great wide, flat boulevard
> things, haven't you? Letting in all that dull, grey
> Melbourne sky (thinks about it)
> Jesus, I hate the place.

He takes out a notebook and positions himself to write at the table, pushing the frying pan aside.

> PAUL. Funny word "Flatette". Not exactly an uplifting
> noun, is it ? Not something to cheer the soul like "apart-
> mont" or "bunga-low" or "pied à terre". Got a nice
> warm feeling about it, don't you think: "bunga-low"?
> Warm, like Noosa beach.

He turns to the toaster again. Holding it close to his chest.

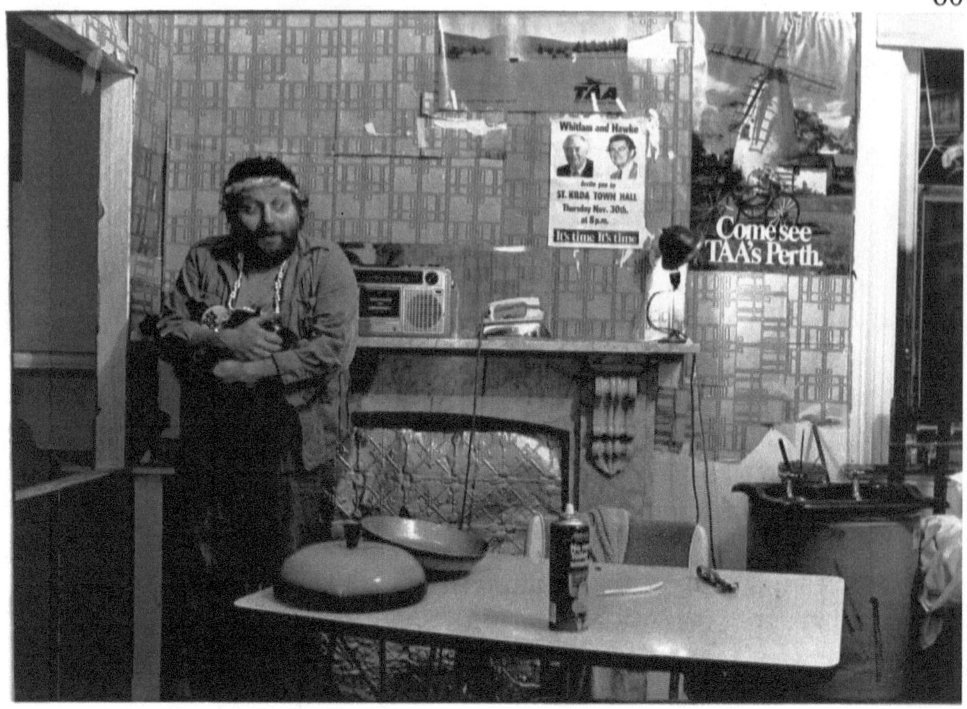

PAUL. Do you remember what it was like to warm?

Suddenly all his frustrations veil up

PAUL. Bugger it!

He viciously pulls at the cord of the toaster until not only the plug, but the power point and the toaster itself sheers away from the bricked-in fire place.

PAUL. (holding the plug limply) Shit !

…Just as CHILLA MAUDLING, the landlord (and a spitting image of CUTHBERT BEAUMGARDINER 72 years earlier), sweeps in.

CHILLA. What's going on ?

At first PAUL looks guilty, then remembers his list of complaints. He suddenly resumes the moral high ground.

PAUL. Oh good, I'm glad you're here - I was just having a shower and the damn hot water ran out!

CHILLA. There's a meter on the tap. You were in there too long.

CHILLA speaks with a kind of repressed but threatening violence.

So PAUL backs off a little, then seizing the toaster again he shakes it aggressively at the landlord.

PAUL. And this bloody toaster hardly heats the room at all. It doesn't work!

CHILLA.(equally firmly) Well it doesn't work now !

PAUL. It never bloody worked

CHILLA. It was working last night.

PAUL. Last night 50 years ago!

CHILLA. Are you calling me a liar ?

PAUL. I'm saying you should knock before you come in here.

CHILLA. I heard banging, I thought you were going to kick the wall down.

CHILLA moves over and stops in front of the "It's Time" poster, sneers up at the photo of Gough Whitlam.

CHILLA. Besides, I want you out of here.

PAUL. Jesus! I only tugged at it a little bit.

CHILLA. Look, you destroy my fireplace, disturb the other guests with your noise and yelling, use up all our hot water, and what's more you're a bloody coward.

PAUL. I beg your pardon.

CHILLA. You're a gutless wonder.

PAUL. Says who ?

CHILLA. Says the two Commonwealth cops who were here just now looking for a certain Paul Bugden, answering your description.

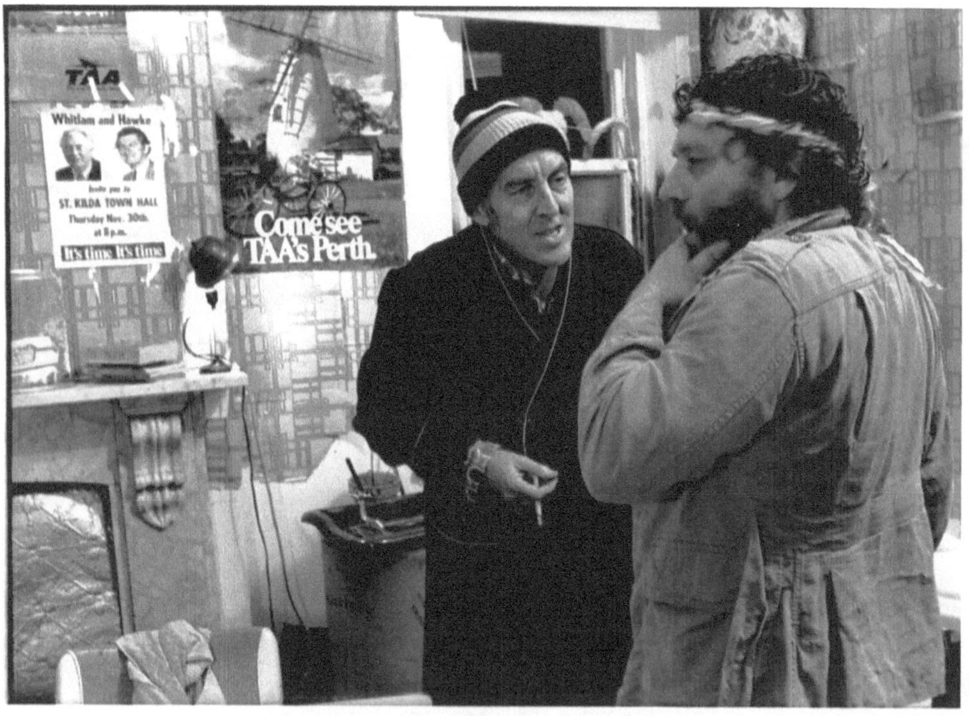

PAUL thinks about it. Hesitating only momentarily.

PAUL. Bullshit. My name's Border, Paul Border.

But PAUL is clearly thrown by the information. He wavers a little.

CHILLA. You're a bloody draft dodger, pal. Too yellow to fight for your country.

PAUL. Look at these eyes… (moving in close to CHILLA)
Do these eyes look 19 years old to you?

CHILLA steps back a bit, recovering his personal space.

CHILLA. So how am I supposed to know how long
you've been a spineless chicken?

PAUL. There's a quarter of a million draft dodgers in
the States right now mate, they can't all be gutless
wonders.

CHILLA. On your bike, Bugden, ya white feather.

CHILLA starts moving in on PAUL intending to shove him out the door,
but PAUL resists.

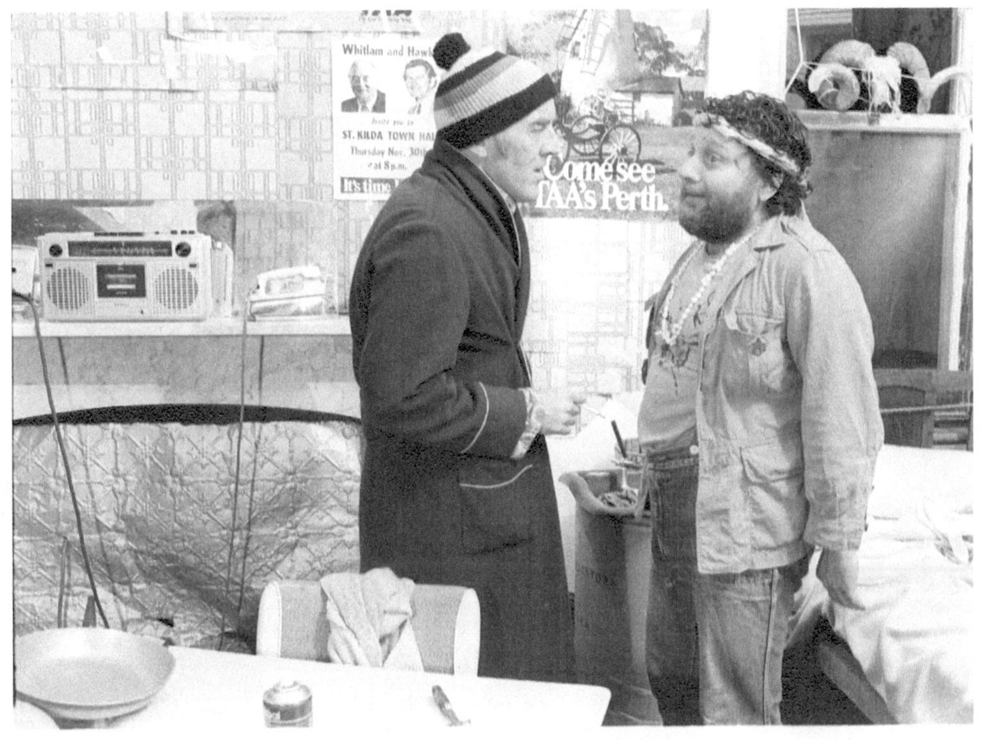

PAUL. My name's Morris, Peter Morris. . . no, alright
its, er Stuyvesant, Phillip Stuyvesant. . .

Paul continues to resist, spread-eagled across the gap of the doorway with Chilla shoving him forwards and outwards.

PAUL. You can't throw me out. I've paid $8 for a night's accomodation.

CHILLA. opens his wallet and counts out 4 one-dollar notes.

But PAUL refuses to take the money.

PAUL. You've signed a contract.

CHILLA. Like hell I have.

PAUL. You oughta be had up anyway, charging $8 for this dump. "Flatette" That's misleading advertising.

PAUL shoves the ad from the paper under CHILLA'S nose. The landlord looks down at it from a certain height.

CHILLA. No it isn't.

PAUL. It says here "Furnished Flatette with kitchen"!

CHILLA. So?

PAUL. So where's the kitchen?

CHILLA. You've got a frypan, you've got a sink.

PAUL. The sink's busted. It's not even connected to anything.

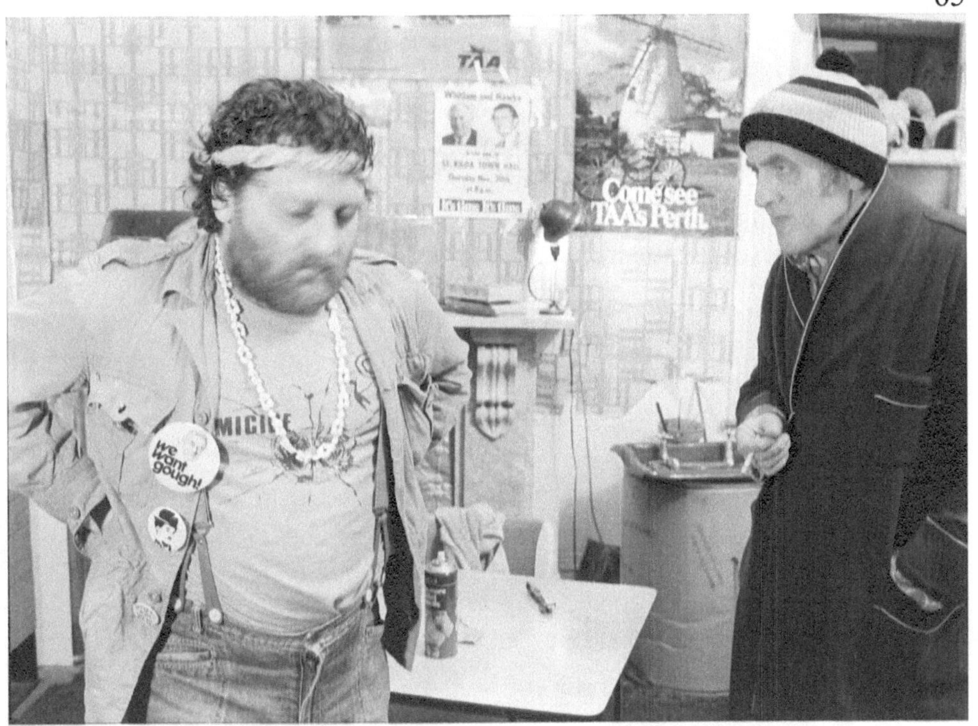

CHILLA. Look, this isn't just another ordinary old boarding house, fella, this place is a former mansion. You're living in what used to be the heartland of the upper crust. 26 Acland Street is more than just an address, it's a status symbol. The place has got history, it's got character.

PAUL (indicating the "body") Well it's got *a* character, that's for sure, and there was nothing in the ad about shared accommodation either.

CHILLA. (defensive) He's not disturbing you is he?

PAUL. Disturbing me ?! The guys so quiet he's practically a corpse !

There's a sharp intake of breath from CHILLA.

CHILLA. I wouldn't say that about him if I were you. Bert's one of our oldest lodgers.

He starts moving in on PAUL again - threateningly, forcing him up against the wall.

CHILLA I'm very fond of Bert. I wouldn't want anything to happen to him. (through clenched teeth) Know what I mean ?

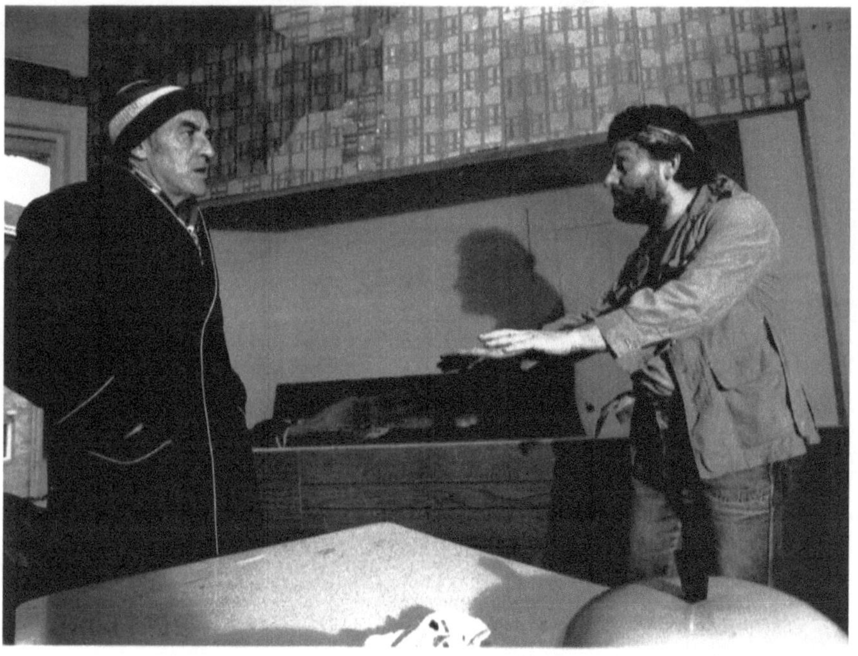

PAUL. (conceding. OK, OK, I don't mind sharing, but Christ, we haven't even been introduced!

CHILLA has backed PAUL into a corner next to the fireplace.

PAUL. (turning to the traps on the mantelpiece above the fire) And look, look at these rats! The size of them! Fercrissake!

CHILLA. (sharply) Rats! They're not rats, they're my pet guinea pigs! (explodes) You've killed Flopsy and Poppet you frigging turd. I want you out of here now !

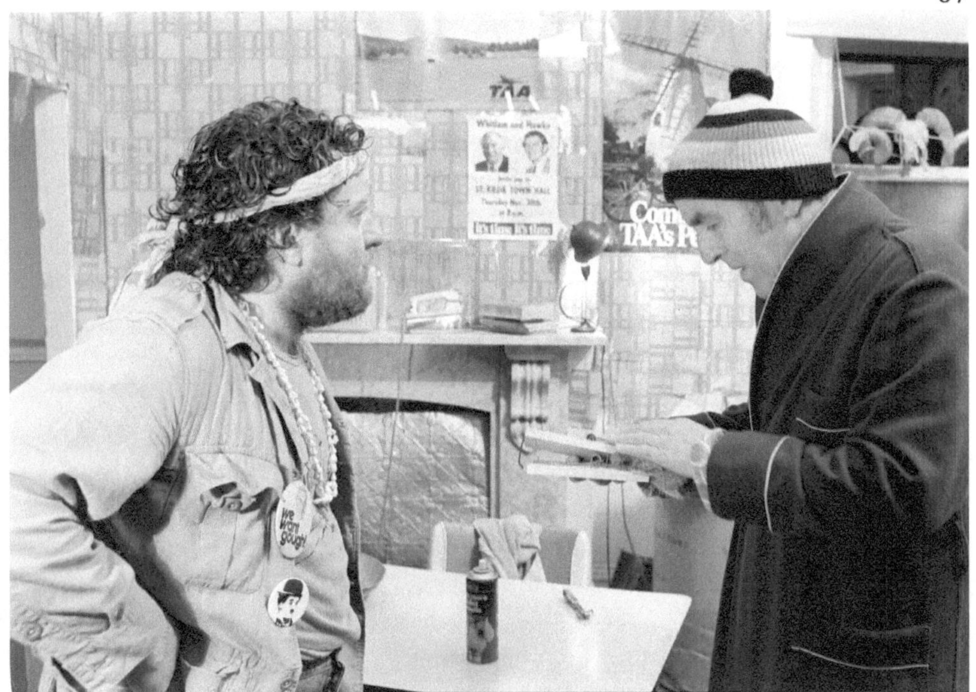

CHILLA tenderly frees the dead "guinea pigs" from the traps and picks them up, cradling them affectionately. Then rubs his hand over the trap where the bodies of the little things enacted their last agonies.

    PAUL. There's no way you're going to throw me out, pal. This is November 30, 1972. In two days time no Commonwealth cop'11 be able to touch me. Gough's going to end conscription. Immediately.

    CHILLA. Don't make me laugh. Whitlam's got no chance. Australians'd never trust a bloody commo to run the country.

    PAUL. Yeah, well maybe that's because the one's doing all the dying haven't even got the vote.

    CHILLA. That's their problem.

    PAUL. Ok, mate you want to kill someone ? Here's a gun. (throws the Memorial baton at him) Just pull the trigger. That doesn't take guts.

CHILLA throws the baton back.

> PAUL. Anyway, haven't you heard ? The war's being "Vietnamised". (he puts imaginary quotation marks around it) They're doing the dying for us. Poor bastards.

CHILLA goes to leave, but now PAUL stops him.

> PAUL. I mean they pull ya birthday out of a frigging lottery barrel, read out the dates on radio and when they've got enough cannon fodder they stop. What sort of way to raise an army is that? On ya friggin' birthday ! I mean happy 19, mate, here's your licence to murder poor mugs in a country thousands of miles away - many happy returns…

CHILLA sniffs something.

> CHILLA. What's that toaster doing on ?

> PAUL. It's heating the room.

CHILLA immediately flicks it off and pockets the electric cord.

> CHILLA. You're separately metered for electricity you realise.

> PAUL (to "THE BODY" - indicating CHILLA) You know, he's blond and over 5'8" it's a wonder he hasn't joined the Waffen SS. (opens CHILLA'S mouth looks inside) Nope. Too many fillings. Sorry, mate, you'd have failed the medical.

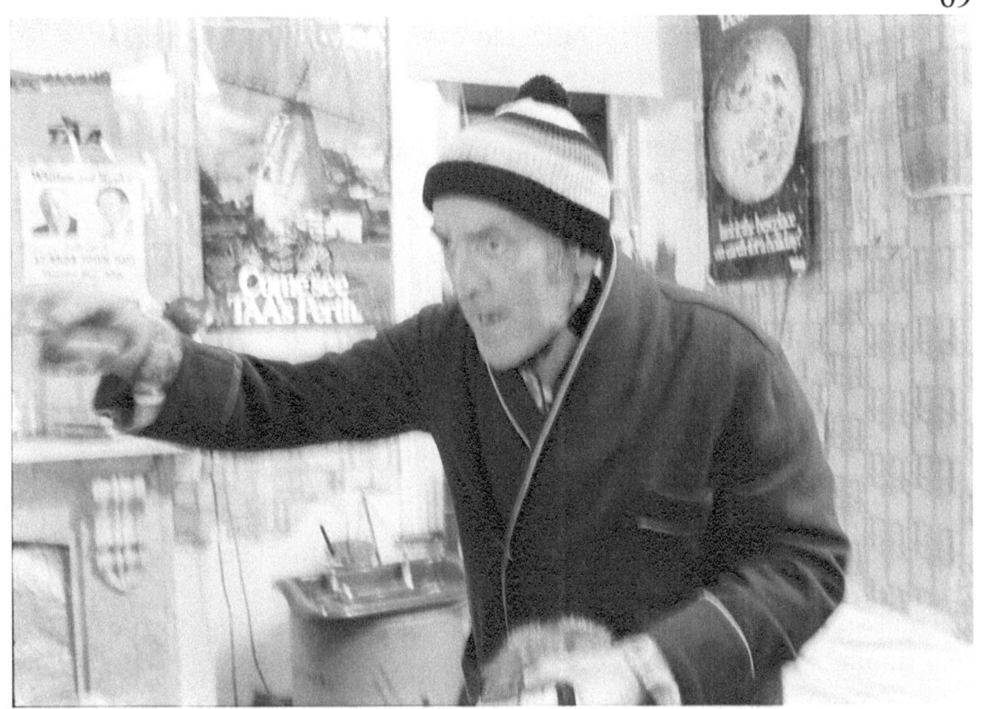

CHILLA.(glowering at PAUL) I want you out of here you bloody dingo. NOW!

PAUL. If you're so pro - war why didn't you dob me in ?

CHILLA. I run a boarding house in St.Kilda, mate, I don't ask questions. And I don't co-operate with the cops.

PAUL No - I guess that'd be real bad for business… round … here …

CHILLA (counting out the notes from his wallet onto the bed) There's $4 back. You've got ten minutes to pack your stuff.

PAUL. What about me deposit?

CHILLA I'm keeping that to fix the fireplace.

But before Paul can protest Chilla addresses "THE BODY".

> CHILLA. See you later, Bert. (patting his top pocket)
> I've got your pension cheque. I'll cash it for you
> tomorrow morning, OK ? (back to PAUL)
> Five minutes!

And CHILLA sweeps out slamming the door.

> PAUL Bastard.

He scoops up the four dollar bills, contemplates them sullenly for a
moment.

> PAUL. Might as well get my money's worth then.

He quickly turns and viciously attacks the fireplace, kicking the heater
and ripping the lino off. Suddenly a yellowed bit of paper drops out from
behind one of the tiles. The unexpectedness of this brings him up short.
He opens the paper out and reads an address at the top.

PAUL. "Johannesburg"? "April 5th 1901"…

PAUL screws up his face.

> PAUL. What is this, a joke ? Did somebody plant this to send me up ? No response from "THE BODY."

PAUL shrugs, he didn't really expect any. He turns back to the letter.

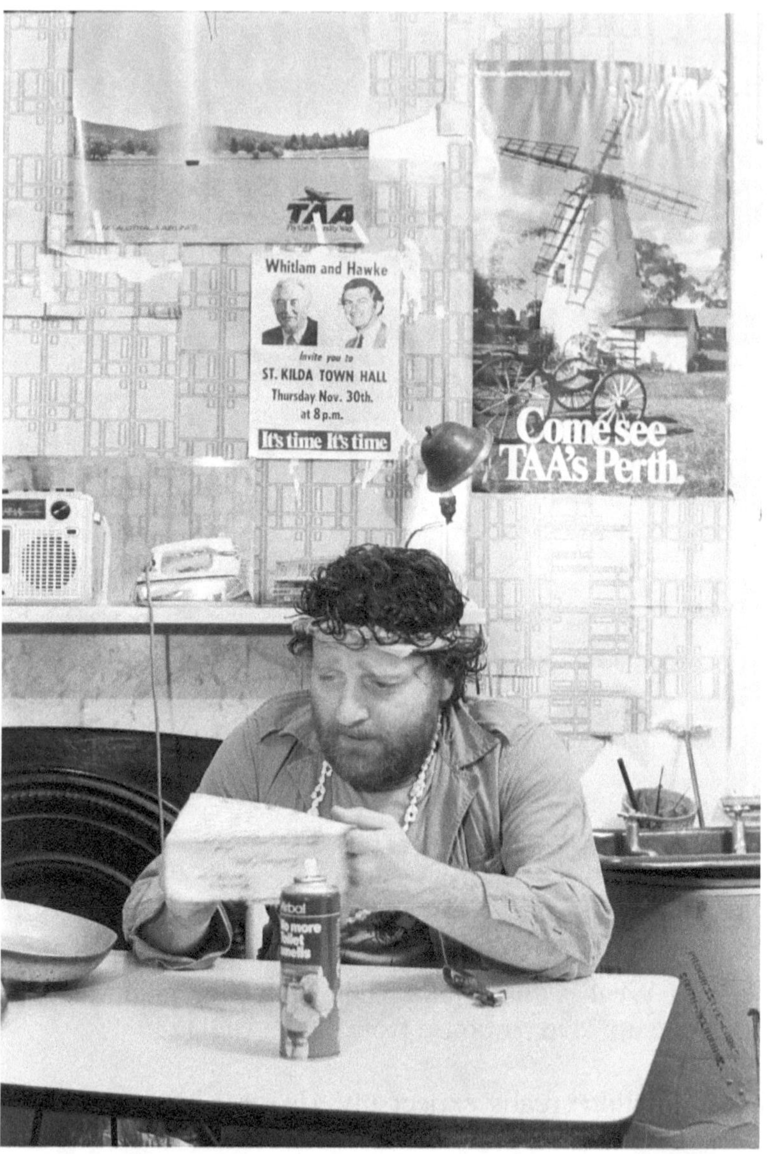

PAUL (reading) "My darling Estelle, already a year of war and I've seen more horrors than we could ever have imagined. I've tried to write many times since our last night together in St. Kilda but somehow the words never came out right. Even this isn't right, but I'm sending it anyway. You were right about the British. In their eagerness to appease the Boers our Empire has left the rights of the native Africans in jeopardy. These blacks are the invisible people and must still carry passes wherever they go. Defeated in the field the enemy have developed an entirely new form of fighting called 'guerilla warfare' and to contain the families left behind we, for our part, have coined another new term: 'the concentration camp'. I fear many of the women herded there will die of enteric fever, and the children of measles. In this, our first twentieth century war disease has killed more people than bullets.

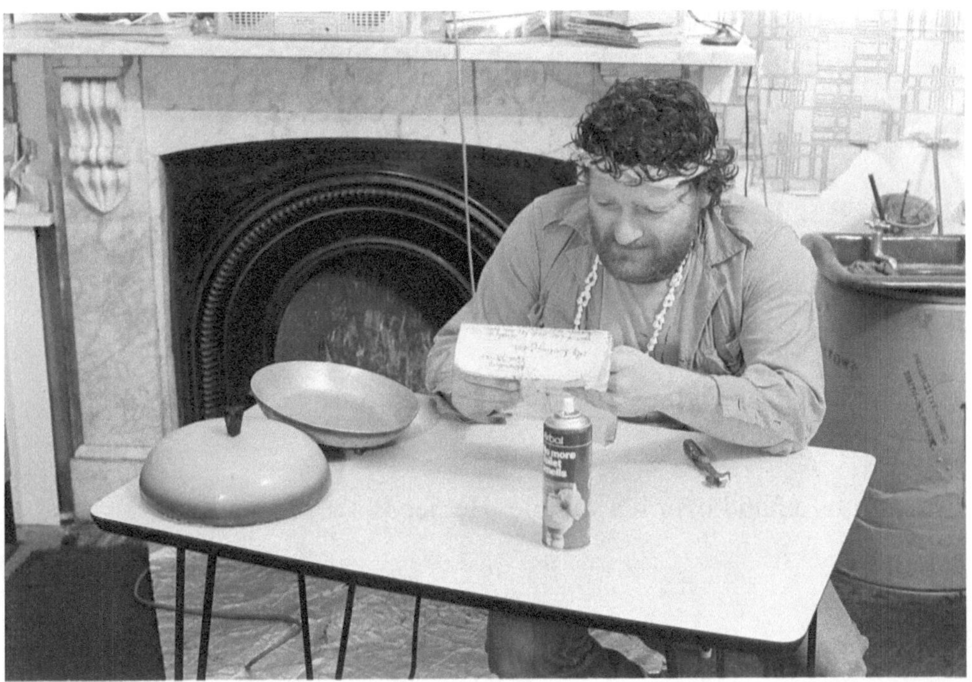

PAUL breaks off reading.

    PAUL. Jesus that's depressing ... sounds just like Vietnam.

He runs a hand along the ornate marble ledge above the bricked in fireplace.

    PAUL. Marble.

He quickly crumples the letter and chucks it back into the fireplace. He glances up at the ceiling roses and other left-over architectural embellishments from a by-gone era.

> PAUL. (cynically) Life must have been real hard for the (not sure what to call them) bunyip aristocracy in those days…

Looking around at the abject mess it's become.

> PAUL. And three generations later it's just another crumbling mansion in "flat city" St. Kilda.

He turns to "THE BODY".

> PAUL. It's not so much the time you're in, but the place you're in it. . . innit eh, mate

No response. He raises his voice so "THE BODY" can hear.

> PAUL. I suppose she must have lived here … this "Estelle".

PAUL rubs a hand over his stubble. He needs a shave.

> PAUL. Not a bad idea for a story, really: disillusioned Aussie soldier comes to full knowledge of how the world works on the bush veld. We could be fighting there again someday. Especially if Bjelke-Petersen keeps promoting the Springboks.

PAUL is hit by a sudden new insight.

> PAUL. Christ, I could get a grant to write something around this … When Gougho gets in there's sure to be lots of cultural incentives: support for the Arts and all that sort of thing. A fella's got to have ideas ready to go.

He bends down and retrieves the crumpled letter from where he chucked it, carefully opening it out again inspired by an idea for a character.

> PAUL. She's 30 odd, beautiful, and runs a "Bachelor Hall" for some bloated exploiter belonging to the Victorian establishment … who's made his fortune in the land boom and wants to ditch his current wife in order to marry… Estelle. At which precise point she falls for this jackeroo from the bush who's seen what happened in the Shearer's Strike and actually *has* a conscience.

PAUL pats his pockets searching for a biro.

> PAUL. Geeze, I better write this down.

He locates a small note pad in his coat pocket and clears a space beside the frypan to set up a "writing desk." He smoothes out the letter beside his pad, uncaps his biro and sits at the table.

> PAUL. It's Jan 11th 1900 - the night before he gets shipped out to South Africa with his artillery unit - in this very house. It's a farewell party and the two lovers have got to talk, to resolve their relationship before he goes. They meet in the near deserted Drawing Room. She says.(writing it down) "Sorry, did I startle you." and he replies "You can't frighten an artilleryman that easily...

PAUL likes the opening, but over the last few moments he hears the sound of an argument coming from some adjacent room (actually ESTELLE and MICHAEL in the Drawing Room Scene unfolding next door). PAUL flings down his biro, and yells out the door. Annoyed.

> PAUL. Is there no bloody quiet to be had in this place?

And he comes back in slamming the door.

> PAUL. Kerrist!

And continues pacing up and down in the tiny space between his bed and the table.

>PAUL. That bloody domestic's been going on for hours in there ! I mean, consider this place, consider the irony of it. This … this home of the gentry trapped now in a sea of flats, a relic of colonialism squashed in by the victims and misery of its own historical greed. A remnant island of the ruling class.

He catches sight of himself in the cracked mirror again, allows a certain self-satisfied smile.

>PAUL. You've actually got it, haven't you, you clever bastard.

He returns to his "desk"

>PAUL. Brilliant, file that one away in the ideas box.

He rips the story so far out of his notebook, attaches these sheets to the letter and carefully folds them and slides them into his coat pocket.

>PAUL. The real secret of political power is to have a good filing system. (second thought) Or to have only one file at a time…

He rubs his hands together.

>PAUL. God this is making me hungry. I've got to eat something or I'll run out of fuel.

He switches on the frypan again and sets about opening a can of tinned spaghetti.

>PAUL. Anyway, can't go down to Gougho's triumphal pre-election party on an empty tummy. I'd be spewing Bundy and Coke all over the place by 10 o'clock.

PAUL'S cooking style is much like the way he writes, he stirs the spag into the frypan with precise, almost frenetic gestures. After a few moments he looks over at "THE BODY" then back at the pathetically thin layer of food in the frypan.

> PAUL. Geeze this isn't going to go far is it ?

He returns to his junk on the floor of the locker and extracts another tin, wrapped still in a paper bag which he doesn't remove, even as he takes the lid off it.

> PAUL. Just a dab of the old… "magic ingredient" to
> fluff it all out and thicken the mixture a little.

PAUL tries to hide the fact, but the brand name "PAL" (dog food) can clearly be seen through a tear in the paper bag. Again we get the precise, erratic, almost spasmodic cooking gestures, but as he shakes the last of his "magic ingredient" into the mixture the can of Pal slips out of the bag and the game is up.

> PAUL. Shit!

He quickly tries to hide it again, but then, realising he's sprung, decides to go with it.
Besides "THE BODY" is hardly watching.

> PAUL. (defensively) Well it's all good native fauna isn't
> it ? Eat locally, think globally. I was only trying to be
> generous. (indicating "THE BODY"). Can't eat alone,
> leave my new flatmate out of it.

PAUL himself is hung between being revolted by it and trying to sell his culinary creation. He sniffs it, and makes YUMMY sounds

> PAUL Mmm mmm ...

But he nearly gags on the smell, quickly puts the frypan back down, and reaches for a tin of pepper.

PAUL. (as he sprinkles) Bit of pepper to sharpen the taste. Bit of toast on the side.

He switches the iron on and places a slice of bread on top of it. Then thinks about it for a moment, opens the lid and unloads the entire contents of the tin of pepper in. Satisfied, he returns to stirring the mixture with confidence.

PAUL. Well - stir the wallaby stew, eh mate ?

But the mixture is warming up and it's too hot to keep stirring with his fingers so he looks around for an implement, approaches the locker and breaks off the handle. It does the job, sort of.

PAUL. Nothing quite like Wallaby bolognaise really - all good roughage- there's nothing un-Pridikin in here.

He gingerly tests a bit, a tiny fragment on the tip of the locker handle , smacks his lips a bit
savoring the taste like a true gourmand.

PAUL. (contemplatively) Mmm … it does lack a certain … je ne sais quoi.

He locates a bottle of chilli sauce and dumps the lot in, followed by an entire packet of salt.

PAUL. OK - so the salt's not Pridikin, but I've got a right to let me hair down haven't I ? On the eve of my freedom.

He sniffs the mixture again and satisfied, he turns gleefully to "THE BODY"

PAUL. You're going to enjoy this mate. I've outdone meself this time.

He bends down to collect a couple of tin plates, then quickly straightens.

PAUL. (shocked, appalled) Who farted ? (to "THE BODY")
Ah geeze, that's stretching mateship a bit thinly isn't it,
pal ? When you're sharing a room … Light a match
fercrissake. We may be down on our luck, pal
(correcting) er, mate, but common courtesies don't cost
much.

PAUL hesitates, sniffs for a moment, looks down at his mixture. A touch
contritely, PAUL strikes a match and waves it over the cooking. He sniffs
again. Still no good. In fact he nearly gags on the smell. So he quickly
grabs the air freshener that he used to "dry clean" his coat and hits the
frypan with a few seconds of spray, drenching its odour. The scent of
pines now floods the room. That's better, He tentatively sniffs the
"wallaby bolognaise" again and
satisfied that it's done, he lifts the frypan and pours half onto the first
plate.

PAUL (offering it) There we go mate. Done to a "t".

But there's no response from "THE BODY". Uncertain, PAUL lowers the
plate a little.

PAUL. All that sleeping - you must be famished.

Still no response.,

PAUL. You're not finicky about roo are ya, mate? All
protein's the same at the cellular level you know. And
roo meat's particularly low in cholesterol.

But still "THE BODY" doesn't respond.

PAUL. (slightly peeved) Suit yourself. That's all the
more for me then...

PAUL establishes himself at the table, puts a hankie in his collar for a
napkin, and gathers the locker handle for a spoon. He faces his creation
for a moment, completely still.

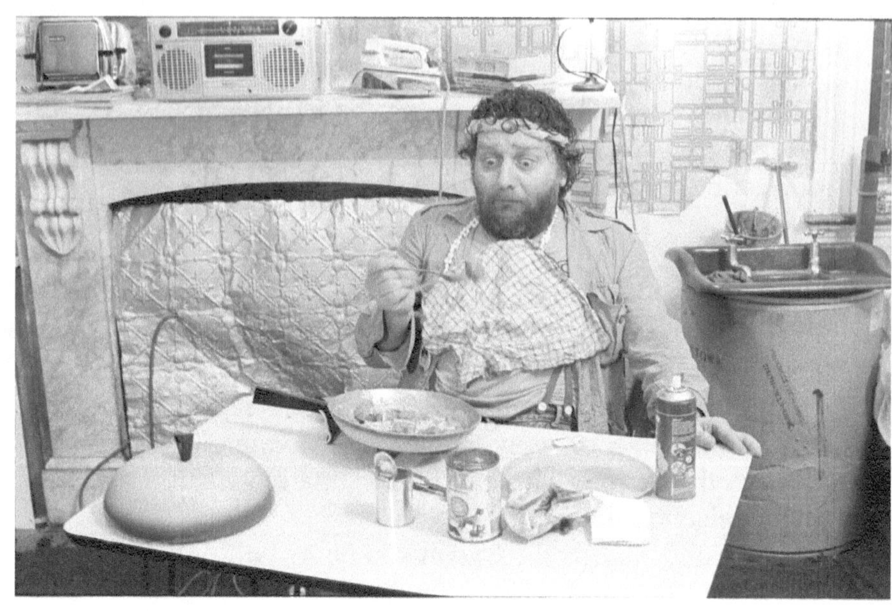

Then he attempts to take a spoonful.

But it really is revolting.

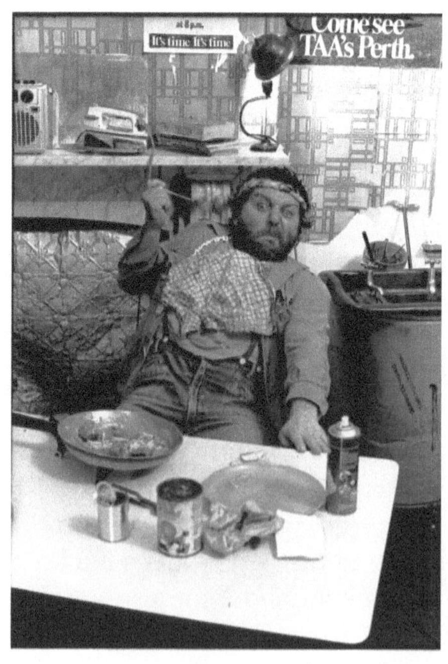

He tries to eat but as he draws the fork towards his mouth his head keeps moving out of the way. How can he admit it? His shoulders drop, he regards the food bleakly, then checks the Pal tin again, reads the use-by date.

> PAUL. Oh, no! It's way past its use-by date. I thought so.(dropping the spoonful back into the frypan) Bloody supermarkets, they outa be shot for selling that stuff. Then again, little doggies don't have the vote either, do they ?

Still seated at the table he shoves the cooking aside, takes out his tobacco tin and savours the butt/joint he found earlier.

> PAUL. Well, here's to canines, cannabis and conscripts. (slight pause).God, I hate being poor. I'm really sick of this … making do. I just want a bloody job like anybody else. There's 80,000 people out of work in Australia right now. 80,000! Christ, Gougho's gotta get in.

He lights the joint, takes a deep drag, exhales, coughs violently.

> PAUL. (through the coughing) No, nope, ' said I'd stop and I will.

He looks around for an ashtray. There isn't one.

> PAUL. The only way you ever discover anything is by breaking an old habit.

Under a bed he finds two chamber pots, one large one small.

> PAUL. (to "THE BODY") Mind if I take the big one, mate ?

No response. PAUL waits.

> PAUL. (warning him) I may still have some Wallaby Bolog…

Still no response.

>PAUL. Alright, OK, you have the big one. I don't want
>to be a dog in the manger. No pun intended. And it *is* a
>long way down the hall, isn't it?

PAUL ashes his smoke in the smaller chamber pot and sets it beside him
on the table. He lines up his biro neatly above his notebook again, ready
to resume writing the great Australian novel.

>PAUL. So he says to her "We never really seem to
>express what we actually feel do we ?" And she replies
>"Is that a question or a manifesto?"

PAUL breaks off at the sound of a dinner gong CHIMING away just
outside his door.
He throws down his biro in disgust..

>PAUL. I DON'T BELIEVE IT ! What is that appalling
>noise !?

Suddenly a young woman is there, just coming in.

>MIRIAM. What's that appalling smell ?

PAUL swings round. Surprised but defensive.

>PAUL. Can't I get any bloody peace around here ?

MIRIAM steps in from the Hallway, tucking the xylophone for the
chimes under one arm and picking up a bucket and clean sheets from
outside his door.

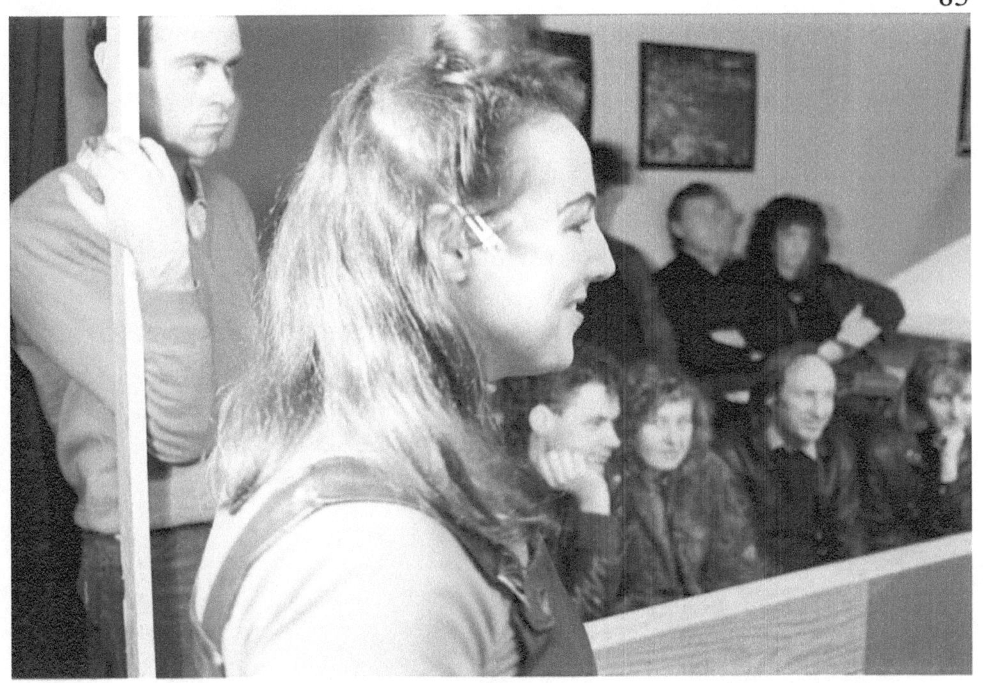

MIRIAM. I've come to do the room.

PAUL. (double takes) I didn't know it was serviced.

MIRIAM. Do you want me to lose my job ?

PAUL. There's nothing in the ad said anything about
"serviced."

MIRIAM. I've got to read the meters.

PAUL. (blocking her) Listen, I always do my own
room.

But she easily brushes past him, jots down the readings on the gas, light,
and power meters.

MIRIAM. You're moving out anyway.

PAUL. (defiantly). That's what you think.

She spots the locker handle and the rancid mess in the frypan.

MIRIAM. (disgusted) Aw, look- look at this muck!

She gingerly picks out the locker handle and wipes it clean.

PAUL. I was only borrowing it.

She fixes it back onto the locker door and spots the chamber pot with the joint ashed out in it.

MIRIAM. (grimaces thrusting the chamber pot out at him) I'm expected to clean this up am I?

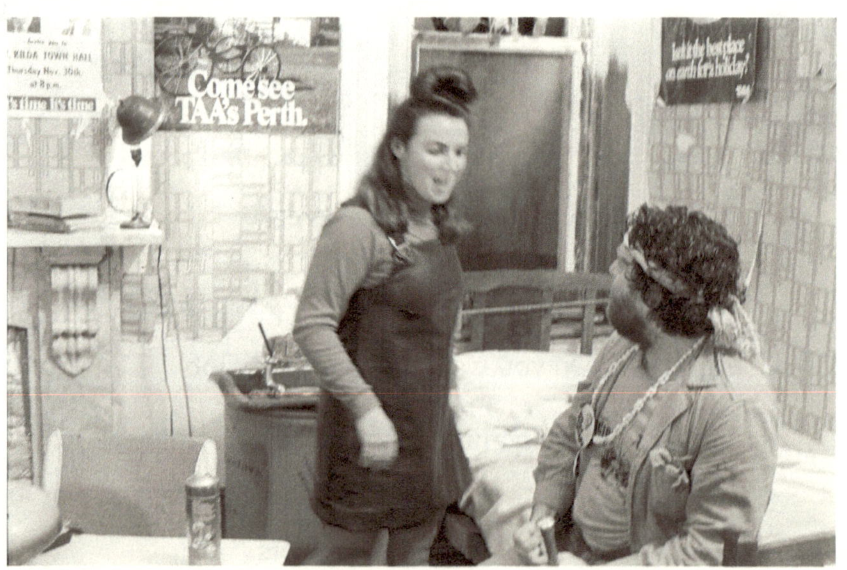

PAUL. (with dignity) There weren't any ashtrays.

She wipes the chamber pot clean with quick, efficient gestures.

MIRIAM. You live like pigs some of you single men.

PAUL feels insulted.

PAUL. I'm no derro love.

MIRIAM finds the tin of "PAL".

>MIRIAM. No - you're a dingo, we all know that. Run,
>run away…

And she plops the tin of pet food into her plastic bucket.

>PAUL. Are you implying I'm a coward? Just 'cause I'm
>a conscientious objector.

She continues cleaning up his mess.

>MIRIAM. You're objectionable that's for sure.

>PAUL. Geeze, news travels fast around here, the walls
>must have ears - as well as rising damp. I suppose
>you're all for the bloody war as well ?

>MIRIAM. I had a brother. He was killed last year in
>Phuc Tuy.

PAUL'S defensiveness evaporates, he's sorry, he shrugs, what can he say.
He touches her arm.

>PAUL. (gently) He didn't have to … you know.

She pulls her arm away from him, not allowing *her* privacy to be invaded
either.

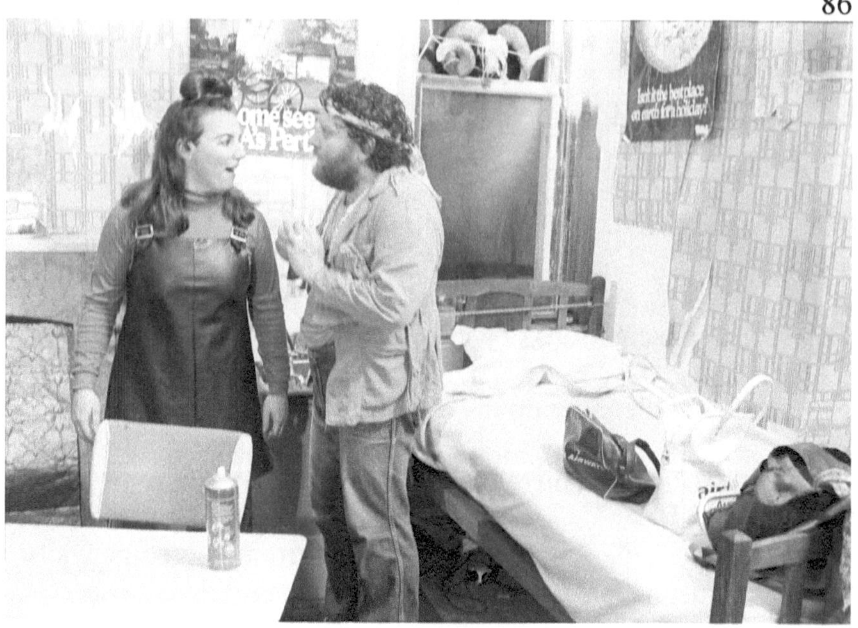

PAUL. I'm sorry. I'm only trying to say what I believe.

MIRIAM. I don't need a draft dodger's sympathy,
thanks
very much.

That hurts.

PAUL. Look, if we don't take a stand a lot more people
like your brother a going to die over there - and for
what ?

MIRIAM. Freedom for a start.

PAUL. Rubbish. What about my freedom - not to kill
people?

With the practiced ease of someone who's done it thousands of times she
rips back his bed covers in order to change the sheets. In a flash he slips
in under them

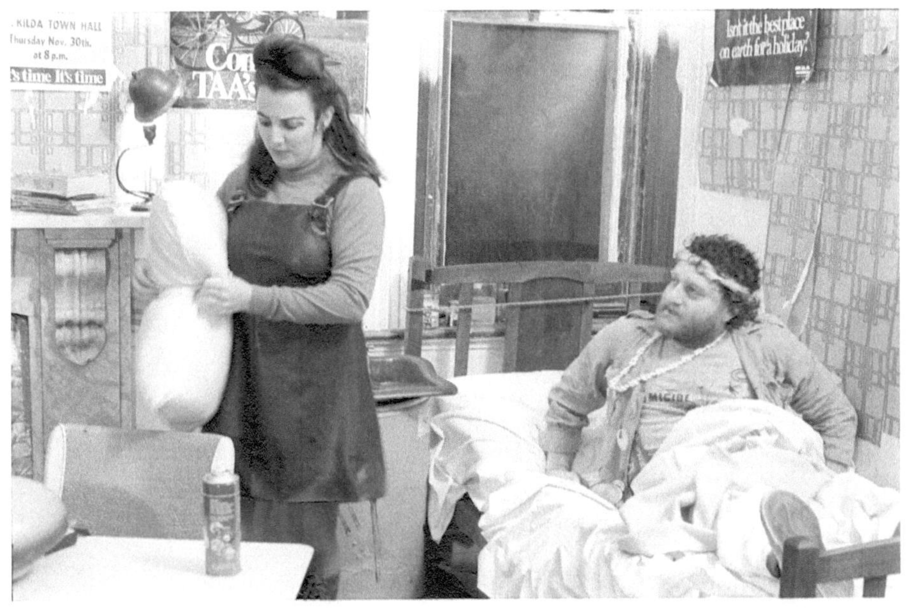

PAUL. Gee you're quick off the mark.

It's happened so rapidly she's more startled than outraged.

MIRIAM. What ?

PAUL. You St.Kilda girls don't muck around do you?

MIRIAM. I'm changing the sheets!

PAUL. Is that what you call it?

She pulls back away, right away from him.

MIRIAM. How dare you!

PAUL. Didn't know you were all on the game.

MIRIAM. (Insisting) I've got to change the sheets.

PAUL. And I've got to know how to talk to you.

MIRIAM. Give it a break, mate.

PAUL. We never really express what we actually feel, do we ?

MIRIAM. Oh fergodsake!

PAUL I can't help being attracted to you.

MIRIAM. Look, I've got a job to do okay ?

PAUL. But I haven't even slept in the bed yet.

MIRIAM. You're out of here. It's for the next guest. Health regulations says I have to.

The mucking around stops. But neither of them move.

PAUL. Well, in that case…

Reluctantly he gets out of the bed.

MIRIAM. (cynically) What ? Throw myself into the arms of some itinerant commo dickhead. You've got to be joking!

PAUL. I'm only suggesting casual sex, I'm not saying we have to fall in love…

She goes to slap him.

MIRIAM. Bastard !!

He interrupts the blow catching her hand

PAUL. Shhh… (indicating "THE BODY" in the adjacent stretcher)
You'll wake him up.

Her face drops, her whole manner changes, she returns to cleaning up.

MIRIAM. What do you take me for?

PAUL. At least I'm honest.

MIRIAM. "Stupid" I would 've said.

PAUL. Don't you believe in free love ?

MIRIAM. I've always found it very expensive.

With quick efficient movements she scrapes his left-over food into her plastic bucket.

PAUL. Hey ! That's my dinner !

MIRIAM. You heard the gong, you can eat in the dining room.

PAUL. Oh yeah ? What's on tonight ?

MIRIAM. (as she continues to clean the fypan) Mince and chips, mince and rice, fried mince and mash, or curried mince on toast.

PAUL. (squirming) I think I've gone off red meat love…anyway I'm going to Gougho's last big gig - before the election. (still trying) Wanta come?

MIRIAM. No thanks.

PAUL. It's only just down the St.Kilda town hall.

MIRIAM. I'm a member of the Liberal Party.

PAUL. Why am I not surprised ?

He anticipates her blow again, sticking his hands up defensively.

PAUL. Only joking - truly, you're a warm and lovely person with a beautiful open smile.

MIRIAM. How dare you !

PAUL. I mean strewth ! You can't assume anything around here can you ? People aren't what they seem. (indicating "THE BODY") He's obviously a donkey voter, you're trying to hold the clock back and I'm just…

MIRIAM. (cutting in she takes his "It's Time" poster off the wall)
And you're just "Waiting For Gougho."

PAUL freezes, blinks at her, jerks his head to one side.

PAUL. Hey that's not bad.

He regards her with a new respect.

PAUL. (with dawning insight) In fact that's bloody fantastic !
"Waiting For Gougho" ! That's what I'll call it. That should let the new cultural bureaucracy know where I stand.

MIRIAM. Call what ?

PAUL. My story.

MIRIAM. (incredulously) You're a writer ?

He pulls the letter and notes out of his pocket.

PAUL. Listen to this:

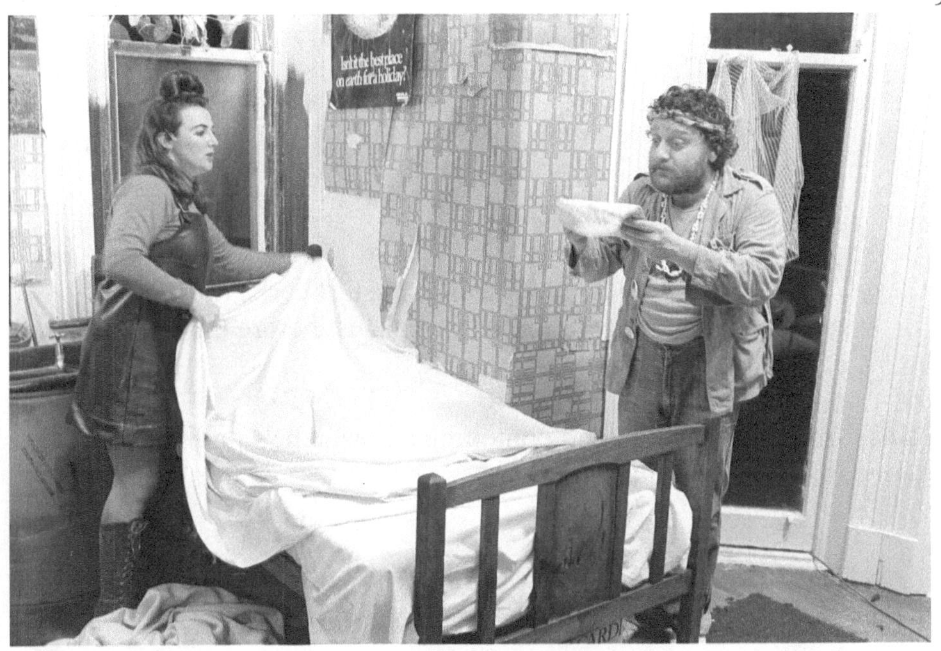

PAUL. (reading) "So when you take your next twilight
stroll up Acland street and round to Alfred Square, my
dear, if your gaze should wander across the bay to those
primeval volcanoes, the You Yangs, remember that
they're-not so different from these round, dry-brown
hills of Africa. And if you linger to see the flashing red
light of Williamstown pier calling out to the gay green
lights of St. Kilda's esplanade, then think of the flashing
red and green, the forever stop/go, stay/leave, pendulum
of my heart. From a million miles away, your ever
loving Michael."

There's a pause.

PAUL. (still reading) "p.s. was it a boy or a girl?"

PAUL sighs quietly and folds the letter returning it to his pocket.
He waits, testing the emotional effect.

MIRIAM. (touched and uncertain) Did you write that?

PAUL. (lies) Yeah, sort of.

MIRIAM. That's … that's very moving.

PAUL. He dies.

MIRIAM. What ?

PAUL. The guy who gushes all that stuff carks it from
enteric fever - over in South Africa. Just before the end
of the Boer War.

He sinks back onto the bed and contemplates what he's just said: an
outcome that's really quite tragic

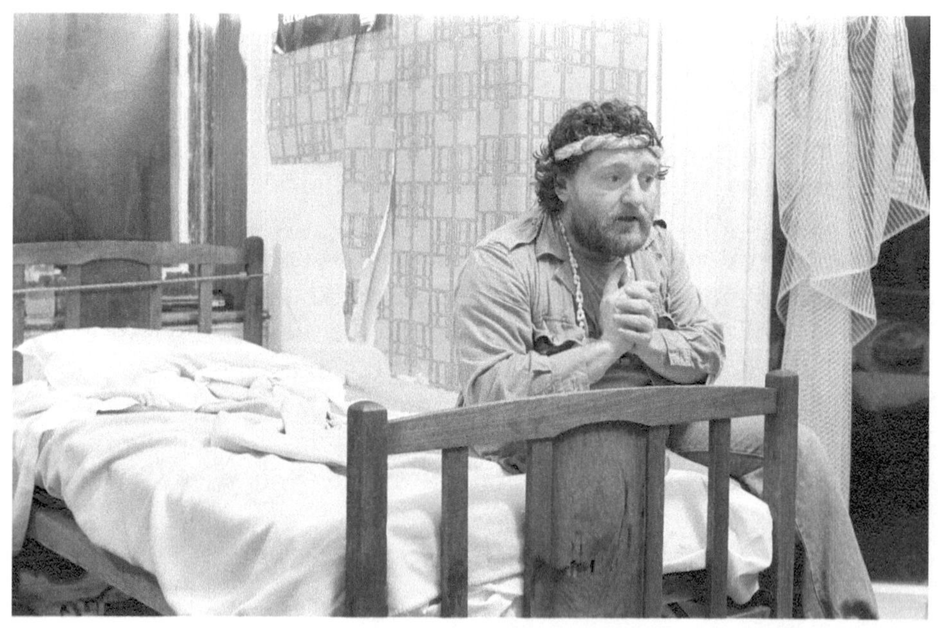

PAUL. A lot of them died of enteric fever. Poor
buggers. More from disease than bullets.

MIRIAM looks blank.

PAUL. (discovering a new piece of the story thread as
he talks) While the woman he's writing it to… inherits a

fortune when her toad-like de facto, the man she's beholden to, dies of a heart attack on learning that the kid she's carrying isn't his.

He looks triumphant. By gosh he's got it!

MIRIAM. That's… that's…(lost for words, literally) I really don't know what to say.

On second thoughts he crumples the letter and throws it into Miriam's bin.

PAUL. Yeah, it's pathetic really. Nobody'd ever want to publish that rubbish.

She shrugs. Can't disagree.

MIRIAM. They don't seem very real to me. If they're your characters.

PAUL. Well, they're more an *impression* of reality, really. I kind of like to exaggerate things for certain effects. You see I'm not just talking about one issue here, like war, or male/female relationships, I'm searching for a whole *new* way of bonding people: on a basis of real equality and mutual respect.

MIRIAM. That's just hippie waffle.

PAUL. Look if society could be organised differently, the problems of aggression and poverty, injustice and violence will cease to exist. They're just the symptoms of what's going wrong. All change has to take place in here (hitting his chest). I'm talking about addressing the *real* causes, the root problem. It's all there in how we relate to each other. That's what a writer does: shows us how to live.

MIRIAM. Yeah, well I'm sorry. I can't relate to that at all.

PAUL. Well, I really pranged-out with you, didn't I ?

MIRIAM. You're weird, you know that ?

PAUL. Weird ? (thinks about it) Yeah, I'm lucky too, I've had a whole
lotta luck in my life and it's all been bad. (slumps back onto the bed)
I could've studied architecture if it hadn't been for this bloody war.

She's finished fixing up the room.

MIRIAM. I think you'd better go now, he's waiting downstairs.

PAUL. Yeah - yeah, go, right.

PAUL starts dumping all his junk from the locker back into his kitbag.

PAUL. All my life I've always been on the verge of saying the right thing and never quite making it, always pushing it too far. Now I've buggered it up completely.

MIRIAM. Please don't go on about it.

PAUL. I'll probably think of the right thing to say to you on Monday

MIRIAM. When you're a long way away. (hopefully)

PAUL. (taken aback) You don't have to sound so happy about it. For a moment there I thought I'd actually found a story and in you maybe I thought I'd found the inspiration to write it. You could have been my Estelle.

MIRIAM. You're not on metho are you ?

PAUL. Give us a break. Tonight it's all champagne where I'm going.
They'll probably even let Liberals in - if you're interested… (still trying)

MIRIAM. That'd be the day.

PAUL. Oh well, here's to optimism of the will and pessimism of the intellect.

He's packed ready to go.

PAUL. See you in one of my next life times, then.

He holds out his hand she declines to take it.

MIRIAM. I sincerely hope not.

Suddenly Cuthbert can be heard yelling out in the Hallway.

CUTHBERT. Martha! MAR-THA !!

MIRIAM tenses, and races out.

PAUL, (yelling back through the door as she closes it)
Oh put a bloody sock in it ferkerrisake ! (opens and yells out through doorway)
There's people actually trying to live in here you crashing bore !

He storms out leaving his bag behind...

A moment later Miriam enters through another door.

MIRIAM. (to the audience) The police have come back.
(takes a quick peek at "THE BODY" reacts horrified)
 You'd better go - quickly!

And she ushers them out.

ACT III
The Gallery 1988

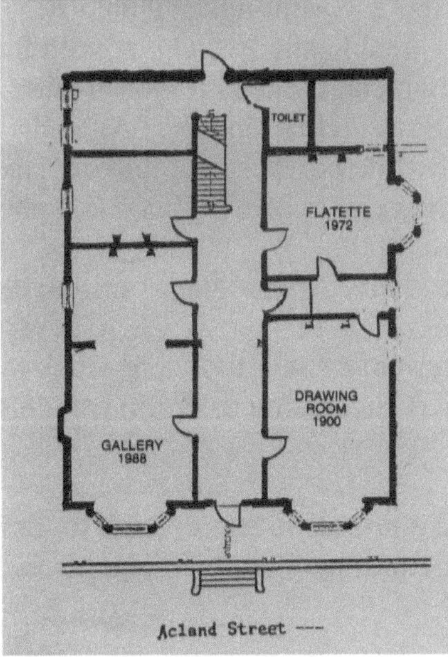

MUSIC again fades up as the audience group we're with move on towards a third room.

After the clutter and filth of the Flatette, the Gallery is a long, bright, open space with chairs arranged around the walls. A banner hanging across the central archway announces that this is an exhibition of "St.Kilda: Then and Now - from the Boer War to the Bi- centennial"

The "Then" part of the room contains a collection of historic paintings, photographs, and memorabilia culled from the St.Kilda Council's art collection, mixed in with which are photographs of people we now recognise to be CUTHBERT and ESTELLE and DEEGAN. Also down that end is a parlour maid's costume circa 1900 hanging from a small hinged screen.

The "Now" part of the room includes fantastic photomontages of a futuristic St.Kilda where the Upper Esplanade and Jacka Boulevard resemble a grotesque parody of Surfers Paradise (Including a Rialto-sized high rise on the corner of Robe Street - gleaming and monstrous in the sunlight).

There are also contemporary paintings and a corner installation entitled "St. Kilda Breakfast" - a table and two chairs with the scattered remains of a particularly untidy meal: half eaten muesli and coke, crumbs of toast, pot of tea, copies of "Smash Hits" and the "Age Gig Guide" scattered around a small line of white powder on a mirror. There's cassette tapes, an overflowing ashtray etc. Also down this end a photo of PAUL BORDER, on his knees at the
tram stop outside Luna Park. Apparently vomiting onto the road.

There's an erratic pattern of yellow footsteps stuck to the floor, each with a different number, as if suggesting a certain (random) order in which to view the exhibition.

After people have had a few minutes in which to take in the exhibition MIRIAM, the cleaner from the Flatette Scene pokes her head through the door.

        MIRIAM. Could you all take your seats please, the
        performance is about to begin.

As people settle into chairs arranged around the walls a clock outside
CHIMES 8pm.

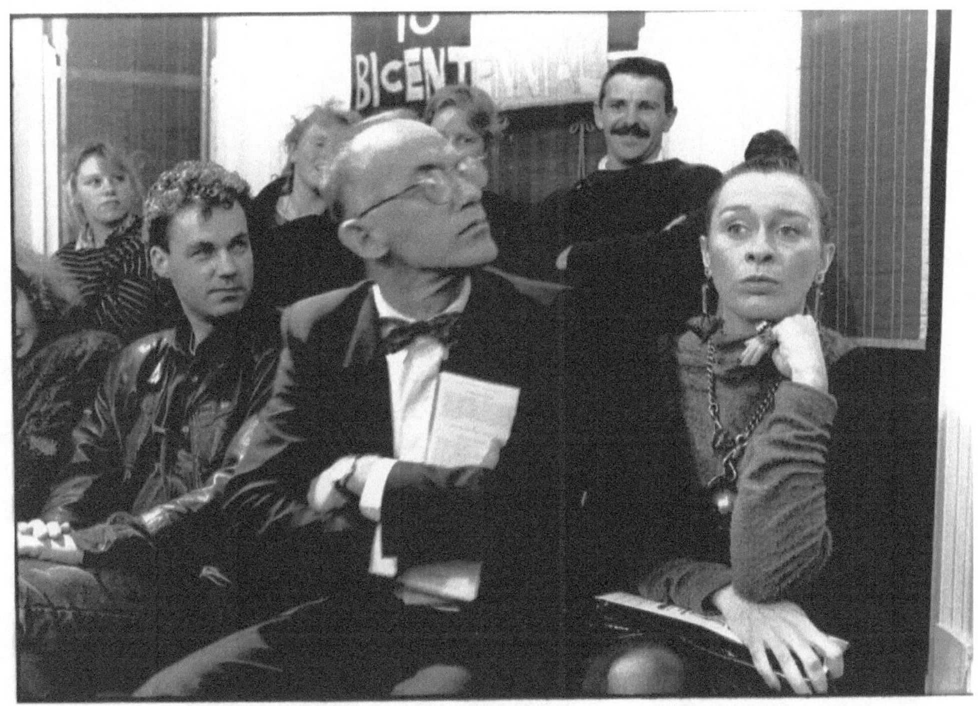

MONIKA and LEON are seated near the door under a large abstract
painting. He's the very image of a modern corporate
manager/banker/architect type - and MONIKA, for her part, is just a
touch overly made-up - dressed to the hilt but failing to look really classy.
Trying just a bit too hard to match the occasion. She's obviously come
expecting a real "arty party".

As soon as LEON hears the CHIMES he reacts.

   LEON. That's strange.

   MONIKA. What ?

   LEON. There's those chimes again.

   MONIKA. It's only a clock, Leon.

LEON. (keenly, curiously) Yes, but it's always followed by this dull buzzing sound. Out in the Hallway somewhere…

MONIKA. I think that's what this button's for. (looking over at it)

She leans over to peer at the sign from her seat just below it.

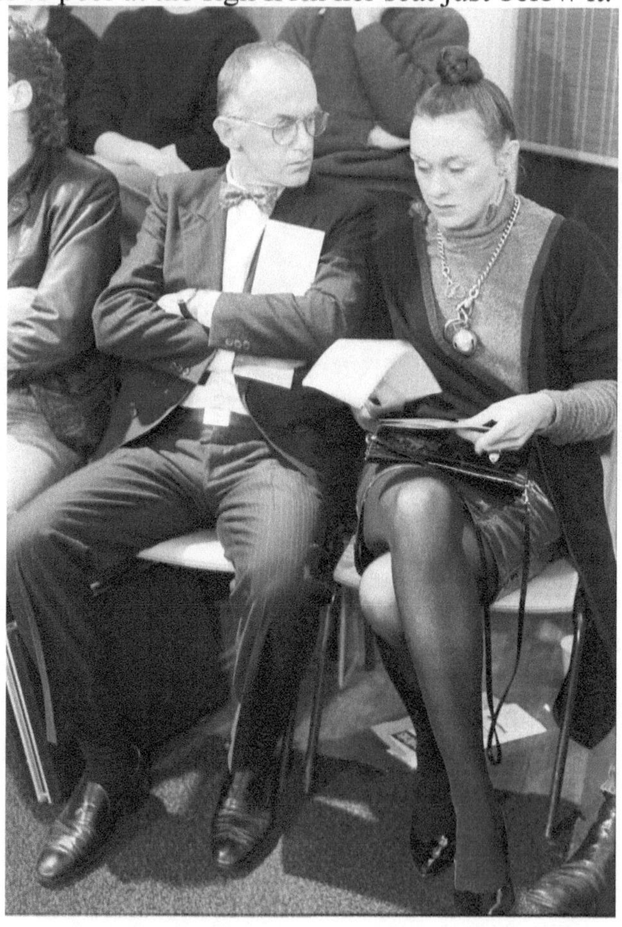

Then she checks in her programme.

MONIKA. (holding out a pair of glasses she refuses to wear)
It says: we're supposed to "press the red button in order to make the room come to life."

So MONIKA gets up and jabs an elegant finger at it…to no effect.

> MONIKA. (pressing repeatedly) It … it doesn't seem to be working.

She stops pressing, stands back.

Nevertheless a BUZZING SOUND is heard off.

> LEON. See - there it is…

> MONIKA. (sinking back into her seat, turning to face him directly)
> Well, but no - I'm not pressing it now. It's not coming from *our* button.

> LEON. (restless, impatient for something to happen)
> Leave it alone then.

She turns to help to the person on the other side of her.

> MONIKA. Could you help me dear ? (indicating)
> Push it…

The audience member tries, but still no buzzing sound.

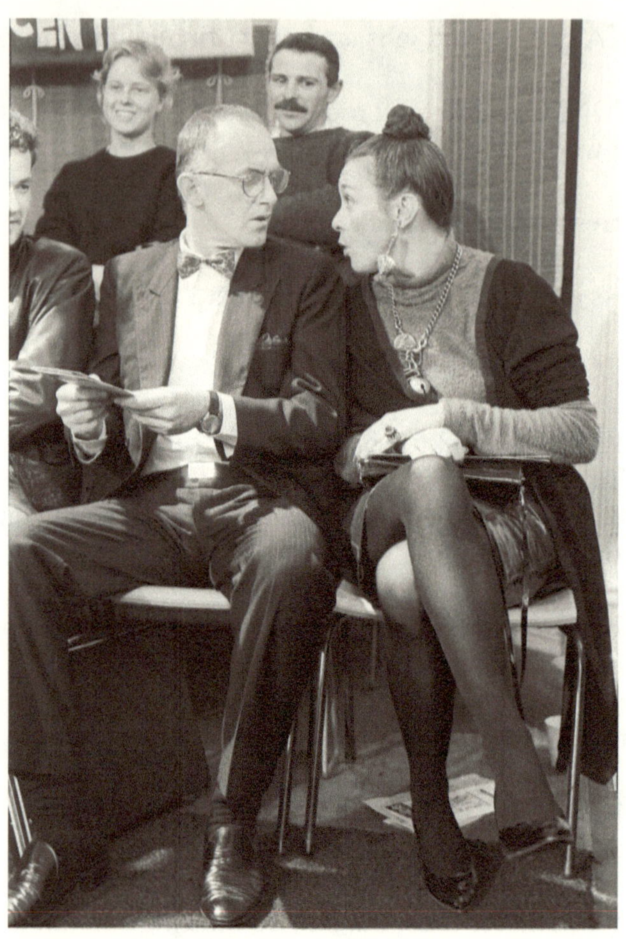

MONIKA. See, it's not just me, Leon. S/he couldn't do it either.

LEON. (in exasperation) Then it's buggered isn't it.

Annoyed, she changes position in her seat, in a huff, re-crossing her legs. LEON for his part is becoming quite impatient.

LEON. (snorts) This place hasn't got its act together at all, I mean, look - (indicating "St. Kilda Breakfast") look at that. The staff here haven't even cleaned up their lunch ! What do they think it is - bush week or something ?

MONIKA is amazed at his ignorance.

>MONIKA. Leon! That's a highly regarded installation
>by Arnold King.

>LEON. (gobsmacked) Installation !?

>MONIKA. Yes, a kind of … frozen performance art
>piece. It is to this play probably what a. . . a still frame
>is to a movie.

>LEON. You mean - people actually pay money for that
>?

He gets up to take a closer look. She follows. Equally curious.

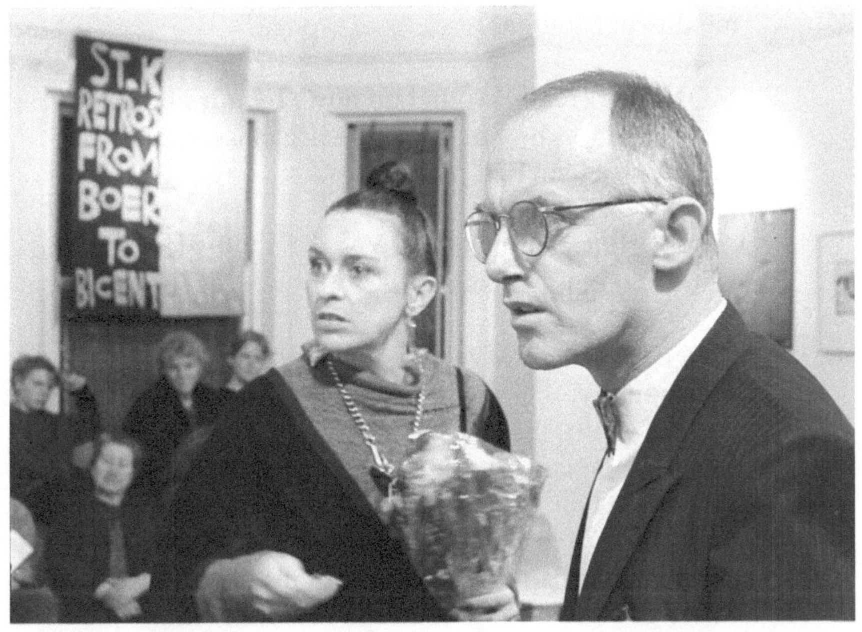

>MONIKA. (dismissively) Only a few thousand dollars.

LEON is aghast.

>LEON. For a mess? … on a table top ?

MONIKA. Well yes, I suppose the mess, yes. (condescending) *And* the way the chair's arranged, the slight angle of the table, the… the…(considering it) level of milk in the muesli bowl, there are an infinite number of variables. It could take Arnold literally hours to produce something like that !

LEON. God! And you think a poor old freelance town planner like me gets paid too much!

MONIKA. It's meant to look like that, Leon, That's the *whole point* ! It's a metaphor … it … it … signifies something of the turbulent social dislocation and ingrained nonchalance of St. Kilda in the late 1980s.

LEON. (objecting to the tone). You don't have to put me down, Monika.

MONIKA. (really wound up now) I *know* about art, Leon. That's why I'm doing the life classes at TAFE. That's why I studied pottery.

LEON. (that reminds him) Yes, a $3,000 electric kiln I paid for and it just sits there.

MONIKA. (defensive) We make pizzas in it occasionally.

LEON. You can't *buy* creativity, Monika.

MONIKA. You admitted yourself that it made a very good Pridikin alternative to those usual old, oil-riddled office BBQs your office keeps inflicting on people.

LEON. Look, Monika, admit it ! This infatuation of yours with expensive courses in cultural toy-making is a not very subtle attempt to blackmail me.

MONIKA. If bureaucrats like you did a little more expanding of your personal horizons, Leon, St. Kilda wouldn't be in the mess it's in today.

LEON. I don't think St. Kilda's in a mess. It's an inner-city real estate opportunity undergoing some pretty exciting social and demographic changes.

MONIKA. Forgodsake, one of your companies has just torn down Luna Park! A absolutely vital local icon.

He thinks that's entirely justified.

LEON. Well, we're going to build a giant waterslide.

MONIKA. And you think that's progress!?

LEON. It'll be solar heated.

MONIKA. Hoh !

LEON. Plus it'll hold 17 times the number of people Luna Park ever did. The timber in that big dipper was rotten to the core. It was a danger to the public.

MONIKA. Your waterslide, Leon, is quite possibly the ugliest thing I've ever seen on a drawing board.

LEON. I can't win, can I ?

MONIKA. It's clear to me now that you have absolutely *no* concept of beauty at all because you know absolutely nothing about ART !

LEON. Oh yeah ?

He cranes his neck around and looks up at the abstract painting immediately above his head.

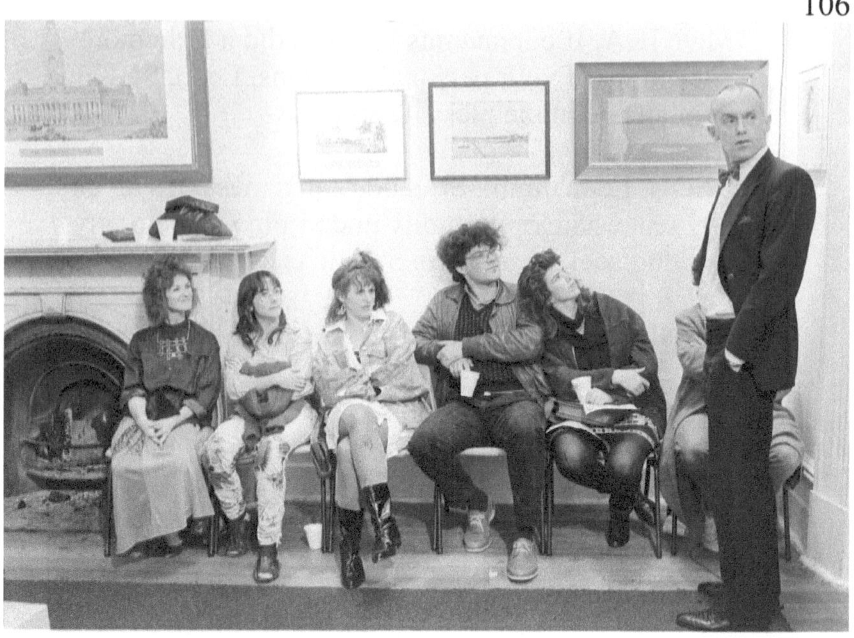

LEON. Well I know that painting's upside down.

He's bends down, peering up at it from an odd angle.

MONIKA. Well, *you're* upside down aren't you ?

Still bent over LEON swings back to face her.

LEON. Wha…?

MONIKA. I mean, look at you.

He realises he *is* upside down, straightens back up and glances at his watch, folds his arms, uneasy.

LEON. This is really pretty exciting, Monika, do we just stand here and get bored to death or what ?

MONIKA. (exasperated) Don't you ever feel the urge to lash out occasionally and plunge into the unknown. ?

LEON. I mean, she said they were going to do their performance business in here. Do we have to make an appointment. ?

MONIKA. (rounding on him) It's a location theatre piece, Leon, almost anything can happen !

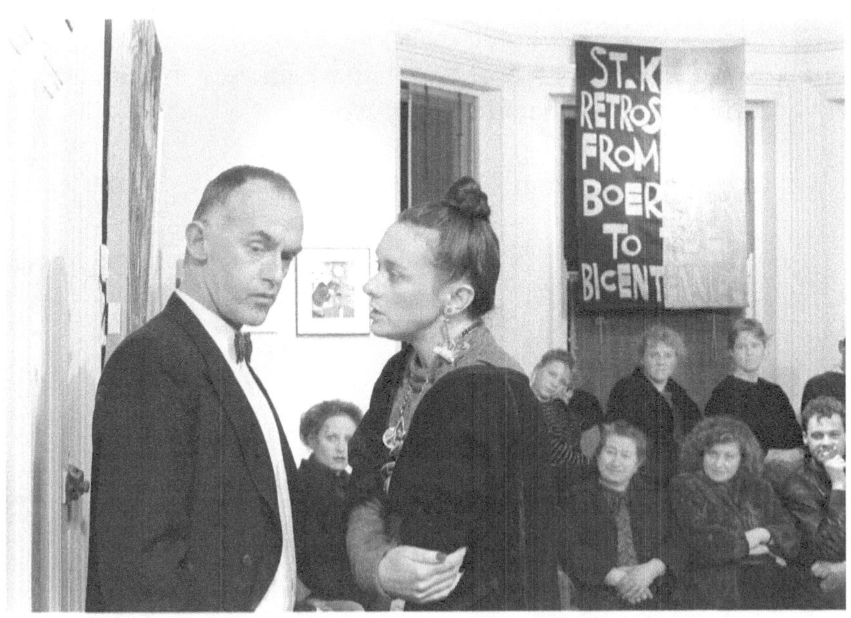

LEON. (completely unenthused) Oh great.

MONIKA again holds her glasses out again in order to read the programme.

MONIKA. We're going to (quotes) "witness an exhibition of dramatic scenes in which several rooms of an old St.Kilda mansion actually come to life." (frowns as she reads on) "Warning to parents, the performance contains language and incidents which may seriously offend…

LEON. (droll) Oh well- that might be interesting.

MONIKA. (putting her programme away) Personally I find most language offensive these days…

MIRIAM comes back in and goes up to the "THEN" end of the room and quickly disappears behind the screen to change into the maid's costume to play the "MARTHA" character from the Drawing Room. MONIKA notices this but LEON is looking the other way - towards the "St.Kilda breakfast installation, still shaking his head at the absurdity.

LEON. Geeze, some people have an easy life. Please themselves when they start work.

MONIKA is nudging him,

LEON. I'd like to see some of these arty types get a real job.

MONIKA. Shh, Leon.

Leon turns back and notices a head behind the screen.

LEON. Hey there's someone now.

MONIKA. Shh- Leon, she's probably one of the cast.

LEON. Why don't you ask her?

MONIKA. What?

LEON. About the button…

MONIKA. No- Leon, this is obviously part of the show now.

LEON. (skeptical) Part of the show ? She's just treating the place like a bloody dressing room.

MONIKA. Oh, be quiet forgodsake!

LEON. Ask her what's happening.

MONIKA. No.

LEON. Go on.

MONIKA. (emphatic) NO !

LEON. We could be stuck here all night.

"MIRIAM" has changed into "MARTHA" now, and comes round from behind the screen with the MIRIAM costume over her arm. She gets a member of the audience to help her adjust the Victorian bonnet on top of her hair.

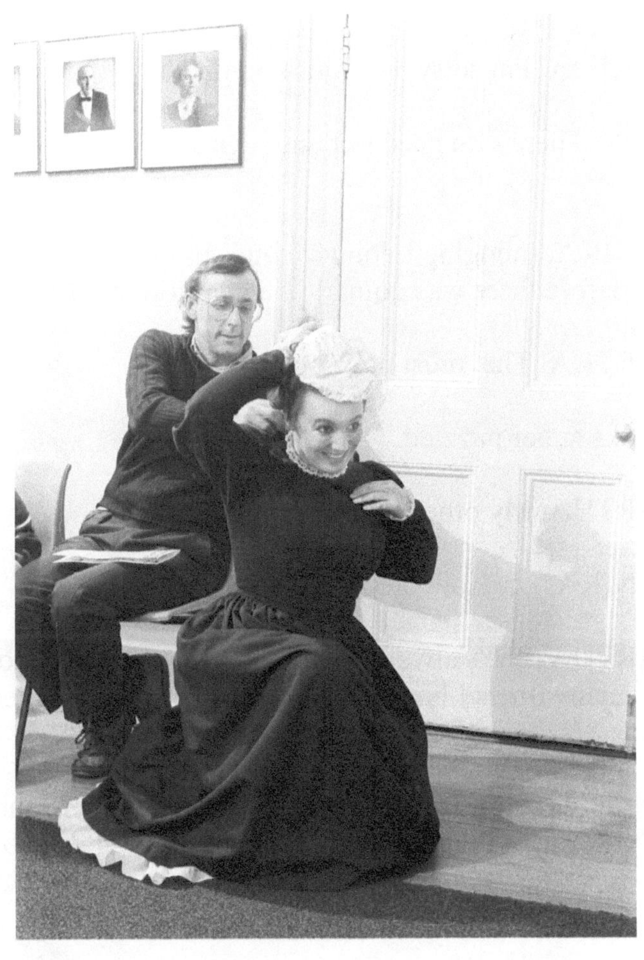

LEON. See- she's not even staying…

This prompts Monika to action.

MONIKA. Excuse me, dear, are you involved with the er… "exhibition"?

MARTHA. (briefly, deferential, in 1900 servant mode) Yes, ma'am.

MONIKA. (not quite sure how to put it) Look, dear, our room doesn't seem to be working.

LEON. Yeah, could we have another one please ?

MARTHA. I'm sorry, sir, I'm running late for my cue.

LEON. There's no need to bung on a servile act for us love.

MONIKA. (nudging Leon to "shut-up") It's just that you said before there was going to be a performance in here.

MARTHA. That must have been "Miriam".

MONIKA looks at her puzzled.

MARTHA. My other character.

MONIKA. Oh…of course.

MARTHA. She's always getting it wrong. I don't know how many times I have to tell her - this is just a gallery space.

LEON makes "lu lu" signs at MONIKA, twirling a finger round his temple. MONIKA tries to ignore him. She nods politely at MARTHA.

MARTHA. We'll try and get you through to one of the other "living rooms" as soon as we can.

MONIKA. (deeply grateful) Oh - thank you ever so much.

LEON. So we just sit here and wait, do we ?

MARTHA. Oh it'll come to you eventually - or…you'll come to it.

LEON (turning back to MONIKA) I can't understand a bloody word she's saying.

MONIKA. Quiet ! Leon

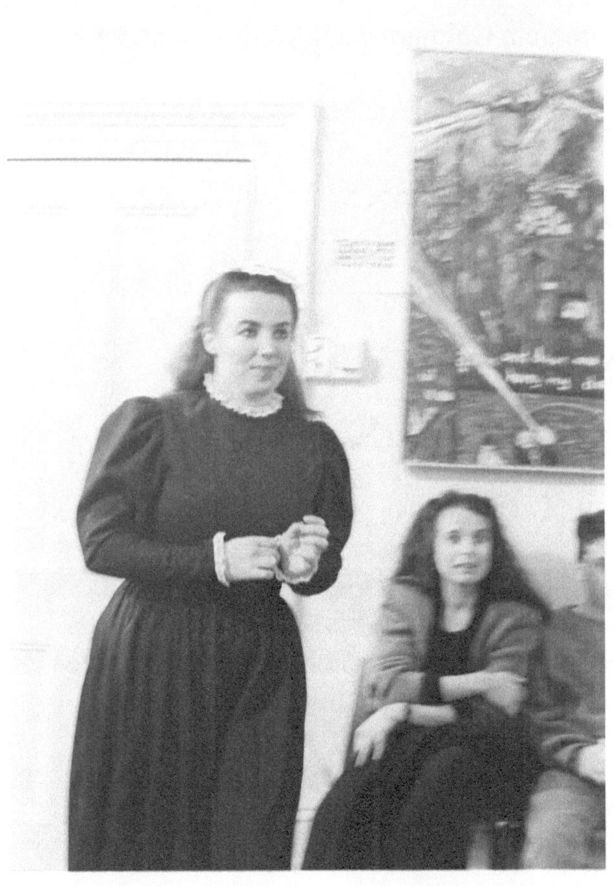

> MARTHA. Why don't you take in the *objets d'art* while
> you're waiting. . .

But in indicating the paintings and exhibits around the room she notices something odd about the painting above Leon's head. As MONIKA babbles on…

> MONIKA. Oh yes, quite, the *objets d'art*. You know,
> sometimes I almost think the whole concept, the very
> *idea* of St. Kilda is an Art *Objet* in itself: the people, the
> buildings - an expressive communal entity.

MARTHA steps up on Leon's chair and quickly turns the abstract painting the right way up.

> MARTHA. Sorry about that, some of our backstage
> staff are on a Commonwealth Employment Grant.

> LEON. (smug, nudging Monika back) See - I told you.

> MONIKA. I suppose even a stopped clock is right once
> a day.

> LEON. Twice.

> MONIKA. What?

> LEON. Twice a day. Once every twelve hours.

> MONIKA. Unless its digital.

MARTHA hangs by the open door.

> MARTHA. Why don't you hire an audio guide - that
> should help you pass the time.

She's indicating a box of headphones and cassette players near the door)

MONIKA. (turning back to him, suddenly enthusiased) Oh, that sounds exciting, Leon.

MARTHA seizes her chance and is gone.

MONIKA. Well, chuckkers then…

She swings back to wish MARTHA farewell.

MONIKA. Break a leg!

But Martha is nowhere to be seen.

LEON. That wasn't a very nice thing to say - "break a leg". We'll never see her again.

MONIKA gets up and goes over to examine the box of headphones.

MONIKA. It's an old theatrical expression.

LEON. Why don't you just say "good luck".

MONIKA. You never say "good luck" in the theatre. It's very bad luck to say "good luck" to an actor. Like "Macbeth". You never say "Macbeth" out loud in theatrical circles. You always call it the "*Scottish Play*".

LEON. Oh well, excuse me, I only know when a painting's upside down.

As MONIKA checks the cash box for audio players and headphones, LEON notices the price.

LEON. God, $5! What a rip-off.

MONIKA. (rummaging in her purse) My shout.

LEON. (searching for his wallet) No, no, I'll pay for it.

MONIKA. I insist.

LEON. I won't let you.

MONIKA. Don't *patronise* me, Leon, please.

LEON. I wasn't *patronising* you. I just happen to earn 8 times what you do that's all.

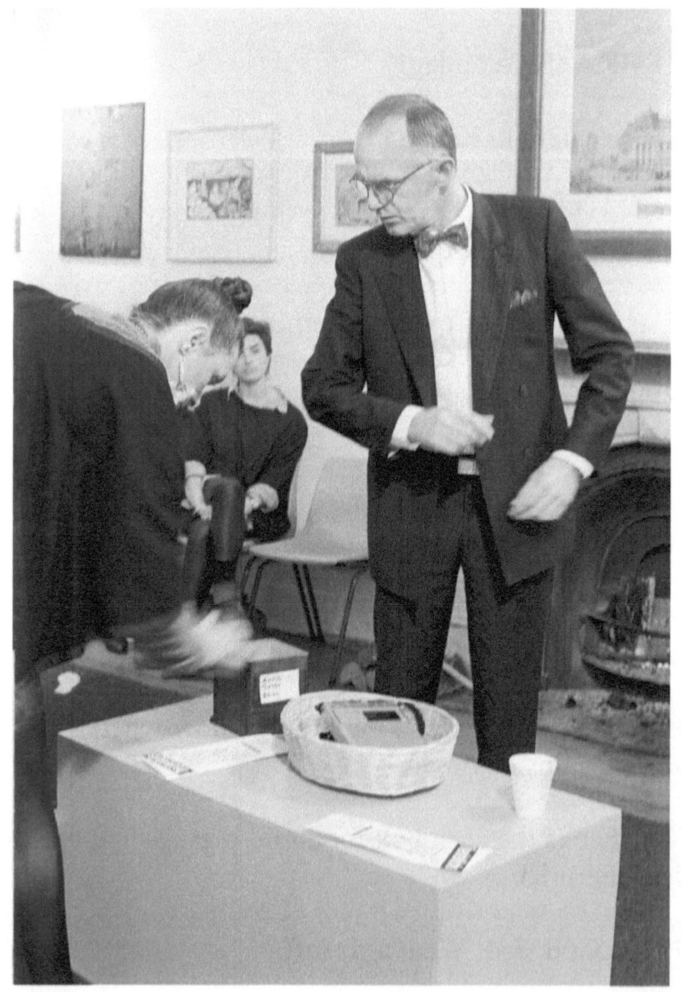

He chucks a lazy $5 note into the box, she takes it out and replaces it with her own.

MONIKA. Oh don't be ridiculous.

So he reluctantly pockets his money, and they struggle into two sets
of headphones joined to the same audio player; which she carries. But the
wires are, like their deteriorating marriage, all tangled up. They never do
quite get it properly sorted out.

Nevertheless, determined, MONIKA takes the opportunity to actually
absorb some of the artwork.

> MONIKA. (glancing round) Pity they changed it into a
> Gallery really. I always thought this old place was much
> more authentic as a seedy boarding house. Real sixties
> grot is so engaging don't you think ? Brick cladding…
> and mini skirts, and platform soles and early Beatles…

> LEON. Oh, yeah, "the early Beatles" I've heard of them
> - they're the ones who get up before the early birds.

She rolls her eyes at this crude attempt at humour, presses the button to
start the tape. We hear it as a voice coming through speakers.

> TAPE (voice over). Welcome to "Walking in St. Kilda-
> Then and Now" a pleasant stroll through the city's glory
> years from the Boer War to our present Bicentennial. A
> special Ministry of Culture presentation. When you hear
> the chimes sound move over to the great big green
> coloured painting in the middle of the room and place
> both feet on footsteps one and two.

The CHIMES play on the tape and bear a distinct similarity to the chimes
heard earlier out in the Hallway.

LEON really chafes at the patronising, almost playschool-like attitude of
the voice on the tape. They're the only ones on their feet. Following the
guide.

> LEON. (glancing uncomfortably around). I feel like a
> real dill standing up here.

> MONIKA. Shh. Leon.

They stand dutifully in front of a large oil painting side by side. She's determined to enjoy herself, takes his hand in hers, he frowns a bit at this but doesn't overtly resist.

ABORIGINAL MUSIC (didgeridoo and sticks) fades up on the tape.

> TAPE (voice over). Originally called "Euroyioke" by the Wurundgeri or Yarra tribe, St. Kilda was built on a hill in imitation of Cannes and other famous mediterranean resorts and was always regarded as a special, almost "magical" place by both Europeans and Aborigines alike.

Now BUS NOISES fade up on the tape.

> TAPE (voice over). In the 1920s, with the coming of buses, the hill was found to be resonant.

> MONIKA. Gee, I wonder if that means there's a big cave under it?

> LEON. I'd like to tunnel down there, rig up a few batteries, put some fluoros in…a bar fridge in one corner…

She disengages their hands.

> MONIKA. Yes. You're like a mole aren't you ? With your head almost permanently buried in the ground.

> LEON. That's an ostrich.

She SIGHS, exasperated.

> LEON. Tell you what though, it'd make a fantastic little fallout shelter.

> MONIKA. War. Is that all you can think about ?

LEON. It's only *the* most crucial global issue of our time, Monika.

MONIKA. You're obsessed aren't you ? I'm sure it all starts with those little boys games you play using sticks for rifles and prancing about thinking you're king of the castle.

LEON. Everybody imagines World War III will be over in a flash, right ? A big nuclear holocaust. Bang - that's it. But they're wrong. It's already started. World War III is going on all over the place right this very moment. A little car bomb here, another terrorist outrage there, a pre-eminent strike over beyond that way…Nobody adds it up for what it really is.

MONIKA. (impatient with his drift, shaking her head, sighing) Sorry, I don't see much point to any of this…

LEON. (insisting) I *really* think we should *seriously* consider building a nuclear fallout shelter.

MONIKA. Oh don't be ridiculous.

LEON. Everyone in Switzerland's got one. Everyone in Israel.

MONIKA. And where, pray, are you proposing to put this monstrosity?

LEON. (simply) Under the kitchen.

MONIKA. I don't believe I'm hearing this.

LEON. Ok - so the bomb doesn't go off - great! We can celebrate in our own little wine cellar. Cool, dark, excellent for keeping reds.

MONIKA. And you complain about the cost of my electric kiln?

LEON. I'm talking about our survival after the next half dozen nuclear reactors blow their stack !

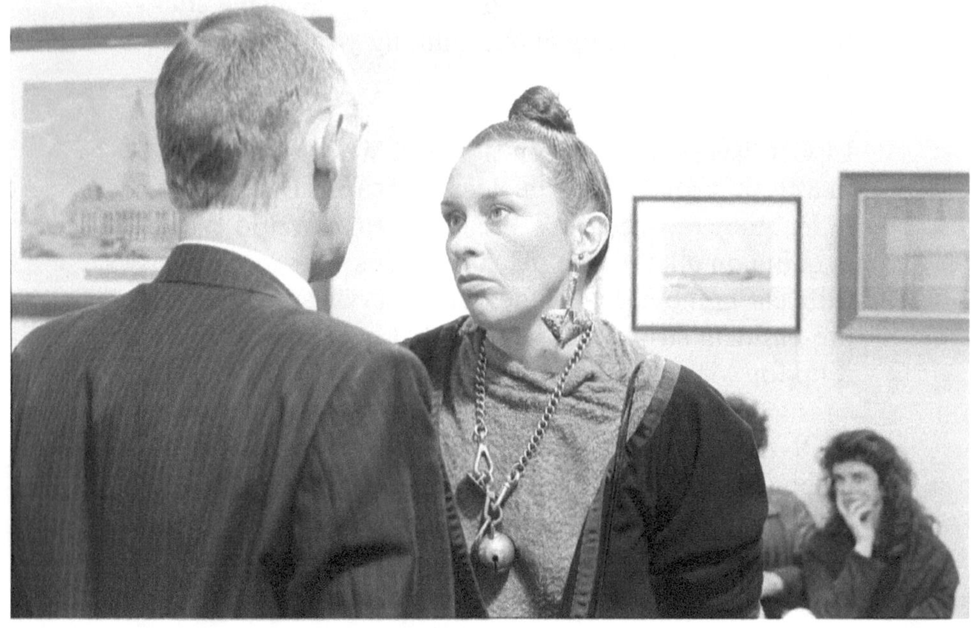

MONIKA. I'm afraid I don't care much for a future I have to share with mutants and cockroaches.

LEON. So - you'd rather be vapourised in the first flash would you ?

MONIKA. You're not building a nuclear fallout shelter and that's final!

And it certainly sounds like it.

LEON. Well I want one.

MONIKA. Over my dead body.

LEON. (mock conciliating) Well that's precisely what it will be if you keep resisting it.

MONIKA. No No No No No.

LEON. I'll let you in after the five minute warning goes
off.

MONIKA. It's not happening Leon, drop it, Now.

LEON. It's my house too, you know

MONIKA. Registered in my name

LEON. I'll do it next time you're in Paris and you won't
even know.

MONIKA. If you keep this up I'm going to walk out
now and I may not even come back from Paris.

LEON. But you can actually *save* yourself. That's the
really incredible thing. You can dig like they did in
every other war and ride the bastard out somehow.
(slight pause). That's my response to the late 1980s.

MONIKA. And a particularly depressing attitude if I do
say so myself.

LEON. It's real, though, isn't it ?

MONIKA. If we all thought like that there'd be no point
trying to stop war.

She snaps on the tape again. He sighs, gives up.

TAPE (voice over). The painting before you is the
earliest recorded image of the St.Kilda area captured by
the Europeans. It shows the track that
later became Fitzroy Street.

They're looking at a semi-rural and somewhat idyllic scene with a row of
crude dwellings along one side of the track and broad paddocks sweeping
away on the other side.

MONIKA considers the painting with the true ritual gestures of the inveterate poseur.

> MONIKA. Yes - it does have a certain sort of …Conrad Martins-y feel about it. Don't you think ? The landscape isn't quite real. Not Australian looking at all. The trees are positively English.

> TAPE. (voice over) Move to footsteps three and four.

Again the CHIMES sound on the tape deck as MONIKA. and LEON stroll across to the relevant footsteps painted on the floor. (Her walk, like her poses in front of various art works are quite…unique.

> TAPE. (voice over). You are now facing a black and white photograph entitled "*Praying To St.Kilda For A Tram.*" December 1st 1972.

MONIKA leans in towards the photograph.

> MONIKA. Am I?

She is still a little blind without her glasses and strains to take it all in. And seems quite unsure about the significance of the title.

LEON screws up his face at the photograph.

It shows PAUL BORDER, the character we've just seen in the Flatette scene, bending over at the tram stop outside Luna Park. It looks a lot like he's dry retching onto the roadway while grasping an adjacent tramways clock for support.

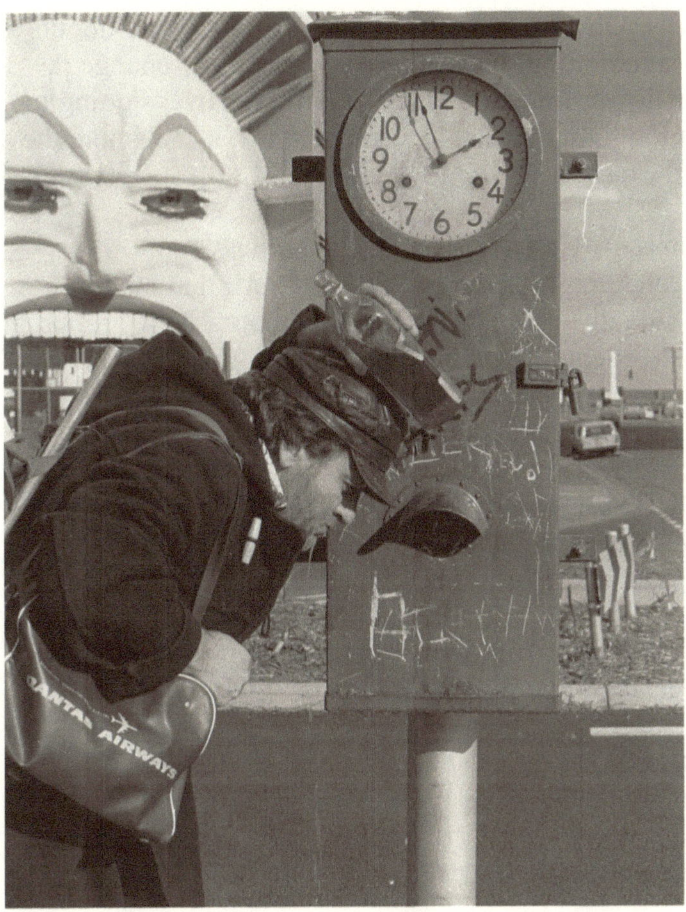

LEON. Praying! (scoffs) He's not praying. He's unloading his Big Mac all over the clock !

TAPE. (voice over) The image shows a typical St.Kilda resident of the early nineteen seventies making his way home after a large political rally in the Town Hall.

LEON Why anyone'd be interested in this rubbish beats me.,

MONIKA. It's a crucial social record, can't you appreciate that ? Once you and your bull-dozers have finished building Surfers Paradise here it's going to be the only memory we've got of the place.

LEON. Oh - we can tart it up with a few round-abouts and a lick of paint, but basically, we won't really change it, deep down. I mean, face it. St. Kilda's always going to be a red light district. Doesn't matter if it looks like the Gold Coast, it's rooted to start with.

MONIKA. How can you be so heartless - so, so…uncaring. It's the community spirit that makes St.Kilda different… the way neighbours stand around in the street chatting to each other for hours. .

LEON. Oh yeah, about what ?

MONIKA. About their…different burglaries, a recent bashing they might have witnessed, or the latest smash and grab at the local chemist shop.

LEON. Yeah, well, you didn't get that sort of thing back in our old home in Glen Iris, thank god.

MONIKA. (explodes) That's because Glen Iris is possibly the most boring suburb on earth !

MONIKA snaps the tape back on.

TAPE. (voice over) Throughout its colourful history St.Kilda has always
attracted transients, "characters", criminals and artists.

LEON. Hoh! What 's the difference.

TAPE. (voice over) "Praying To St.Kilda For A Tram" is the work of local lens-person, Miriam Sanderson who worked as a cleaner in several St.Kilda boarding houses while quietly compiling a striking visual record of the hobos and petty gangsters who inhabited the bayside city in the early 1970s. When this photo was taken St. Kilda had descended into a dysfunctional slum, its former family mansions converted into crumbling boarding houses and its seedy backstreets - the rubbish strewn sites where locals lived their drab grey lives in tattered overcoats. While Fitzroy Street never really improved Acland Street did undergo a modest gentrification at the beginning of the 1980s so that the city's major thoroughfares soon became as different as night and day.

LEON. (stabbing a finger at the tram stop photo) I mean, look, look at him with his duffle coat and travel bag. (snorts) Qantas Airways ! He's going nowhere. Fast.

MONIKA. Your prejudice is just ignorance, Leon.

LEON. (sulkily) Well you said you wanted to know how I felt about things.

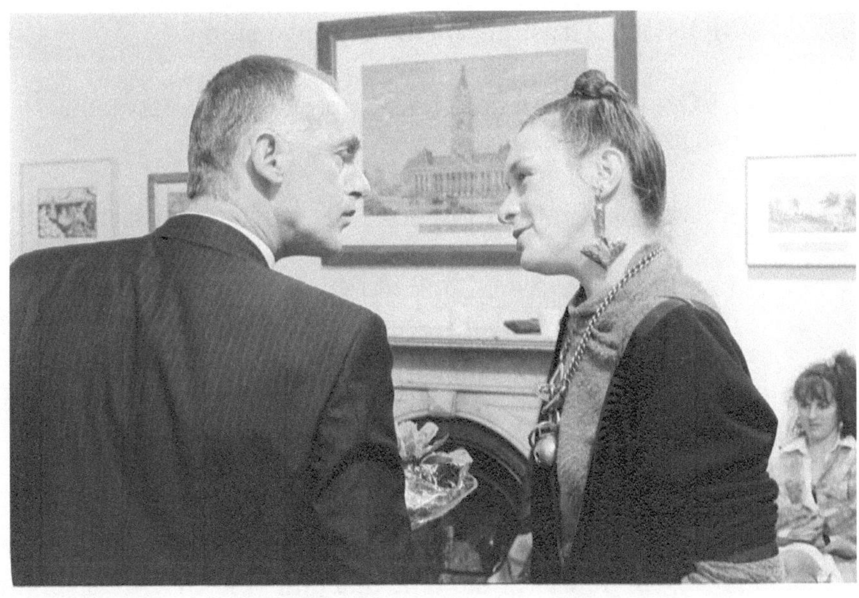

MONIKA. You know, you strike me as the sort of person who'd memorise all the Trivial Pursuit questions just so you could win something.

LEON. (defensive) I found them very educational.,

MONIKA. (shocked) You *did* read them !

LEON. Only a couple of times.

She gives up.

MONIKA. Wind the tape back.

LEON. What ?

MONIKA. (curtly) I missed the last bit, would you
wind it back please.

LEON frowns at the device.

LEON. There doesn't seem to be any rewind button on
this thing.

MONIKA. (frustrated) Oh that's just stupid !

LEON. I suppose they figure people might cheat and
use it twice or something.

She lets out an exasperated sigh, takes the tape and presses "play" again.

TAPE. (voice over) Look, do you want to go on with
this, or would you rather have your domestic in private.

MONIKA and LEON react. They look around. Where did that come
from?

MONIKA. Who said that ?

LEON glances anxiously at the tape machine, the CHIMES sound again
and the voice resumes its normal, neutral tone as if nothing had happened.

TAPE. (voice over) Move over to footsteps 5 and 6

Tentatively they do so.

TAPE. (voice over) The next painting entitled "Agent Orange Sunset " depjcts the rear end of the famous Palais Theatre with various palm trees rendered to look like the mushroom clouds that follow a nuclear explosion.

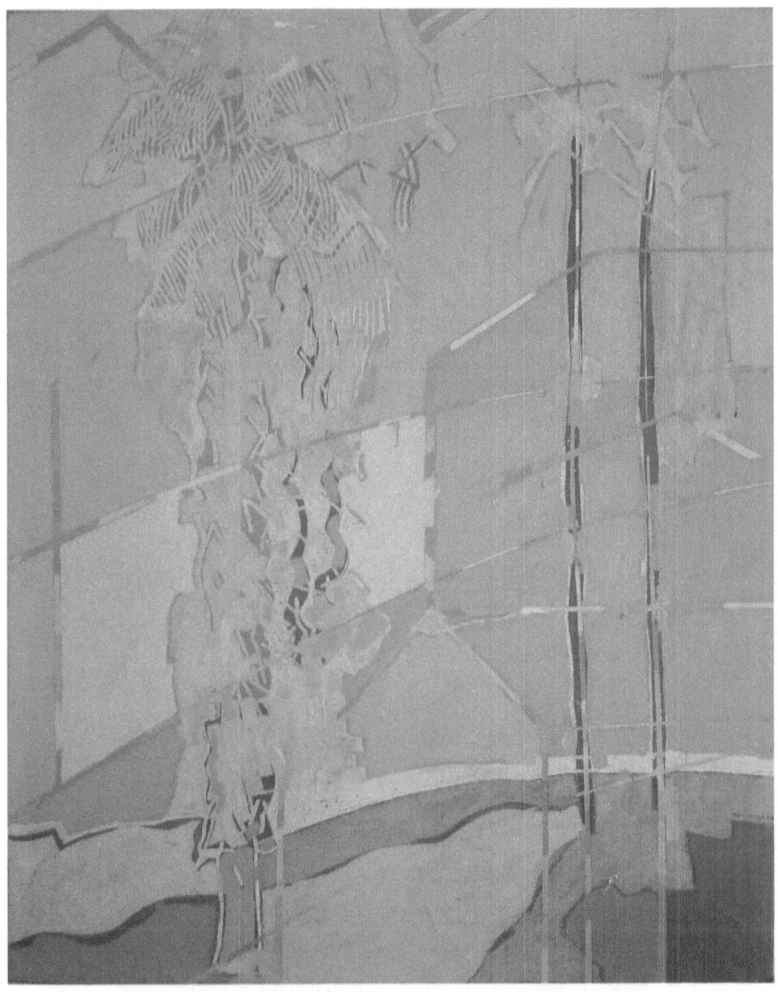

LEON. Gawd, our three year old could've painted that.

MONIKA. Look, Leon, I asked you to come here because I wanted to engage you in my world

LEON. (non-comprehending) You're a family therapist fercrissake!

MONIKA. That doesn't mean I can't be inspired in my work by art, and consoled by it in my personal life, I can also possess it if I want to. I work very hard for what I earn, I need some compensations.

LEON. Oh so - art's a humanising force is it ? That's interesting, Hitler was a painter did you know that ?

MONIKA. (pointedly at Leon) Hitler was an architect.

LEON. He failed his finals.

MONIKA. He wasn't such a hot shot on the forward planning side of things either.

LEON. Alright, I'll shut—up then.

There's a tense pause.

MONIKA. I brought you here so we could talk.

LEON. About your world.

MONIKA. About us!

LEON. (sighs) Here we go…

MONIKA. About "we" as a couple, the "you" and "me" of it. About our relationship.

LEON. We haven't got one - it doesn't exist.

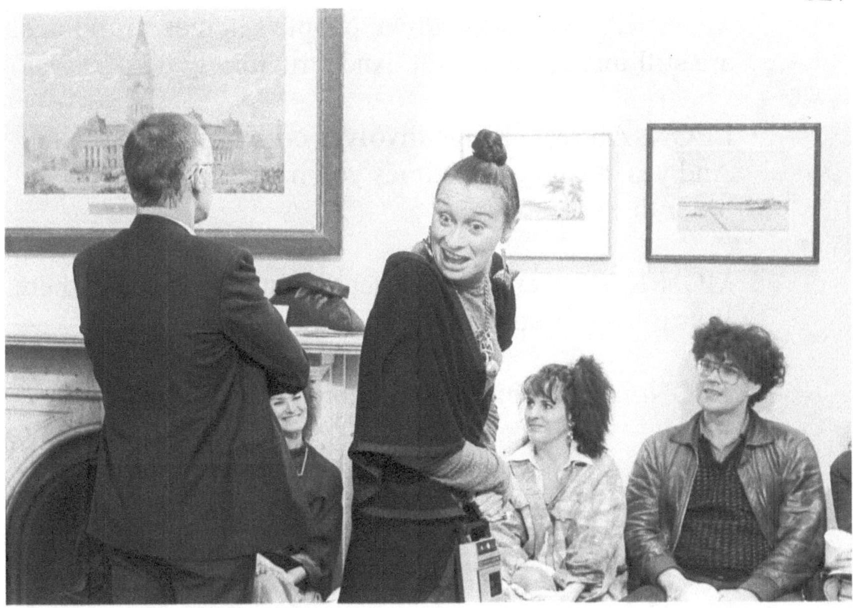

MONIKA. Oh that's just great. That's just 10 years together down the drain is it ?

LEON. Look - I'm just an ordinary old GPS guy who grew up in the eastern suburbs and went to Melbourne Uni and made a reasonable go of creating exciting new spaces for people to live in; and to be perfectly frank I don't feel comfortable residing in St. Kilda. I never wanted to move here in the first place.

MONIKA. Forgodsake ! You're one of the people who are completely changing it ! And you don't even like the place!

LEON. Whoever said you had to like your work?.

MONIKA. Don't you see ! That's what's wrong with you. You're destroying this place because deep down you have absolutely no feeling for it.

LEON. We're creating more parks - more open space

MONIKA. By tearing down people's homes. Buildings that are still incredibly useful. And structurally okay.

LEON. All real change involves compromise, Monika. And yes, alright, sometimes you have to destroy in order to create.

MONIKA. I seem to have heard that before somewhere. Was it Mein Kampf?

LEON. Is there any point in going on with this ?

MONIKA. You never want to talk about it, do you ? Men are all the same. Never discuss what's really going on in that pump they call a heart.

LEON. Look, I *did* want to come here tonight.

MONIKA. Good.

LEON. Obviously we have to talk about it.

MONIKA. Well, *that's* progress.

LEON. So, I'm glad I came, alright ?

MONIKA. Fine.

LEON. And deep down I *do* like you.

MONIKA. Don't strain yourself.

LEON. As a matter of fact I… (reaches down into his expensive leather briefcase) I bought these for you …

He pulls out the most magnificent bunch of roses.

She's genuinely touched. Doesn't quite know what to say.

LEON. (holding them out, sheepish) I…got them on the way home from work.

The anger vanishes. She takes them.

LEON, You haven't forgotten have you ?

MONIKA. What ?

LEON. (slightly hurt) You *have* forgotten,

MONIKA. What ?

LEON. The 26th of January?

MONIKA. Invasion Day?

He slumps further, then it hits her.

MONIKA. Our anniversary ! Oh Leon I'm so sorry…
How could I forget?

LEON. Pretty easily by the sound of it.

MONIKA. Well we haven't celebrated it for a long
time.

LEON. Can you believe it's ten years already ? Since
we first shacked up together?

An awkward pause. He puts his hands in his pockets. Looks down.

LEON. And we never got married so…

MONIKA. That's very sweet of you.

She sniffs them.

MONIKA. They smell lovely !

LEON. (snorts) They ought to they cost the bloody earth !

She smiles.

He holds up the tape recorder questioningly?

She nods.

He presses it on.

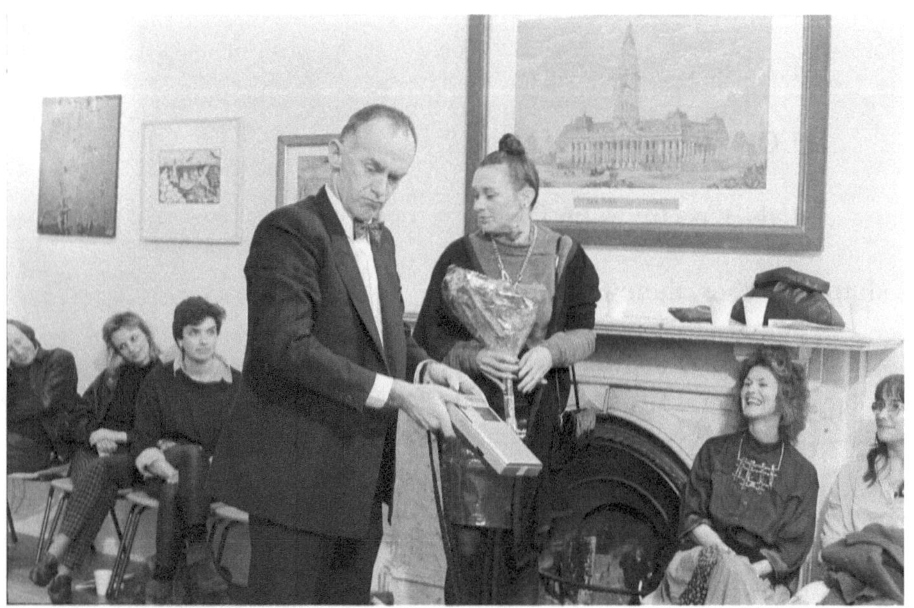

TAPE. (voice over) Move over to footsteps 7 and 8.

Again the CHIMES SOUND

TAPE. (voice over) The next personality in our little walking history - if you can be bothered to listen - is Dr. Cuthbert Beaumgardiner who bought this house for his mistress, Estelle Lawson, in 1895.

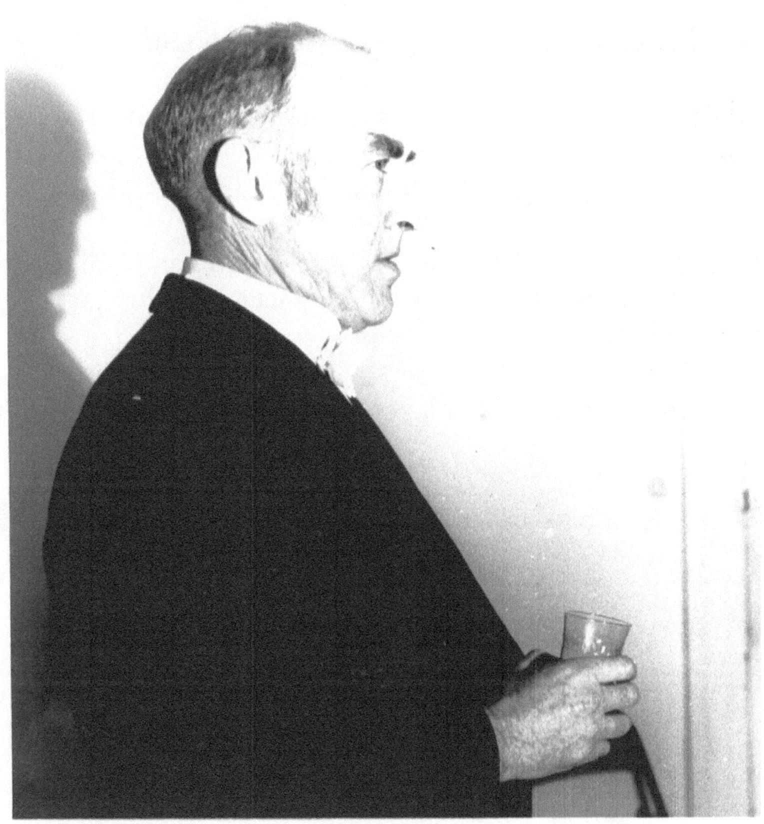

TAPE. (voice over) Because of a strange scandal associated with this relationship, the house also became known as "Beaumgardiner's Folly." He is typical of the self-made merchant classes who built St. Kilda in the 1880s, when the centre of Melbourne was not regarded as a fit place to live. Indeed records show that the central business district was never quite free of the smell of human or equine excrement

MONIKA has become increasingly fidgety.

MONIKA. I don't think I need to hear much more of this.

She goes to switch it off.

TAPE. (voice over) Please don't do that.

MONIKA. (looking around again) Who said that ?

TAPE. (voice over) I did - please don't switch me off.

The TAPE has become tired and emotional sounding.

TAPE. (voice over) Do you realise how dull and tedious it is reading off these dry historical facts day after day, hour after hour ?

LEON is examining the cassette player, turning it over, jabbing at the stop button.

LEON. It won't seem to go off. Is this some kind of joke ?

TAPE. (voice over) All the time - the same ridiculous conclusion: "St. Kilda was originally settled because of the shit elsewhere. quote, unquote.

Finally Leon unplugs his headphone, the voice stops.

LEON. Just what the hell is going on here ?

MONIKA frowns at the bunch of flowers Leon had given her. Sniffs them again.

MONIKA. (reacts, shocked) These roses are plastic !

LEON (quickly examining them, as surprised as she is) What ?

MONIKA. (with dawning awareness) Perhaps … this is it, Leon, perhaps the show has already started.

He glances quickly round, they are still the only ones on their feet.

LEON. You mean - *we're* the show !?

The lights begin to flick on and off wildly.

LEON rips off his headphones and slams them down into the floor.

LEON. Well stuff that for a joke !

There's an instant BLACKOUT. The Gallery, is suddenly plunged into darkness.

MONIKA. (voice over)Now look what you've done.

LEON. (voice over, uncertain, wavering - like a kid
caught in the act) I didn't do anything.

The Hallway door CREAKS open quickly and CUTHBERT is instantly framed there, silhouetted against the light in the Hallway.

CUTHBERT. (voice over) Estelle ? Is that you ?

He swings the door shut behind him and comes fully into the Gallery making the room completely dark again.

CUTHBERT softly approaches MONIKA from behind. Lovingly rapping his arms around her, mistaking her for ESTELLE.

CUTHBERT. (voice over) I thought you were hiding
from me,

LEON. (voice over) Who is this ?

MONIKA (voice over - mistaking CUTHBERT for
LEON) Leon - don't … please.

There's the sound of a passionate embrace.

MONIKA. (voice over - reels back gasping for air)
What do you think you're doing?

CUTHBERT. (voice over) Cherie, I was so worried when I couldn't, find you at the party. May I…kiss you…my love…

MONIKA. (voice over) Leon - Your breath - it stinks.

LEON. (voice over) There's nothing wrong with *my* breath.

In the darkness CUTHBERT pulls up short. Now *he's* confused

CUTHBERT (voice over) Eh ?

MONIKA. (voice over - pulling herself free) Good God ! What have you been drinking?

CUTHBERT. (voice over) Rather cheap Portuguese sherry I'm afraid.

MONIKA. (voice over) Leon - who is this speaking ?

CUTHBERT. (voice over) Who's Leon ?

LEON. (voice over) I never kissed you.

MONIKA. (voice over) Well somebody did.

CUTHBERT. (voice over) Look, I apologise for the sherry but it's partly your fault, my dear, I did warn you not to serve it.

LEON. (voice over) Who the hell is that?

MONIKA. (voice over) Would you please get your hands off me.

LEON (voice over) I haven't touched you! Nor since the lights went out.

CUTHBERT (voice over - puzzled) Estelle ?

> MONIKA. (voice over) Who's Estelle ?

CUTHBERT realises his mistake.

> CUTHBERT. (voice over) Madam, I do so humbly beg your pardon.

> LEON. (voice over) Who *is* that speaking, please

> CUTHBERT. (voice over) I'm most frightfully sorry.

> LEON. (voice over - alert, and threatening) Listen, pal, get your grubby mitts off my wife.

> MONIKA. (voice over) De facto

In the darkness LEON hits CUMBERT. There's the sound of the two men struggling.

> LEON. (voice over) How dare you,!.

> CUTHBERT (voice over groan of pain) Ow !

CUTHBERT is sweating, but contains himself)

> CUTHBERT. (voice over) I was under the mistaken apprehension that you were my mistress.

> MONIKA. (voice over) I beg your pardon ?

> LEON. (voice over) Stop feeling her up you pervert !

> CUTHBERT. (voice over) It was thoroughly unconscionable of me.

LEON and CUTHBERT continue to thump into each other. There's the sound of people being hit. LEON goes to punch CUTHBERT, just as MONIKA swings her handbag wildly and hits LEON by mistake

LEON. (voice over) Monika that's me

CUTHBERT (voice over) Ogh, Ough, Ah, Gopf…

CUTHBERT doubles over clutching his stomach and staggers back out into the Hallway, a mass of bruises and strangled oaths, He slams the door shut behind him and, just as mysteriously, the LIGHTS come on again.

MONIKA. straightens herself up. Smoothing out her clothes.

LEON stares malevolently at an amused, MALE MEMBER of the audience.

LEON. Oh - big joke, eh ? You think it's funny assaulting my de facto wife?

MONIKA. Leon- it wasn't him.

LEON steps back angrily tearing off his coat, flinging it down. The further away he gets the more aggressive the stance.

LEON. Check his breath .

MONIKA. Are you serious.

LEON. I'm going to lay charges.

MONIKA. It can't be him.

LEON. Why not ?

MONIKA. His hands are too small.

LEON throws a contemptuous look at the suspect audience member and eases his knuckles out of their tight fist. But soon seizes on the bloke next to him.

LEON. Well was it *him* then ?

MONIKA. How should I know!? It was pitch black. I had headphones on.

LEON. There's something pretty weird going on here. Are you sure this place is kosher.

MONIKA. It was originally built by a very devout Jewish family.

LEON. (losing his patience) No, since then, I mean is it a knock shop ?

MONIKA. I beg your pardon ?

LEON. This is St. Kilda after all.

MONIKA. (gobsmacked) What?

LEON. You said it had 18 bedrooms.

MONIKA. So ?

LEON. So - massage parlours come in some pretty strange shapes these days.

MONIKA. This building is sponsored by the Victorian Ministry of Culture.

LEON. I bet the only culture this place's ever seen is penicillin.

MONIKA. I'm amazed and appalled at you

LEON. Well I hate history !

MONIKA. Obviously a large part of your problem.

LEON I mean look, look at me, I need a shave, I haven't been home to change my clothes.

MONIKA. I'm sorry, Leon, it was doomed from the start wasn't it ?

LEON. (feeling some sympathy) That's alright, it's not *all* your fault..

MONIKA. Oh that's very generous of you.

LEON. I'm trying to say I'm sorry.

MONIKA. Love means never having to say that, Leon.

He looks at her uncertain, a small smile creases his face.

LEON. Touché.

And again the heat goes out of their argument.

MONIKA. It 's funny really -

LEON. What ?

MONIKA. Well, here we are tearing each other apart and 24 hours ago all I could think of was holding your warm furry body next to mine, and listening to . . . to . . .

LEON. To the semi trailers going past on Beaconsfield parade ?

MONIKA. Listening to Jason talking in his sleep and thinking - wouldn't it be nice to have a little girl.

LEON. We've got two kids already. We can't afford any more.

MONIKA. Yes, but little girls are so much easier. They hardly ever complain.

LEON. Jason and Romney are more than a handful.

MONIKA. I'm 35, Leon, this may be our last chance.

LEON. I much preferred it when we were fighting
about other people's lives.

She stares at him open mouthed, hardly believing what she's hearing.
She's obviously hurt, he tries to make amends.

LEON. I mean there's no guarantee it'll even be a boy…
er girl … see, even I'm confused.

But she's still hurt. He tries another topic.

LEON. So - you obviously approve of this place do you
?

MONIKA. I *am* on the organising committee. I've got to
do something with my spare time - now that the boys
are both at kindy.

He still refuses to bite.

LEON. Personally, I wouldn't give two bob for the
place.

MONIKA. Yes, well it's a *community* centre isn't it ? It
belongs to everyone- you'd hardly understand the
concept.

LEON. (noticing the banner) I see you've accepted bicentennial money.

MONIKA. (stressing it) *And* from the Department of
Youth Sport and
Idealism. And the international year of Motherhood.

LEON. Isn't that part of the problem you're always railing against ? Government funded festivals celebrating some ludicrous date on the calendar ?

MONIKA. Well yes, it would be nice if they invested in people for a change…

LEON. Instead of Taj Mahals?

MONIKA. And mass produced fun.

LEON. But funding is funding.

MONIKA. We don't accept money from South Africa.

LEON. Oh - I can just imagine the Krugerrands flowing into this palace. You know they closed down 26 cheap flatettes to put your precious works of art in here.

MONIKA. Forgodsake, this is the last house left standing in Acland Street, if it has to be a Gallery in order to survive then so be it.

LEON. And that's your idea of progress is it ? As long as it suits yours truly.

MONIKA. I'm not saying it's uncomplicated, Leon, but it is a question of taste, a question of proportion, of access. People have to feel involved in the change.

LEON. Somebody has to have the initiative.

MONIKA. Well it can't be imposed from above

LEON. Then nothing would ever happen

MONIKA. The trouble with your initiatives, Leon, is that they have no soul.

LEON. No soul ? We're changing a seedy old red light district into a very desirable place to live.

MONIKA. For those who can afford it.

LEON. It was a slum, Monika. We've done our demographic and psychographic surveys, we've had an Environmental Impact Study. The results show that St. Kilda Paradise is what people want.

MONIKA, Which people ? What figures ?

LEON. Did you fill out the questionaire we put in every mail box?

MONIKA. You know we've got a "No Junk Mail" sticker.

LEON. Then you can't complain, can you ?

MONIKA You think a computer can evaluate what a home means to someone who's rented it for 30 years? Or what lead in car exhausts does to a child's brain ? Do you have any concept of visual pollution ?

LEON. Ah yes. The sun setting over the Westgate Bridge with the its rays breaking through bronze-red clouds like a giant Anzac badge, that's my idea of a visually stimulating image

MONIKA. That bronze red colour is photochemical smog.

LEON. Well look at these people (indicating Paul Border). Is that your idea of a suitable neighbor ? Vomit all over the footpath. Needles in the gutter. Burglaries every second day of the week. People too afraid to walk in the streets at night.

MONIKA. At least in St. Kilda there *are* people around on the streets at night. To be quite honest I was more worried living in Glen Iris.

LEON. So this is your idea of a more pleasant place to live ?

MONIKA. Most of those problems are brought here by outsiders - by yobbos from other suburbs.

LEON. Hoh !

MONIKA. I work with the victims remember, I'm the one at the coal face, I'm the social worker.

LEON. You're just putting bandaids on it, you're not solving anything.

MONIKA. What's exciting about this place *is* it's cultural diversity. It's the mixture of people that makes it unique. Here we've still got a suburb on the cutting edge of change. What you're proposing to do is merely fill it full of yuppies.

LEON. I like yuppies.

MONIKA. Have you seen Lygon street lately?

LEON. We're a two car, two income family, stable jobs, kids in private kindergarten, *we're* yuppies. How can we be bad for a place?

MONIKA. If it's not statistical you don't understand it do you ?

LEON. In the 1950s everybody drooled over the idea of having a brick veneer on their own little quarter acre block. With a hills hoist in the backyard. Then petrol got expensive and suddenly everybody wanted to live within an easy bicycle ride of the office.

MONIKA. That's because they found something they never got in the suburbs. The discovered a sense of community.

LEON. (protesting) We're giving them a village atmosphere !

MONIKA. But in pulling down historic buildings and forcing prices up you destroy the very things that make it attractive in the first place. Look what happened to Carlton - it went from bohemian to trendy to dead.

LEON. What are you saying Monika ?

MONIKA. I don't think I want to live here anymore.

LEON is astounded.

LEON. But we've just gotten used to the place.

However MONIKA seems resolved.

LEON. I mean I was always the one who wanted to leave.

MONIKA. Yes, well now I want to go too.

LEON. Well I'm sorry, but I actually like the idea of being able to walk to work.

MONIKA. I think we should attempt a trial separation anyway

LEON. Are you saying all this because I don't want another kid ?

MONIKA. No.

LEON. Well why then ?

MONIKA. Do I need a reason ?

LEON. But… but… we can't split up.

MONIKA. Why not ?

LEON. We'd have to sell the flat.

MONIKA. It's in my name.

LEON. Only because I couldn't get the first home buyers grant.

MONIKA. I wouldn't tell too many people about that Leon.

LEON. It's my money in there too.

MONIKA. You'll get your money back.

LEON. Yes, but I can't afford to buy another flat here not by myself.

MONIKA. Well whose fault is it that property values have gone through the roof. Literally.

LEON. All my capital is tied up in the business .

MONIKA. Perhaps Robert Holmes à Court will make you an offer.

LEON. You can't spring this on me, Monika, just out of the blue like this.

MONIKA. Well now you know what it's like to be evicted.

LEON. Oh this is stupid. We're just going round in circles.

MONIKA. Then its time for a break isn't it ?

LEON. Look, Monnie, please, be reasonable.

MONIKA. Don't call me Monnie!

LEON. (raising his voice) Well stop raising your voice then!

MONIKA. (louder) I'm not raising my voice

LEON. There's no need to get hysterical.

MONIKA. (hysterically) WHO'S HYSTERICAL ????

LEON. YOU'RE DRIVING ME STARK RAVING GA GA.

There's a silence. She starts rummaging her handbag/

LEON. What are you doing ?

No response

LEON. Monika, please…not till the new financial year at least.

MONIKA. I'm can't stand it a minute longer.

LEON. Can't we talk about it?

MONIKA. What do you think's been going on for the last half hour? The last half dozen years of my life ?

She gives up rummaging.

MONIKA. Oh no

LEON. What… what's the matter ?

MONIKA. I can't seem to find the keys to the Volvo.

LEON. Don't tell me they've picked your purse as well !

LEON rounds on the previously suspect phantom pasher.

LEON (rolling up his sleeves) Righto, pal, on ya feet, empty ya pockets

MONIKA. Its alright, Leon, I can whistle for it.

LEON. (shocked) Not while you've still got anything to do with me you can't.

MONIKA. It's one of those clever little "Key Finder" thingos. I'm always losing it.

MONIKA WHISTLES and two answering BEEPS from two different "Key Finders" come back at her.

She whistles again, and again there's the two answering BEEPS.

She puts on her glasses and looks in the direction of the second answering beep. She's already located her own set of keys in her handbag so…

LEON. Somebody else's got your car keys out there ?

MONIKA. (surprised, delighted) Cyril ! Hullo- I didn't realise you were here.

LEON. Who's Cyril ?

MONIKA. I told you, Leon, Cyril is the model for our life classes.

She turns to a member of the audience.

MONIKA. Cyril this is Leon. . .

LEON is aghast.

> MONIKA. I gave him one of these little key-finder thingos as a birthday present - didn't I Cyril ?

> LEON. You mean, you've seen this person with all his clothes off ?

> MONIKA. (as if he's really dumb) That's what life classes are all about Leon.

LEON looks "CYRIL" up and down. Curling a lip

> LEON. But…that's the most disgusting thing I've ever heard!

> MONIKA. I'm not interested in what you think anymore.

> LEON. And you give him birthday presents?

> MONIKA. Only as a small gesture of my appreciation. They're so useful, aren't   they Cyril ? I'd be really lost without mine.

> LEON. I feel a bit week in the knees.

> MONIKA. You never understood my passion for painting have you ?

> LEON. Well its becoming a little clearer now.

> MONIKA. What would you know about the thrill that passes through my body when I dip a brush in oils and spread the first colours onto canvas?

But LEON'S mind is focused on only one thing.

> LEON. What's he like in the nude?

MONIKA. How dare you .!

LEON. (viciously) Did you get off on it ?

For answer she simply slaps him across the face. He staggers sideways holding his jaw and collapses into a seat at the "St.Kilda Breakfast" installation.

LEON. Thanks, I needed that. (adjusting his jaw) I…I don't know what came over me.

MONIKA. (horrified) You can't sit there, that's a piece of sculpture!

LEON. Just think of it as Life intimidating Art.

MONIKA. Leon - you're making a prize idiot of yourself

LEON. Must be this house. It seems to have a strange effect on people.

She stands there for a moment looking round. Indeed it does. Slowly, inevitably she sinks into the other chair at the "breakfast" table.

He feels the table top with both hands.

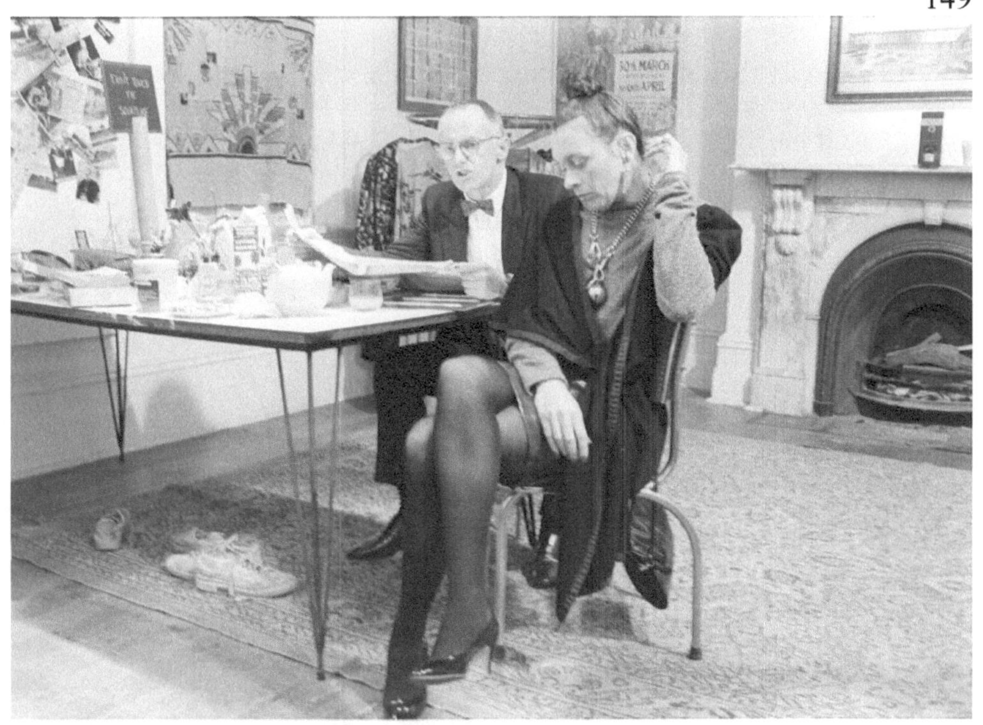

LEON. You know, we should get a table like this for our kitchen. Laminex. Very practical.

MONIKA. There's enough of your clutter in there already.

LEON. We can move all that into the fallout shelter.

MONIKA. There isn't going to be any shelter !

LEON. I wouldn't mind a table to cook at you know. It'd be handy.

MONIKA. There isn't enough room in the kitchen for a table.

LEON. You can put the chairs in underneath.

He stands and moves his chair under the table.

LEON. See they don't stick out much.

MONIKA. We'd never get the frig door open.

Suddenly Leon notices a line of white ' powder on the mirror, frowns, tastes a bit on the tip of his finger.

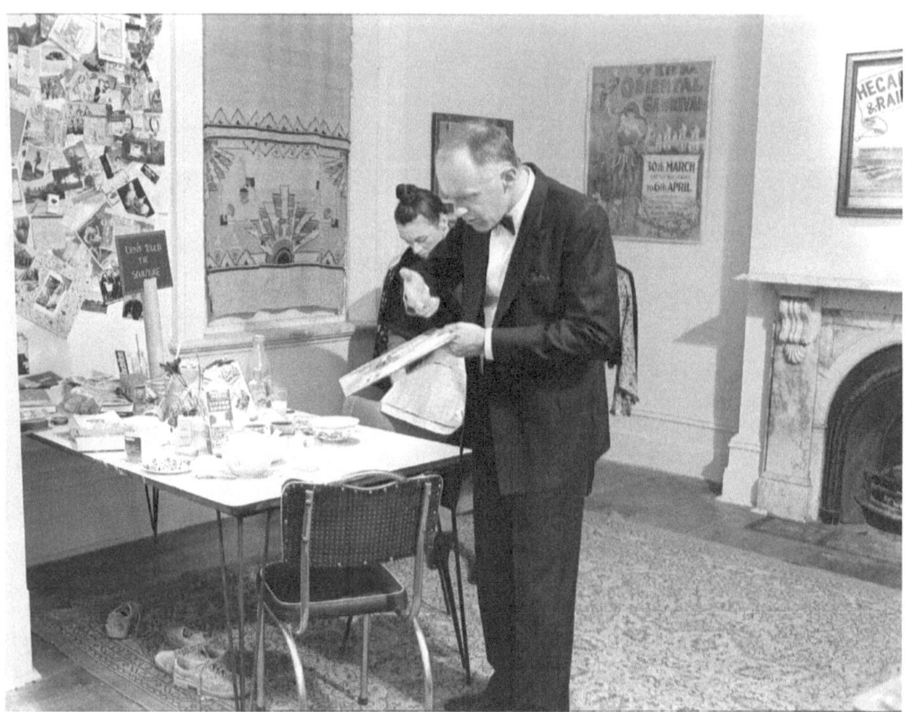

MONIKA. Don't touch that !

Leon reacts to the taste.

LEON. Bloody hell ! I'm going to ring the police.

MONIKA. It can't be illegal, Leon, it's a work of art !

He heads determinedly for the door. She snaps at him
MONIKA. Leon !

He hesitates

        MONIKA. If you go out that door don't ever come
back!

He glares at her, fuming, takes a deep breath and slams out !

        MONIKA. (yelling after him) Well good riddance !

It takes a moment for her fury to settle down.

        MONIKA. (calmly) I'm sorry about that Cyril. Thanks
for not…you know, saying anything…he's a bit old
fashioned about all that. Do you do home visits ? I
forgot to ask you about that I'd love to paint you in my
lounge room some time.

She scribbles her address in a small notebook

        MOINIKA. Why don't you pop over one day next week.

She tears out the page and is just handing it to Cyril when the door swings
open and a crestfallen, head down, humbled Leon, shambles back in.

        LEON. Look Monnie, I'm sorry about …(all that)

He glances up from the floor just as Cyril is taking the note from her.
MONIKA freezes. LEON strides over and seizes it. He quickly reads it .

        LEON. Bitch !

And he storms out again.

        MONIKA. Leon !

She goes to chase after him.

        MONIKA. Leon !

ACT IV
The Hallway.

People from all three rooms now merge into the dim, candle-lit Hallway. There's a grand staircase at one end leading from the upstairs rooms down to an ornate front door with stained glass panels. Doors from the three ground floor rooms (Drawing Room, Gallery and Flatette) open out onto this central corridor.

Here MONIKA, along with the three combined audience sub-groups, discovers the figures of DEEGAN, CUTHBERT and ESTELLE all frozen on the steps as if they have just emerged from the Drawing Room Scene (as per the end of ACT I). And so we seem to have returned to the time frame of 1900 again.

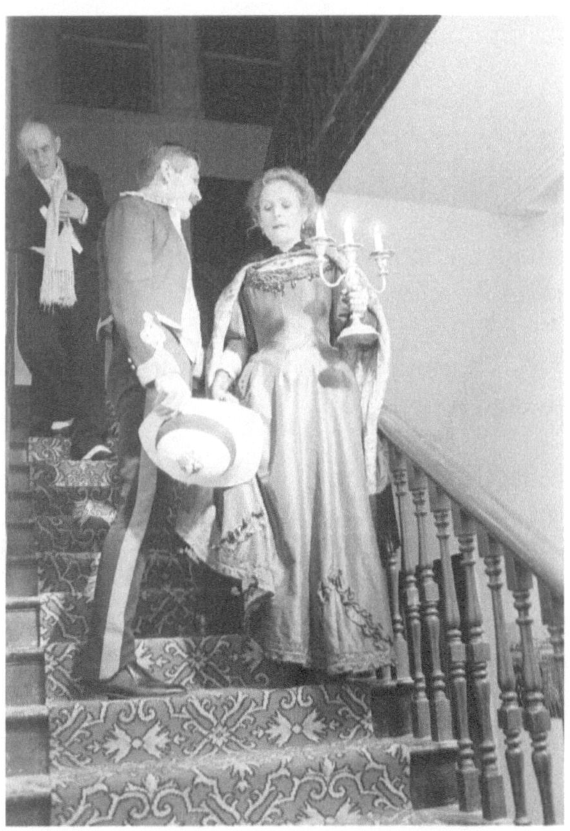

ESTELLE is holding a lit candelabra and stands motionless in the act of heading down the stairs, trailed by DEEGAN and CUTHBERT who remain frozen on the steps above her.

Meanwhile, LEON emerges from underneath the stairs where he has been looking for a phone to call the police.

> LEON. You'd think there'd be a public phone somewhere…

> MONIKA. (taking in the characters on the stairs) Oh look, Leon! This must be the play we've been waiting for.

> LEON. Oh great - great timing, Monika. Looks like they're all about to leave. Brilliant!

MONIKA spots a prominent red button about half way up the stairs. She reaches for it.

> MON1KA. And there's another one of those funny little buttons, let's see if this room works…

> LEON. Leave it alone, fercrissake, what's the point in only seeing the end of the damn thing ?

> MONIKA. I'm not going to let your drippy mood stop me from enjoying myself.

> LEON. Well I'm calling the police and then I'm getting out of here - I mean even the bloody tram home's a No 69!

He finally spots a phone in the middle of the Hallway - on the counter where the old booking office for the boarding house used to be.

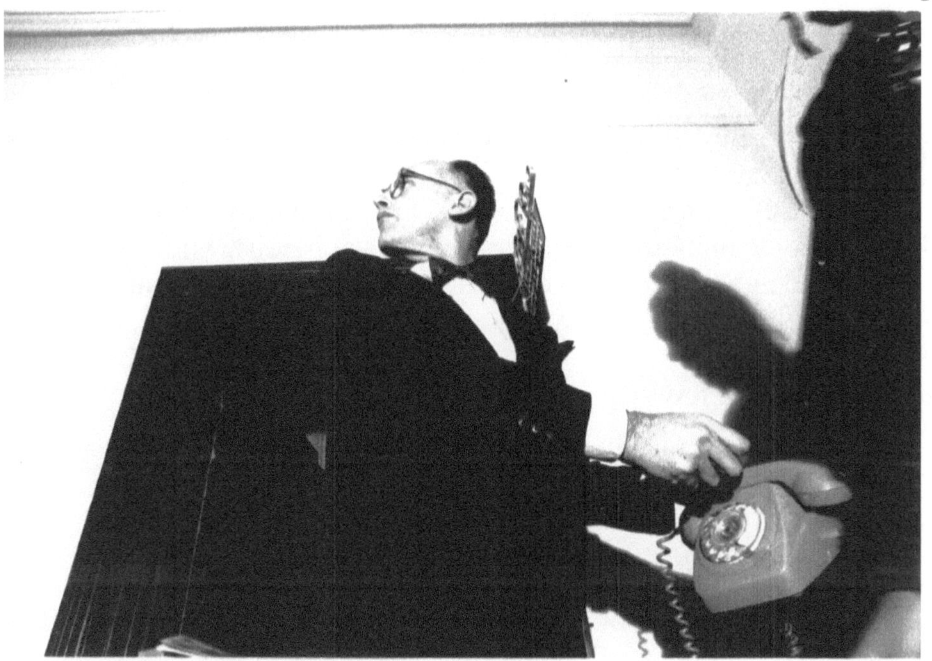

MONIKA, determined, pushes the button and a BUZZER SOUNDS
which immediately brings DEEGAN, CUTHBERT and ESTELLE back
to life.

>   CUTHBERT. (clutching his heart) Estelle - wait: Where
>   are you going ?

>   ESTELLE. I'm going upstairs to pack, Cuthbert, and
>   then I'm leaving this place.

>   CUTHBERT. But - how can this have happened ?
>   What did I do wrong?

>   ESTELLE. If you can't work out the answer to that then
>   it really is finished,
>   Cuthbert. So let it go. It's over.

She pushes past him. Continuing up to her bedroom.

>   CUTHBERT. How can you have formed such a liason
>   with the cad? (sudden anger) Behind my back!

CUTHBERT and DEEGAN follow after her. She stops again, looking down on both of them.

>ESTELLE. You're the one who encouraged him to stay, Cuthbert. Remember? I can't recall the number of times you sent him with a cab to collect me from the theatre, or some dinner you failed to show up at because you were out on a "call' or too busy with some card game at the club.

She continues on a few steps…

>CUTHBERT. But Estelle - wait, please…I'll give you the house, anything, anything.

>ESTELLE. I can't stay chained to this place forever, Cuthbert. I've felt like a prisoner here long enough.

>CUTHBERT. But where will you live ? You've no income of your own and I can't see him supporting you - he's off to war on Saturday.

>DEEGAN. I'm taking Estelle to my cousin's house in North Melbourne. (turning to her, putting it to her directly) And, if she'll wait for me there, we might even settle on some patch of scrub outback where you can actually see the stars at night and believe there's some purpose to it all.

>ESTELLE. I said we were leaving, Michael, I didn't say we were leaving together.

That's a bit of a shock.

>DEEGAN. What?

>ESTELLE. I need some time on my own, that's all.

>DEEGAN. But, darling, Sophie would love to have you.

ESTELLE. I'm sorry, Michael, I want to he in a position to make my own way. Decide my own future.
Maybe…then I'll be ready for a life under the stars.

And again DEEGAN, ESTELLE, and CUTHBERT go into frozen mode on the stairs…

… Just as PAUL BORDER appears at the top of them, heading down, carrying his duffle bag. He's hotly pursued by MIRIAM who carries a torch, putting him in the spotlight.

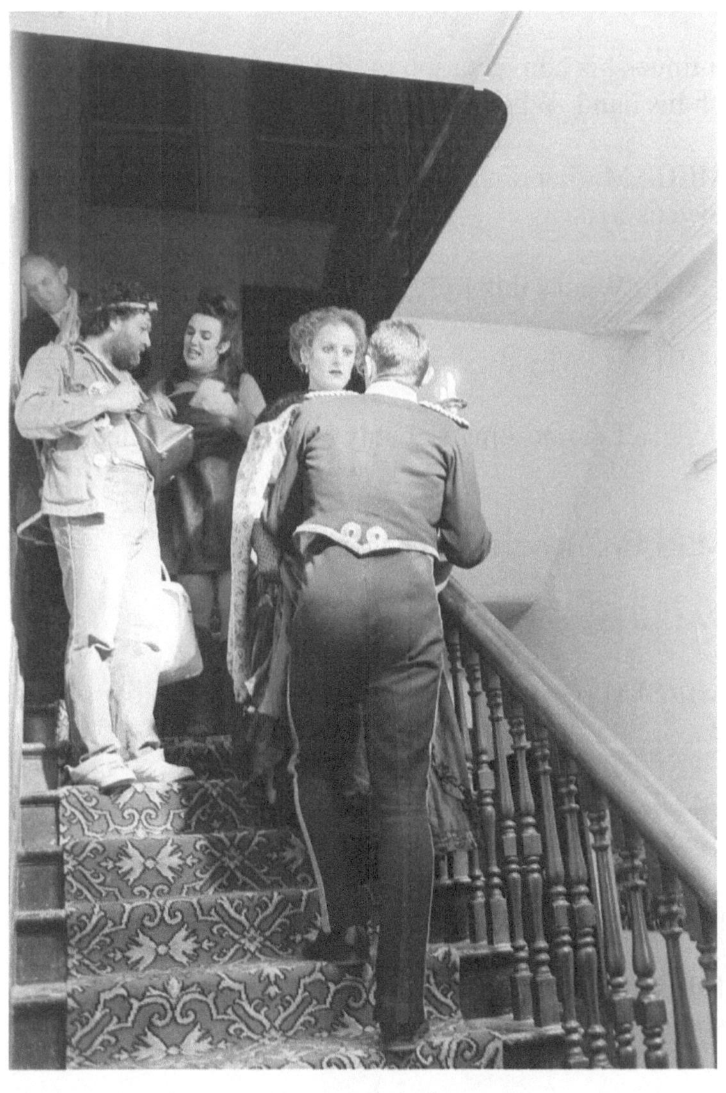

MIRIAM. Hey wait a minute- where do you think you're going ?

PAUL. I'm getting out of here in case he does ring the cops.

Meanwhile LEON has finally found the number in the phone book…

LEON. Hullo - is that "Dob In A Dealer " ?

MONIKA. Oh, shush! Leon

LEON continues his conversation on the phone *sotto voce*. Covering his mouth with his hand. Whispering his discovery of cocaine.

MIRIAM. (handing PAUL the Bill) Listen, mate, you owe us $10.

PAUL. What's this for ?

MIRIAM. Why do you think the lights have gone off ?

PAUL. I dunno - he probably hasn't paid his electricity bill

MIRIAM. Because you haven't paid yours,

PAUL. I've only been here half an hour

MIRIAM. He takes the difference out of my pay alright ?

PAUL. Well, you're the one who chooses to stay here. I don't know why the hell you put up with it.

Miriam hesitates to tell him…

MIRIAM. Maybe I've got a project. Maybe I'm doing some research.

PAUL. Oh yeah - prying into people's lives no doubt. Robbing them of their privacy.

MIRIAM. I'm only trying to preserve something.

PAUL. Preserve what ?

MIRIAM. A way of life.

PAUL takes in the dim, tatty Hallway. Visibly underwhelmed.

PAUL Don't think it's a way of life I'd care to remember much thanks, love.

And he heads on down the steps, moving past ESTELLE, DEEGAN and CUTHBERT as if they're not there.

MIRIAM. Well, let me get a photograph of you then. I'll waive the bill.

PAUL. A photo ? Of me ? (incredulous) What, so you can hand it over to the cops, help them update their file ?

MIRIAM. Won't be much use to them will it ? If your hero Gough wins on Saturday.

This brings PAUL up short. She does have a point there.

MIRIAM. (seizing the moment) Look I'll pay you 10 bucks for it. Call it quits, alright ?

PAUL is obviously tempted.

MIRIAM. I'll just fetch my camera…

PAUL. (but finally reneging) I'm not paying 10 dollars and that's final!

But MIRIAM has already disappeared back up the stairs. Throwing his hands up in despair PAUL accidentally bumps the red button again. There's a BUZZING SOUND as the 1900 characters come back to life.

CUTHBERT. But why, Estelle, why ?

PAUL and ESTELLE have suddenly arrived at the same step on the stairs. His ears prick up at the name. He takes out the old letter he's just found in the fireplace.

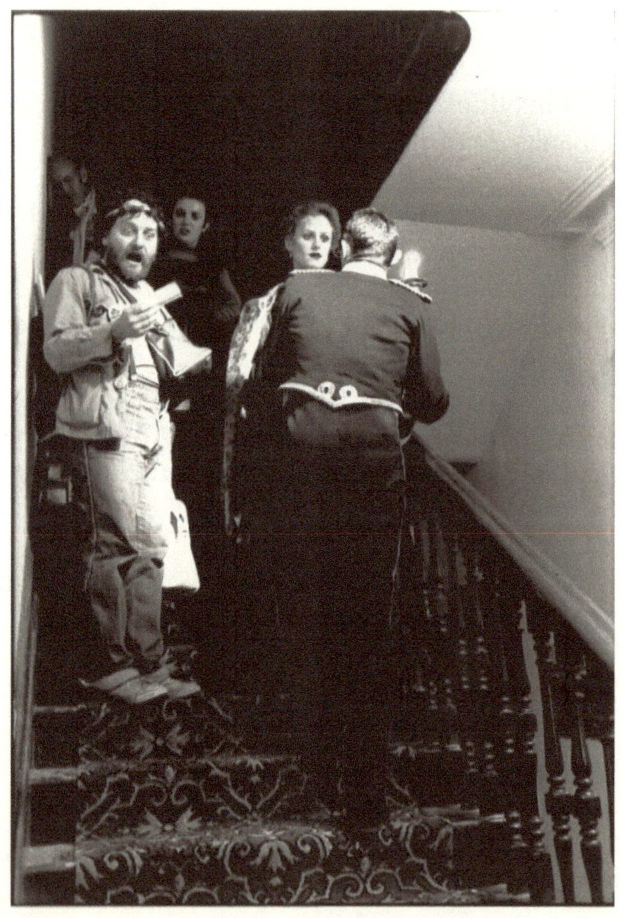

PAUL. Estelle ?

PAUL starts to realize who she is. The character in the letter…

ESTELLE. Because life's too short, Cuthbert.

PAUL observes her closely. She remains unaware of him.

PAUL. My god ! You really are beautiful.

DEEGAN. I'm sorry - none of this is making much sense to me. I'm afraid I've got a boat to catch.

He heads off down the stairs towards the front door.

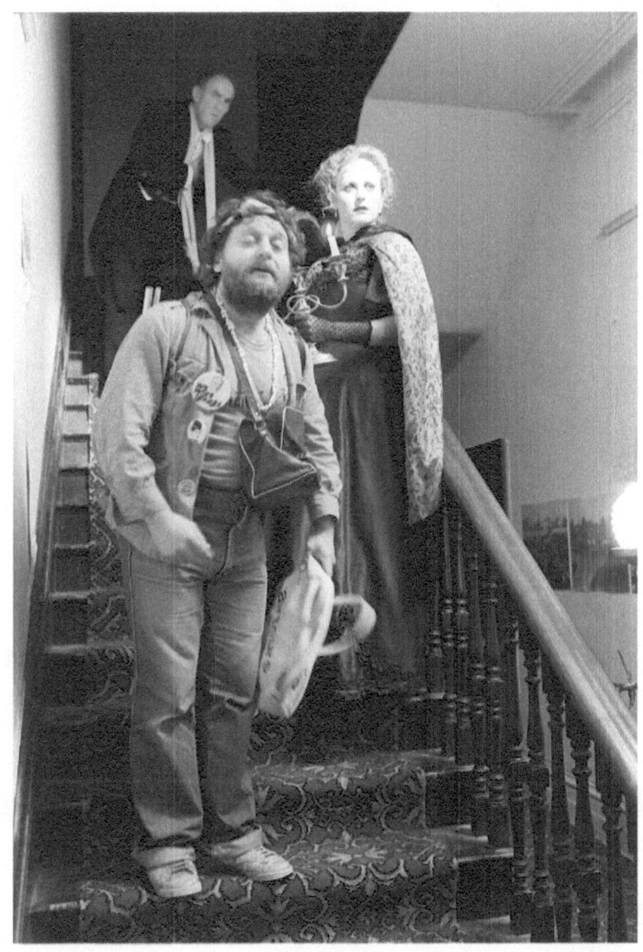

PAUL. (addressing him directly) So - you're just going to walk out on her are you ?

DEEGAN slows, but keeps moving towards the front door. The audience make way for him. Among them is MONIKA now totally immersed in the drama of it all.

> PAUL. (calling him out) Leave her in the lurch to explain about the baby?

DEEGAN hesitates with the front door open.

> MONIKA. (thrilled) Oh, this is more like it, Leon. This is what we came to see.

DEEGAN comes hack from the front door, uncertain.

> DEEGAN. You mean, it's *my* child. . .?

> CUTHBERT. (news to him) Child ?

> ESTELLE. I didn't tell you, Michael, because I didn't want to complicate things.

> CUTHBERT. (flabbergasted) COMPLICATE THINGS ! ?

> DEEGAN. You admit this now, and still you refuse to come to my cousins house ?

> ESTELLE. Well, if you persist in your overseas adventure it's all theoretical what I do isn't it ? I can't plan my life around the off chance you may or may not he back in six or twelve months time.

> PAUL. Anyway, love, as soon as Gougho gets in you can always claim the single parents' benefit.

> DEEGAN. I'm getting out of here.

And DEEGAN continues on out through door.

CUTHBERT (confronting Estelle) You're telling me you've actually had congress with the wretch!

PAUL. It's the sort of info that gives you a heart attack, mate…sorry about that.

PAUL follows ESTELLE who follows DEEGAN, wanting to explain…

ESTELLE. Michael… (wait)…

Finally MIRIAM has her camera and is chasing after PAUL

MIRIAM. Just one shot…

Behind MIRIAM. CUTHBERT is the last one out, but he crumples over, clutching his chest so that he almost kind of stumbles through the door after them, slamming it behind.

CUTHBERT. (outside) Heart Attack !

With all the characters gone there's a momentary silence.

But this is broken by a the VOICE of the HOUSE which reverberates through the Hallway as if from somewhere above. The VOICE sounds much like the one on the Gallery tape recorder.

HOUSE. (voice over) Right, stop, hold it right there…

By now, with both the torch and the candles gone, the hallway is in almost complete darkness adding to the disembodied nature of VOICE of the HOUSE.

HOUSE. (voice over) I think I've seen enough…

MONIKA has hopped up onto the bottom rung of the stairs to get a better look at the dramatic exits.

MONTICA. (slight surprise) Oh. The stairs creek.

HOUSE. (voice over) Well you would too, if you were as old as I am.

MONIKA reels back in shock, looking round for the source of the VOICE.

MONIKA. (feeling the one next to her) Leon - it's, it's… coming from the walls!

HOUSE. (voice over) This is the house speaking.

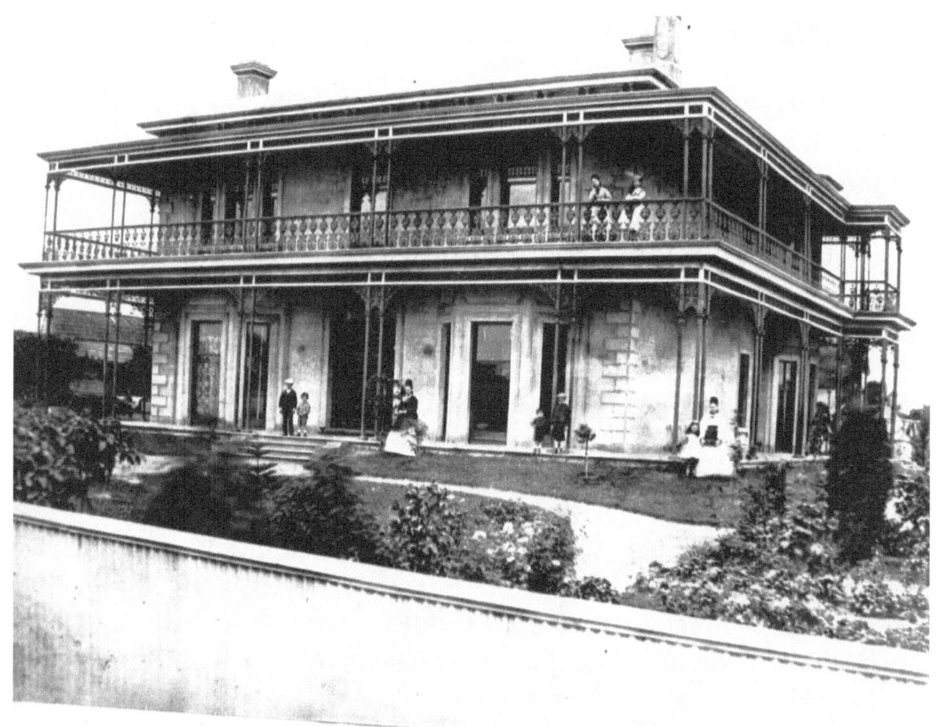

Through the dim light of the Hallway a slide of "Linden" in 1870 appears on the wall at the top of the stairs - perhaps reflected almost three-dimensionally through the smoke that now also seems to waft in from somewhere outside as if plunging the Hallway into an ethereal haze. Members of the Michaelis family (who originally built the house) are arranged on two levels. Facing the camera. The Eric Satie Waltz (*GYMNOPEDIE # 1*) that DEEGAN was playing earlier on the piano at the beginning of the Drawing Room Scene fades up behind the VOICE…

MONIKA. It's. . . it's like an apparition. .

LEON. Oh, come on, that's just a slide forcrissake!
Anybody can do that.

MONIKA is still carrying the audio cassette player from the Gallery. She regards it now with intense suspicion.

MONIKA. Some element - some *thing* has penetrated
the cassette player.

LEON. Well, you should've handed it back in.

In the background the CHIMES from the Hall clock start counting out 10 O'CLOCK.

HOUSE. (voice over) One hundred and sixteen years
I've been hanging around on this plot of ground
belonging to the Wurundjeri nation, wondering what the
devil you lot are going to turn me into next. I mean, am
I a mansion, a boarding house, or an art gallery ? Not
that I'm not grateful to still be here - don't get me
wrong. Life as a community cultural centre isn't all that
bad long as you don't mind getting your guts ripped out
by an army of plumbers and central heating experts. I
mean, let's get our act together chaps. You just keep
making the same mistakes generation after generation,
don't you ? You strut your stuff here for a few short
hours like some waking dream of somebody else's
nightmare, pretending your pathetic little lives are all so
goddamn bloody important, and all so weighted down
with angst about who's coming and who's going and
who's paid the goddamn electricity bill. I mean, come
on, I've got a good 150 years left in me. I'd like to see
any of you humans manage that on your fancy Pridikin
diets.

LEON (fighting back) Unless we pull you down!

MONIKA rounds on him.

MONIKA. Oh sush! Leon, he's talking about *us*, now.

HOUSE. (voice over) Ghosts can't hurt bricks and mortar.

LEON. I'm no ghost, mate, I can switch you off any
time I jolly well
like…

HOUSE. (voice over) I think you'll find if you tried to
switch me off you'd be making a (voice rising) *very big
mistake!...*

LEON. We'll soon see about that !

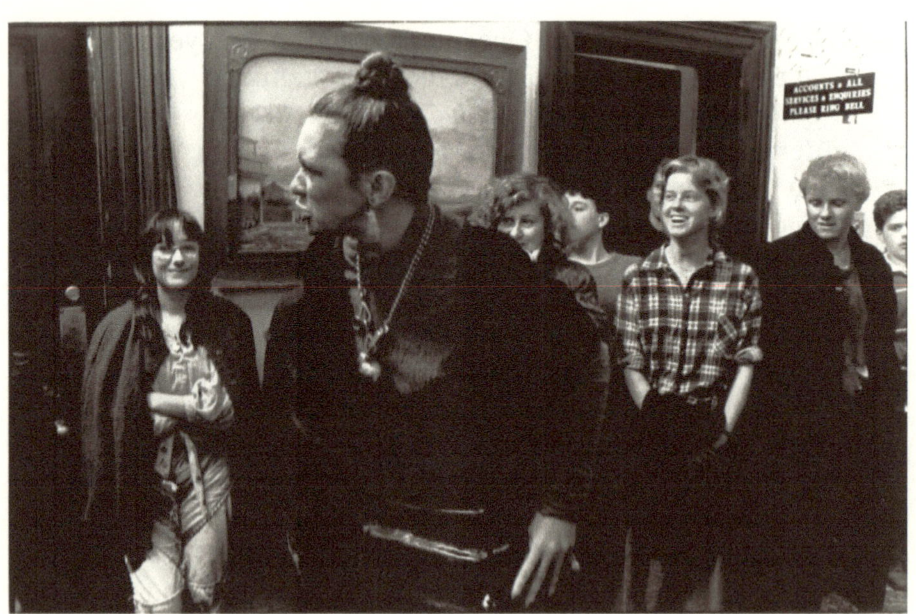

MONIKA. Leon, don't! The house is giving us a key to
the future.

LEON. In future, Monika, you and I are speaking
through our lawyers.

He moves forward to press the red button half-way up the stairs.

MONIKA (screaming at him to stop) Leon! Stop!

But he presses the button and instantly LEON and MONIKA freeze on the steps.

The lights slowly fade to black over the deep BOOMING LAUGHTER of the house…

PROGRAMME

WRITER'S NOTES

The building in which this play is staged has gone from Victorian Mansion to Boarding House to Cultural Centre. The story is an invention based on impressions of the life of a grand mansion in St Kilda from the Boer War to the Bicentennial. Its bricks and mortar enshrine our history and the lives of its inhabitants pass like shadows, wondering if there's such a thing as real progress after all, or whether life is just a case of "you can't always get what you want." It's not so much the place you're in, but the time you're in it. Or, as Monika would say, "Only the journey matters."

SPECIAL THANKS

Adrian Gough; Chris Reidy; Another Planet Posters; Chris Minko & Albert Littler -
Operative Painters & Decorators Union;
Jean Tattersall, 3RRR-FM. Gavin Quinn, Richard Kersly, Paul Craft, Jimi Baeck, Melbourne Moomba Festival Ltd.;
Fred Vaines - Woodruff Farms Pty Ltd.
Paul Cavell, Michael Trudgeon, Connie White.
Jean-Marc Dupre and Emmanuel Santos -
Open Space Productions.
Martin Kingham - Building Workers' Industrial Union.
Daryl Pellitzer, Tony Leonard, Martin Grant,
Nick Dell'Oso, Vida Horn, Michael Vale, Jos Duivenvoorden, John Macdonald, Jean Menzie, Leslie Wilson, Andrew Eddy, Mandy Bede and
the Riley Collection State Library of Victoria.

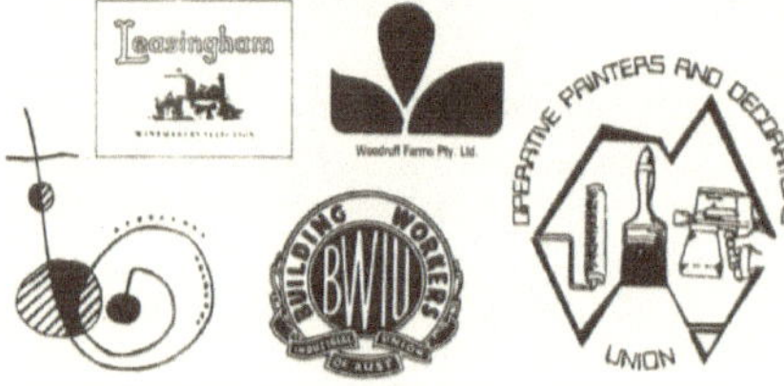

THEATREWORKS BOARD OF DIRECTORS

John Bell, Tony Briscomb, Paul Davies, Ann Galt, Dick Gross, Elaine Miller, Graeme Stephen, Shirley Sydenham, Michael Nation (observer).

WHAT'S NEXT

TheatreWorks' next show for 1986 is a Bill Garner comedy specially commissioned by the company to open its new theatrical space at 14 Acland Street, St Kilda.

Cake is a comedy which peeks behind the closed doors of an actors' agency, a place where artistic aspirations, egos and hard business come face to face with hilarious results.
Opens October 30th.

Typesetting: Liz the Typesetter 417 7608
Printing: T & S Press 417 6150
74 Smith Street, Collingwood, 3066

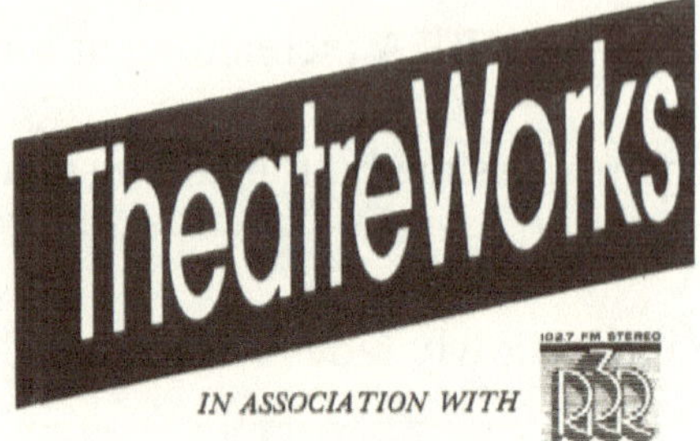

Each scene runs for 30 minutes.
There will be an interval of 20 minutes
after the second scene.

THEATREWORKS GRATEFULLY ACKNOWLEDGES ASSISTANCE FROM THE THEATRE BOARD OF THE AUSTRALIA COUNCIL, THE VICTORIAN MINISTRY FOR THE ARTS, THE COMMUNITY EMPLOYMENT PROGRAM AND THE CITY OF ST KILDA

THE CAST AND DIRECTORS

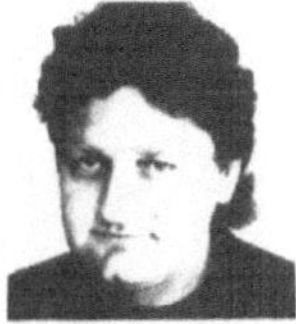

PAUL DAVIES · Writer/Director/Actor

Paul was first attracted to the idea of live performance when he won a smiling competition. Since then he has co-produced the film *Exits* with Carolyn Howard and Pat Laughren, and has collaborated on the feature screenplays for *Traps* with John Hughes and *Southern Aurora* with Mark Shirrefs. *Living Rooms* is the third play in a trilogy of suburban surrealism which began with *Storming Mont Albert by Tram* and *Breaking Up in Balwyn*, all written since he joined **Theatre-Works** in 1982.

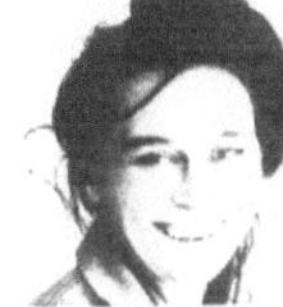

CAROLYN HOWARD · Director/Actor

Carolyn was a director of Open Channel and is a founding member of **TheatreWorks**. She has played lead roles in many **TheatreWorks** productions. On screen she acted the main female role in *Exits* and also performed the lead role of Vera in Kathy Mueller's *Everyday Everynight*. More recently she appeared in Clair Jaeger's *Spy in the Family* for the ABC.

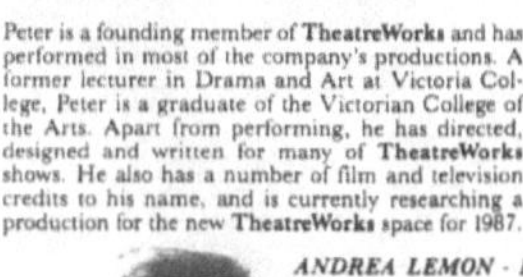

PETER SOMMERFELD · Director/Actor

Peter is a founding member of **TheatreWorks** and has performed in most of the company's productions. A former lecturer in Drama and Art at Victoria College, Peter is a graduate of the Victorian College of the Arts. Apart from performing, he has directed, designed and written for many of **TheatreWorks** shows. He also has a number of film and television credits to his name, and is currently researching a production for the new **TheatreWorks** space for 1987.

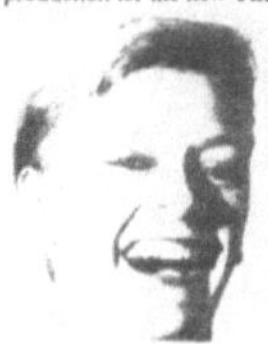

ANDREA LEMON · Director

Andrea joined the Home Cooking Theatre Company in 1982 and has performed in, written, designed and directed various productions, including *Not Still Lives* and *Looking In Looking Out*.

She is currently writer-in-residence at St Martins', and is writing a secondary school show called *A Change of Face* commissioned by Handspan Theatre Company.

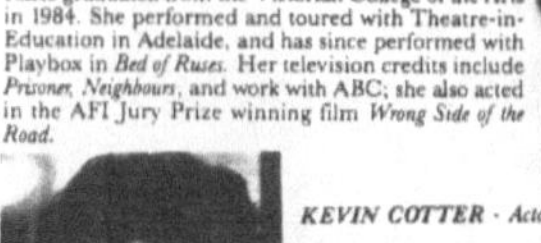

ROSIE TONKIN · Actor

Rosie graduated from the Victorian College of the Arts in 1984. She performed and toured with Theatre-in-Education in Adelaide, and has since performed with Playbox in *Bed of Roses*. Her television credits include *Prisoner, Neighbours*, and work with ABC; she also acted in the AFI Jury Prize winning film *Wrong Side of the Road*.

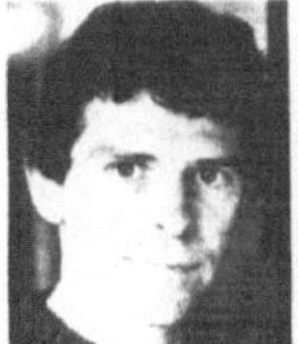

KEVIN COTTER · Actor

Kevin graduated from the National Theatre Drama School in 1984. He has performed in various graduate productions from Rusden and Swinburne, including the David Cox film *Time of Day*.

Kevin was the founding director of the Heywood Community Theatre, and has performed both in their productions and others, including the National Theatre production of Chekhov's *The Seagull* where he played the role of Trigorin.

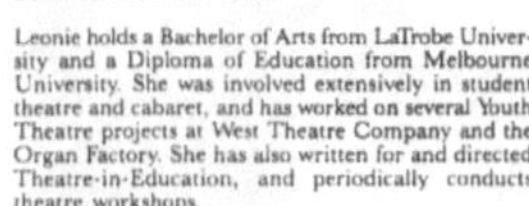

LEONIE HURRY · Actor

Leonie holds a Bachelor of Arts from LaTrobe University and a Diploma of Education from Melbourne University. She was involved extensively in student theatre and cabaret, and has worked on several Youth Theatre projects at West Theatre Company and the Organ Factory. She has also written for and directed Theatre-in-Education, and periodically conducts theatre workshops.

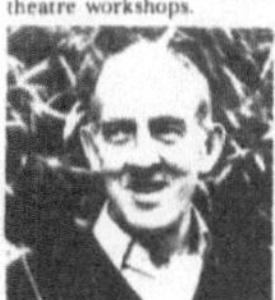

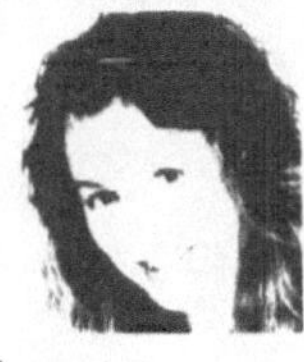

CLIFF ELLEN · Actor

Cliff has an impressive list of film and television credits to his name, including *Petersen* and *Phar Lap*, and *The Sullivans* and *Prisoner*. He has also performed in many Playbox productions, including *The Marriage of Belle and Boo* and *Unsuitable for Adults*.

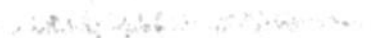

⬛⬛⬛⬛⬛⬛⬛⬛⬛⬛⬛⬛⬛⬛⬛⬛⬛

THE DRAWING ROOM

Estelle	–	Rosie Tonkin
Deegan	–	Kevin Cotter
Cuthbert	–	Cliff Ellen
Martha	–	Leonie Hurry

Directed by Carolyn Howard

⬛⬛⬛⬛⬛⬛⬛⬛⬛⬛⬛⬛⬛⬛⬛⬛

THE FLATETTE

Paul	–	Paul Davies
Chilla	–	Cliff Ellen
Miriam	–	Leonie Hurry

Directed by Peter Sommerfeld

⬛⬛⬛⬛⬛⬛⬛⬛⬛⬛⬛⬛⬛⬛⬛⬛

THE GALLERY

Monika	–	Carolyn Howard
Leon	–	Peter Sommerfeld

Directed by Paul Davies

⬛⬛⬛⬛⬛⬛⬛⬛⬛⬛⬛⬛⬛⬛⬛⬛

Consultant Director:	Andrea Lemon
Publicity & Promotions:	Graeme Stephen
	Kate Shaw
Design & Production:	Peter Aland
assisted by:	Janice Drewe
	Susan Weis
Administrator:	Wolfgang Wittner
Outgoing Administrator:	Amanda Smith

IN MEMORY OF MARY BETTY DAVIES
1929 - 1986

CRITICAL RECEPTION

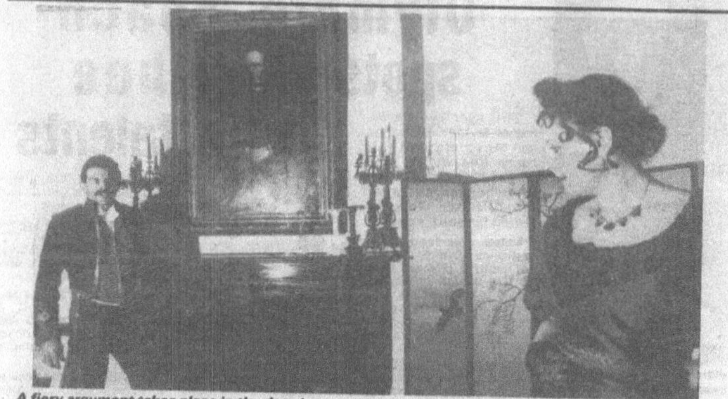

A fiery argument takes place in the drawing room between jackaroo Degan, played by Kevin Cotter and mistress of the house, Estelle, played by Rosie Tonkin.

Living Room comes alive

By LIDIA GIARRATANA

Walking into Linden, a great Victorian mansion in Acland St, St Kilda it is easy to forget that you are living in 1986 rather than 1900.

It seems that you are in a time warp and that you're walking into some rich history book.

The mansion is draped in d Victorian elegance and arm which helps make Paul Davies' play "Living Rooms" come to life.

The play doesn't s **UO** until the audience calls for its commencement.

Upon arrival, you are assembled in the gallery. When it's close to starting time, the host escorts the audience to the drawing room where the first scene takes place.

A member of the audience is asked to press the chime which brings the room to life.

The first scene in the drawing room is made up of a 1900 love affair between an idealistic jackaroom named Deegan who is bound for the Boer war. Deegan is played by Kevin Cotter and the sophisticated mistress of the house Estelle, is played by Rosie Tonkin.

As the audience moves to different room for each scene, time also changes.

The next scene in the gallery, is one that involves the audience.

Linden has become a public gallery and an exhibition of St Kilda's history with objects d'Art on show.

Just when you think there's been some kind of technical hitch, two actors come to life from the audience like figures in a painting.

It's 1988 and a modern couple is arguing over a frozen living art piece. Before long, their argument becomes one concerning their own problems.

The actors, Monika played by Carolyn Howard and Leon played by Peter Sommerfield, pretend to be a part of the audience and with mounting irritation, are waiting for the scene to start.

An intermission with coffee and cake is followed by the third scene, which takes place in a seedy flatette next door.

It's the eve of Gough Whitlam's election to government and the boarder, Paul played by director Paul Davies, stumbles across an old letter written by the jackaroo to the mistress.

As he concocts an elaborate past for the house, he is distracted by noisy characters he believes he has created.

Eventualy the characters from all three periods meet in the hallway and the arguments between past, present and future rise to a pitch until the house intervenes.

Living Rooms, produced by Theatreworks is witty, humorous and quite profound.

The play is being staged at 26 Acland St, St Kilda until Sunday 7 September, although it looks likely to be extended.

Times are 8.15pm with another show on Saturday's at 5pm.

Tickets range from $5 to $14.90.
Inquiries: 535 4879.

THE

NUMBER 6815

AUSTRALIAN

TUESDAY JULY 22 1986

40 CENTS* Freight extra

Theatre

Living Rooms
by Paul Davies
Theatreworks
St Kilda, Melbourne

HELEN THOMSON

Theatreworks does its bit for St Kilda

THEATREWORKS has been in existence for six years, building a reputation for innovative and enjoyable performances which do not necessarily rely on conventional theatre space. Their *Storming Mount Albert by Tram*, for example, was performed in a travelling tram.

This time they are to be found in a Victorian mansion, Linden, in Ackland St, St Kilda, roughly between the cake shops and the brothels. *Living Rooms* is about the suburb and the building in which it is performed, the house a precise symbol for St Kilda's chequered history.

Writer, actor and director Paul Davies has ingeniously constructed a play which breaks down the normal constraints of place and time in theatre. On entering the enormous hallway, audience members are given a program and a colour-coded set of instructions. The starting point for the evening's entertainment will be one of three performance areas, from which they will later proceed to the other two.

In each of three rooms, simultaneously, a scene is performed. By the end of the evening everyone will have seen all three, but in a different sequence. They will also have been told the history of Linden and some of its inhabitants, though not necessarily in chronological order.

In the splendidly furnished, candlelit drawing-room, seated around the walls, we witness a passionate scene between an idealistic jackaroo and his lover on the eve of his departure for the Boer War in 1900.

In the room next door another scene is being performed: this time it is 1972, on the eve of Gough Whitlam's election to power. Linden has become a seedy boarding-house divided into squalid "flatettes", in one of which a hippie draft-dodger finds an old letter tucked behind a boarded-up marble fireplace. It is from South Africa, from the now disillusioned Boer War soldier we have seen (or will see) farewelling his lover in the earlier scene.

In the third scene it is 1986, and we sit in the public gallery which is what the present-day Linden has become. Paintings and photographs of St Kilda's history line its walls, and a modern couple join the audience waiting for the performance to begin. Gradually a quarrel develops, until the couple realise that they themselves have been the performance.

Finally we all line the huge hallway while on its stairs a surreal encounter between all the participants takes place, and the house itself speaks to us.

Paul Davies has not adopted the stance of neutral historian: his play, in different ways, argues against the current trend towards a re-gentrification of St Kilda, while also making a case for the restoration of its grand houses for public use.

His cast — himself, Rose Tonkin, Kevin Cotter, Cliff Ellen, Leonie Hurry, Carolyn Howard and Peter Sommerfield (the latter two also co-directors) — put on fine performances in this inventive, intriguing work. This is community theatre at its best, socially relevant, artistically challenging, thought-provoking in the contemporary issues it raises.

CENTRE STAGE
AUSTRALIA

SEPTEMBER 1986
$3.00

☆☆☆

And now, having saved the best until last, we come to the latest in a series of location theatre pieces from the extraordinary Theatreworks, the eastern suburban Community Theatre Company. Theatreworks is the Company who created *Storming Mont Albert By Tram* some years ago, the play which took place along the route of the No. 42 Tram. Their most recent event, *Living Rooms* (August 17-September 13) takes place in Linden, a restored Victorian mansion at 26 Acland St., St. Kilda. The house (and its history) is both the subject of the drama and, at the same time, one of its central characters.

Linden has gone from being the resort home of Sir Cuthbert Baumgarten at the turn of the century, to being a somewhat seedy boarding house in the seventies, and now — in the late eighties — it's a local Cultural Centre, complete with Art Gallery. Writer Paul Davies has written three scenes (played simultaneously — three times per evening! — to an audience subdivided into three sections) each of which depicts imagined incidents of life in three different rooms of the house at three different periods in its "lifetime". As well as linking certain threads in the story of some of the characters who lived and loved in the house, each piece takes a particular line on the overall theme of Conservation.

This is a warm issue in St. Kilda (to which area Theatreworks has recently moved from its earlier home in sedate Canterbury) where the imperative to tear down and "develop" the very sites in which the play is performed is vigorously opposed by the determination to restore and preserve them.

Apart from the incredible precision required to mount this production as smoothly and coherently as they have, and the skills to perform the material with the energy and cunning that they have displayed, Theatreworks have also had the wit to exploit that most marvellous amalgam of theme, atmosphere, location and contemporary relevance so vital to the success of community theatre. *Living Rooms*, in short, has been without doubt the most interesting show in town for some nine weeks. And the fact that they have been able to run it that long is the best news of all: it would seem that this community theatre has begun to find its audience. ★
Geoffrey Milne

M·E·L·B·O·U·R·N·E

■ Theatre

LIVING ROOMS

It's difficult to write about this play as the audience didn't exactly watch it, and writing about the unseen is always a challenge.

'Living Rooms' takes three events in time, houses them in a St. Kilda mansion and lets them run wild.

The complexity of how these events relate to each other is captivating and enchanting — so much so that you could view the events in any order and still understand. But let me start — the first scene we saw took place in the drawing room of 'Linden', the house, a relic of the days when St. Kilda was inhabited by Melbourne's upper-crust. It is 1900, a year before Federation, and we see an idealistic republican and liberal mistress struggling to resolve their relationship only days before the republican is due to leave to fight Britain's war with the Boers.

The audience was seated around the room like flies on a wall, mesmerised as the drama unfolded and the players' reality became ours. Because we were so close to the action, we could not help but be drawn into it — yet still remain disparate. There was some confusion as to whether we were supposed to be in the room with the players when one performer drew us into the conversation, yet this distracted only slightly from the act as a whole.

For the next scene we moved to the Gallery and into 1988. There we all sat, amongst photo's, paintings and objets d'Art, waiting. And it wasn't until the conspicuous professional couple sitting opposite us started complaining about how long the play was taking to get started did we realise that the play had actually started. There they sat, she with her gaudy voice and screeching jewellery and he with his stone face. They skidded around the room and bounced off each other, threatening, cajoling, building up into a frenzy of idealistic arguments about St. Kilda, their relationship and the meaning of art. These two roped the audience well, the town planner accusing me of molesting his wife and the social worker giving her address to the 'nude model' amongst us.

And the interval.

Folowing the break we went into the flatette. Here we saw a burnt-out hippy on the eve of Gough Whitlam's election in 1972, trying to scratch a living out of nothing. Whilst cooking a meal of canned spag and Pal, he comes across a letter written by our young republican to his lover. And amidst the onslaught of his bigoted landlord and the sexual innuendos of the maid, the hippy pieces together a 'short poem' of what happens between these two turn of the century lovers.

The final scene takes place in the hallway when the characters come together and erupt into a surreal volcano of events that becomes so bizarre that the house itself is forced to intervene, which only makes the whole thing more surreal.

Because of the play's construction, some of the others in the audience saw the three scenes in a different order, and simply speculating upon how those people would perceive the chain of events afterwards is enough, let alone having actually participated in the play itself.

Written by Paul Davies and performed by Theatreworks, 'Living Rooms' is an accessible and stimulating

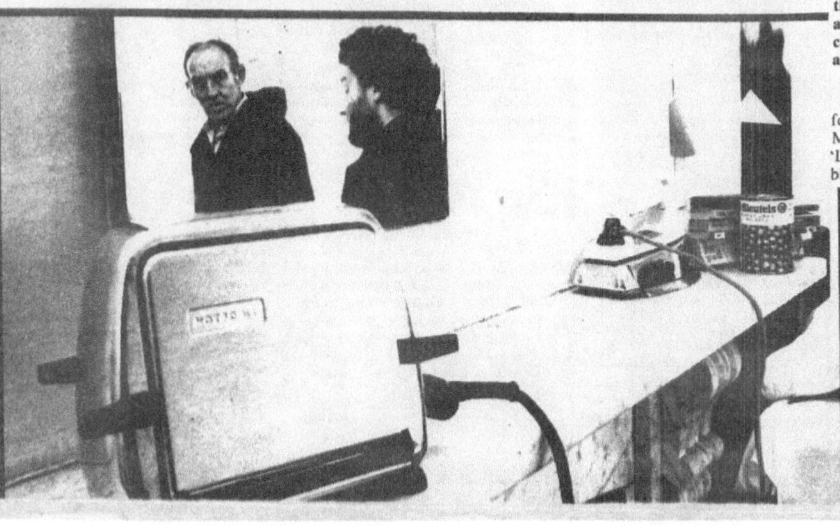

theatre piece tha
and personal qu
compels the au
and belong. Goo

'Living Room
for a limited sea
Monday throug
'Linden', 26 Acla
bit pricey ($10.9

Confluence of time in living rooms

By JACQUI MACDONALD

THEATREWORK'S committment to original Australian drama is well reflected in the production of Paul Davies' *Living Rooms*.

This piece of innovative location theatre deals with the tragedy of misused moments.

Davies' premise is that idealists' values at the turn of the century and during the Whitlam years were never realised, leaving a vacuum of empty rhetoric.

In the first scene we find ourselves lured into the confines of a small and squalid flatlet, choked with the odors of stale incense and smoke.

It is the eve of the 1972 election and Paul (Paul Davies) is "waiting for Gougho".

Whitlam is to be the saviour of this cruel, oppressive world that allows such creative artists as Paul to rot in poverty.

Paul becomes distracted by the discovery of a 19th century letter tucked away in the fireplace.

He elaborates on its intrigue and creates a cliched, romantic scenario set in the same house.

In the process he finds his attention diverted by arguments of his self-created characters in the next room.

Having written this witty and lively part himself, it would be difficult to say Paul Davies misinterprets his character.

But I feel this part deserves a less contrived characterisation than Davies gives.

The couple described in the letter live out their lives through Paul's script.

Together they had once shared an ideal and a disgust of upper class values.

She is the mistress of a wealthy socialite and the lover of an idealistic jackaroo.

While Estelle (Rosie Tonkin) and her lover Deegan (Kevin Cotter) find themselves searching for a way to express their feelings they challenge each others changing ideals.

Tonkin carries the sophistication and self-righteousness of Estelle with style and subtley reveals her moments of self-doubt.

Deegan's macho, romantic, "I'm your man"-type speech and his impassioned cry of "I was once an idealist" lacked all the grace it sought.

As the poor boy from the country, out to show the world, Cotter is strong and convincing.

But it is in the gallery with Monica (Carolyn Howard) and Leon (Peter Sommerfield) that the play finds its strength.

Monica the new-born artist is becoming disillusioned with Leon, St Kilda's town planner, as the two discuss the worth of a "frozen living performance art piece".

The year is 1988 and the mansion has become a cultural centre.

As the couple wait for the performance to begin we find ourselves witness to their building frustrations and personal problems.

It is only after they have revealed their inner most hostilities that they realise they are the performance.

The walls begin to lose their barriers of time and the mansion's moments of history meet.

The gallery scene is full of quick, witty and sharp lines delivered with flair by Howard and Sommerfield.

In particular, Sommerfield gives a shrewd characterisation of Leon with his obvious gift for straight man comedy.

By the final scene the conflicts of past, present and future have escalated to the degree that the times meet only to be intervened by the mansion itself.

The plays' attraction is in its unconventional movement from era to era and its innovative setting.

The acting is generally energetic and convincing and the script is sharp and extremely witty.

It makes its point well while being lighthearted and original.

Living Rooms is being performed at "Linden", 26 Acland St, St Kilda. Tickets can be booked through BASS.

Tuesday, August 12, 1986

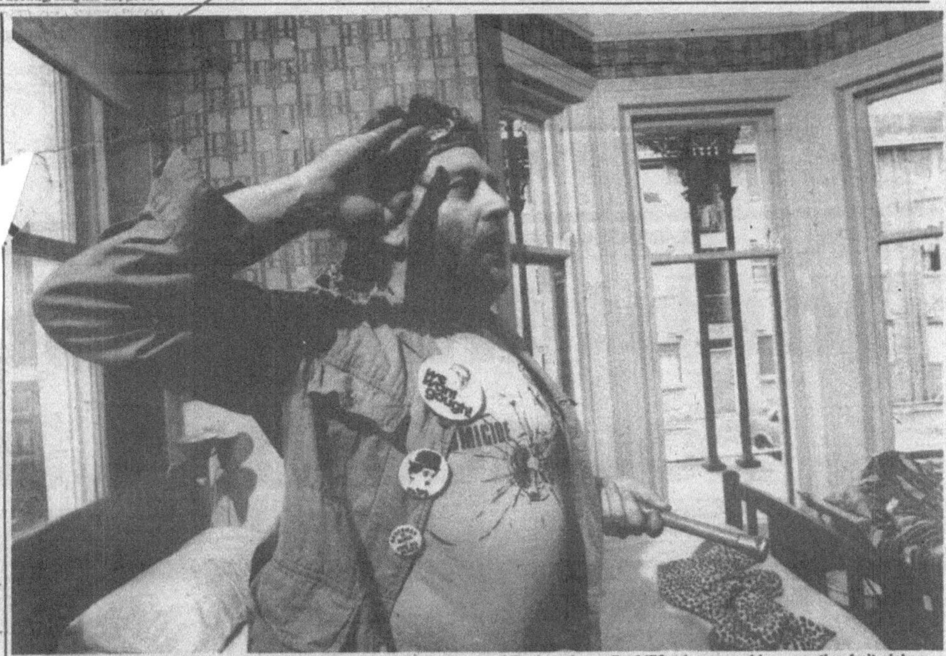

PAUL Davies, writer and director of "Living Rooms", plays the part of Paul — the radical '70s dope-smoking, creative fruit picker.

Slightly different touch to live theatre, with room to move

THEATREWORK'S commitment to original Australian drama is praiseworthy in the production of Paul Davies' ''Living Rooms''.

This piece of innovative location theatre deals with the tradegy of misused moments.

Davies' premise is that the value of idealists at the turn of the century and during the Whitlam years were never realised, leaving a vacuum of empty rhetoric.

In the first scene we find ourselves lured into the confines of a small and squalid flatette, choked with the odors of stale incense and smoke.

It is the eve of the 1972 election and Paul (Paul Davies) is "waiting for Gougho".

Whitlam is to be the saviour of this cruel, oppressive world that allows creative artists like Paul to rot in poverty.

Paul becomes distracted by the discovery of a 19th century letter tucked away in the fireplace.

He elaborates on its intrigue and creates a cliched, romantic scenario set in the same house.

But in the process finds his attention diverted by arguments of his self-created characters in the next room.

Having written this witty and lively part himself, it would be difficult to say Paul Davies misinterprets his character.

But I feel this part deserves a less contrived characterisation than Davies gives.

In the second scene we move into the mansion's drawing room in the year 1900.

The couple whom the letter describes act out their lives through Paul's script.

Together they had once shared an ideal 'and a disgust of upper class values.

She is the mistress of a wealthy socialite and the lover of an idealistic jackeroo.

While Estelle (Rosie Tonkin) and her lover Deegan (Kevin Cotter) find themselves searching for a way to express their feelings they challenge each others changing ideals.

As the poor boy from the country, out to show the world, Cotter is strong and convincing.

But it is in the gallery with Monica (Carolyn Howard) and Leon (Peter Sommerfield) that the play finds its strength.

Monica the new-born artiste is becoming disillusioned with Leon, St Kilda's town planner, as the two discuss the worth of a "frozen living performance art piece".

The year is 1988 and the mansion has become a cultural centre.

As the couple wait for the performance to begin we find ourselves witness to their building frustrations and personal problems.

It is only after they have revealed their inner most hostilities that they realise they are the performance.

The walls begin to lose their barriers of time and the mansion's moments of history meet.

The gallery scene is full of quick, witty and sharp lines delivered with flair by Howard and Sommerfield.

In particular, Sommerfield gives a shrewd characterisation of Leon with his obvious gift for straight man comedy.

By the final scene the conflicts of past, present and future have escalated to the degree that the times meet only to be intervened by the mansion itself.

The plays' attraction is in its unconventional movement from era to era and its innovative setting.

The acting is generally energetic and convincing and the script is sharp and extremely witty.

Living Rooms is being performed at "Linden", 26 Acland St, St Kilda. Tickets can be booked through BASS.

JACQUI
MACDONALD

Something more than a history lesson

NOT quite knowing what to expect, or what is expected of the audience, may seem a risky way to increase the atmosphere of excitement and anticipation in theatre.

But I found the "location" aspect of theatre in this Theatreworks production, fascinating to say the least.

The venue chosen for the production, the grand old St Kilda mansion, "Linden" was the perfect setting for the three-scene play which explores St Kilda's development and decline over the past 86 years.

All three scenes are performed simultaneously in separate rooms: the drawing room (1900), the flatette (1972) and the gallery (1988).

The audience is divided into three groups, each going to a different room and different time in St Kilda's history.

It matters little in which order one travels through

THEATRE

LIVING ROOMS
By Paul Davies
Presented by
Theatreworks
Linden,
26 Acland Street, St Kilda
Review: KAREN MURPHY

the time zones: each scene is entire in itself but adds perspective to the others.

I travelled backwards through history, starting in 1988 and finishing in 1900.

The first two scenes, 1988 and 1972, were excellent, both for the mixture of provocative social comment and wry humour in the first, and for the great sense of idealism portrayed in the second.

The third scene, involving the mistress of the house and an idealistic jackaroo bound for the Boer war, left me cold. This is a pity because it could well have been the most emotive scene of all.

The dialogue in this scene wasn't sharp enough and some good ideas are left hanging.

The costuming is perfect and all performances - particularly Cliff Ellen in the flatette scene and Peter Sommerfield in the gallery - are impressive.

The final scene in the hallway involves all the characters and the entire audience, and runs the gamut of Linden's history.

The characters continue the scenes the audience has already witnessed and the involvement of cross-dialogue is both funny and creates an impression of a timewarp.

The argument between past, present and future rises in pitch as each accuses the other for the bewildering state of things until, finally, the house intervenes.

And it works. I thoroughly recommend *Living Rooms*, not only for its dramatic qualities, but also as an entertaining history lesson.

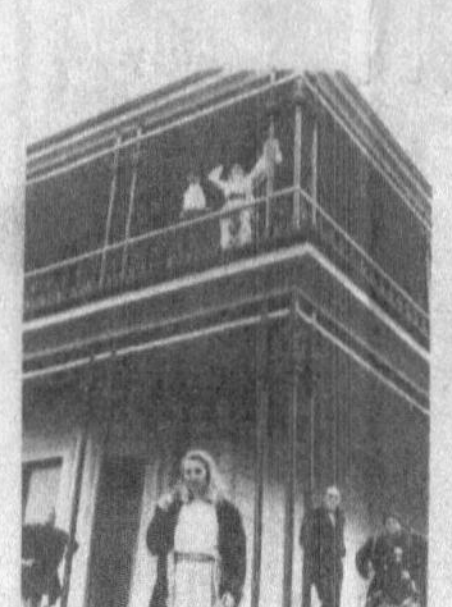

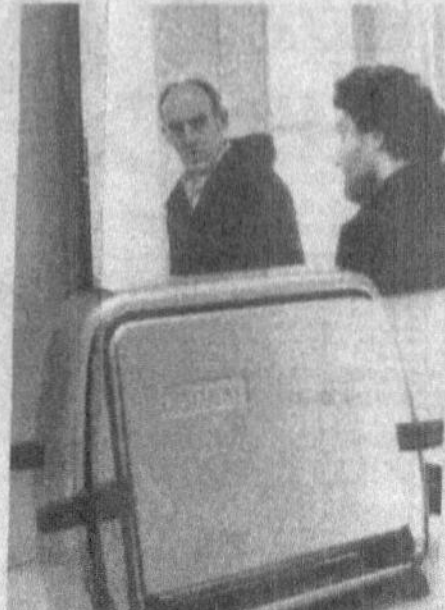

Theatre on the move

Playwright Paul Davies believes that Australia had the chance to become genuinely independent in 1900 and 1972. We missed the boat on both occasions, he feels.

His latest play, *Living Rooms*, has two scenes which try to capture the sense of idealism that existed at those times. One scene is set on the eve of federation, during the height of the Boer War, and the other on the night of Gough Whitlam's election to power.

"They were key moments in Australian history, in that people felt genuine change was about to happen. What we got was a brief period of change, followed by a long period of conservatism," he says.

Davies wants his play to focus on these "lost opportunities". To project into the future, a third scene is set in 1988. While the concept of independence is still there, the idealism is not.

"The issue of progress is the key focus of the play," says Davies. "The third

SALLY HEATH talks with Paul Davies whose play, "Living Rooms" will be performed by Theatreworks at an old mansion in St Kilda from July 17.

scene argues that some change is necessary, that you can't hold onto the past all the time. The values that are incorporated in the change are important: change involves compromise."

History will surround the audience and players in the old mansion where the play is being performed. The house, Linden, is a reminder of St Kilda's origins as an exclusive seaside resort.

As the suburb declined, Linden, like so many of the grand houses, was converted into boarding rooms. The house has now been bought by the St Kilda Council to be used as a cultural centre.

"It occurred to us that encapsulated in the very building that we would be using was all this history," says Davies. "It is a physical and architectural account of the kind of changes that have gone on in St Kilda."

It was in fact the opportunity to use Linden that prompted the idea of Davies' play.

The play itself is performed in three separate rooms, a drawing room, a boarding room and a gallery space, and works almost like a "living museum". The audience step into a scene in a room, while simultaneously the other two scenes are being played out elsewhere.

The order in which the audience see the three scenes is unimportant: actors and themes are common to all. Finally, audience and performers from the three different periods meet in the hallway.

The company stumbled into performing on location partly because they had no theatre of their own. Their previous productions were performed on a tram and in a pub.

They discovered that "location theatre" could work and that there were

unexpected spinoffs.

"We discovered a new sense of excitement and danger that isn't present in a normal theatre. There is the sense that anything can happen once you're in that less controlled environment."

Frequently the unexpected did happen, especially with tram shows. Some drivers went so slowly that the actors had to improvise; people boarded the tram, not realising it was a play.

While not so vulnerable to the unforseen, the same random influence will be at work with *Living Rooms*.

Davies: "The skill is to get things happening at the right time because the play is occurring simultaneously in three different rooms.

"The actors have to be perfect in the timing of their performance because they are moving from room to room."

The random element involved means the play is always renewing itself. As Davies points out, "no two nights were ever the same with the tram show".

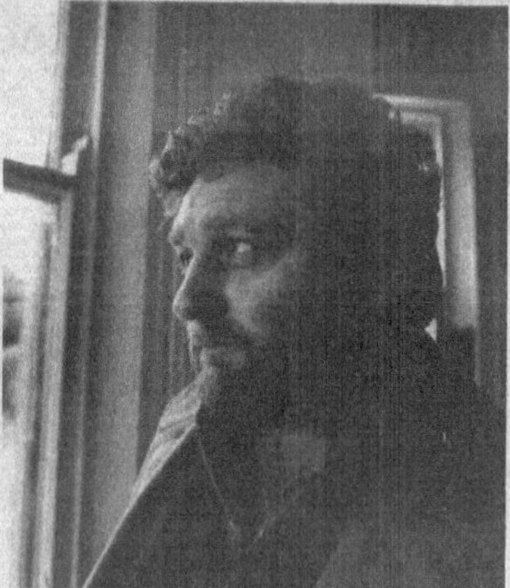

Paul Davies: "The skill is to get things happening at the right time . . ."

Star Observer - Fri. 4/7

TheatreWorks in a Living Room

After *Storming Mont Albert by Tram* and *Breaking up in Balwyn*, TheatreWorks's Paul Davies has come up with another *location theatre* triumph. This time his unconventional setting is a magnificent Victorian mansion, "Linden", which has a history as chequered as that of St Kilda itself

Living Rooms consists of three scenes in three separate rooms. The audience reclines in the full original splendour of a drawing room in 1900 to witness the end of the love affair between an idealistic jackaroo bound for the Boer war and the sophisticated mistress of the house.

Moving from the drawing room into a seedy flatette next door, it is the eve of Gough Whitlam's election to government. A boarder stumbles upon an old letter, tucked under the lino covering up the original marble fireplace. Inspired by this, he concocts an elaborate past for the house.

The setting for another scene played simultaneously is the public gallery which **Linden** has now become, restored to match its former glory. An exhibition of St Kilda's history in *objets d'art* is now on show. A present day couple, deliberating over the exhibition become aware that they are somehow on show themselves.

Eeventually, characters from all three periods actually meet in the hallway and things become faintly surreal. The argument between past, present and future rises in pitch as each accuses the other for the bewildering state of things until, finally, the house itself intervenes . . .

Living Rooms by Paul Davies presented by TheatreWorks at "Linden", 26 Acland St, St Kilda
Mon - Sat, 8pm from 17 July
Tickets $14.90/$10.90
Concessions available, Mon eve, Sat matinee only.

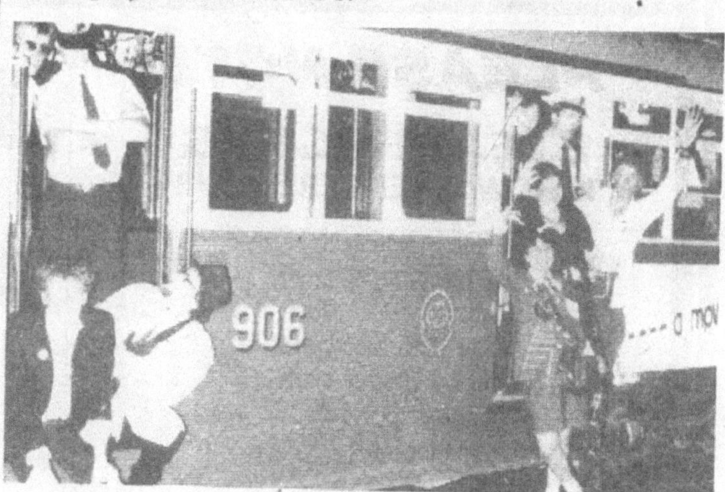

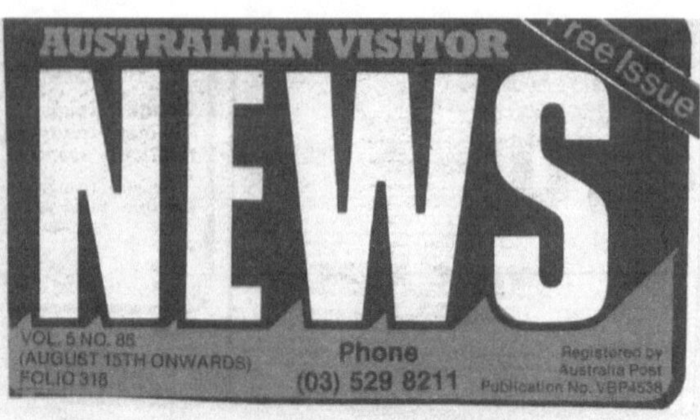

AUSTRALIAN VISITOR NEWS

Free Issue

VOL. 5 NO. 86
(AUGUST 15TH ONWARDS)
FOLIO 318

Phone
(03) 529 8211

Registered by
Australia Post
Publication No. VBP4538

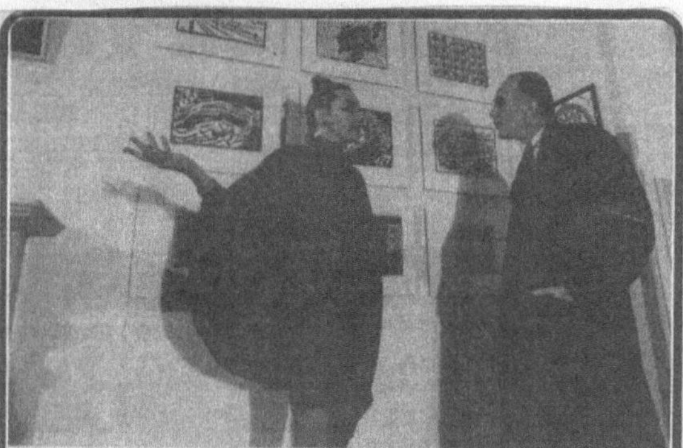

★ *Monica (Caz Howard) and Leon (Peter Sommerfeld) argue about art, life, relationships, redeveloping St. Kilda, and nuclear fallout shelters in Theatre Works' Living Rooms at Linden.*

Last of the mansions

LINDEN is one of the last of the great mansions that dominated the once-fashionable St. Kilda beachfront this time last century. But times changed; the families who built houses like Linden moved east and the mansions with their landscaped gardens and esplanade-views were either torn down or divided up into a dozen seedy flatettes.

Now times are changing again and the "yuppies" are moving back into St. Kilda, doing up those little terrace houses that are left, and Linden has been bought by the St Kilda Council, to spend her old age as a community arts centre.

But right now Linden has come alive as an animated museum thanks to Theatre Works' Living Rooms — If Wall Could Speak . . . by Paul Davies.

Theatre Works and Davies has earned a reputation for "location theatre", performing 'Storming Mont Albert by Tram' on a moving 42 and 'Breaking Up In Balwyn' on board a yarra River ferry. 'Living Rooms' is another excellent use of "alternative theatre space."

Davies has taken Linden's three major periods — as a turn-of-the-century family mansion, an early -70s boarding house, and a late -80s art gallery — and fashioned three separate stores which are played out in three separate rooms.

The audience, divided into three, sees the three self-contained, but interrelated stories in a different chronological order as the groups move from room to room and activate the museum "display cases" in each well-dressed setting.

While not a documented history of Linden itself, the three stories present an expressionist version of the history of houses like Linden in the St. Kilda area, and of the suburb itself.

They also reflect some of Davies' concern for the area — the fear that, now the area is popular again, developers will tear down the Lindens and create another Surfers paradise with a Miami marina — and Theatre Works' own reasons for abandoning the eastern suburbs, where it was based for so long, in favor of St. Kilda.

The first period is 1901 — in the elegant drawing room, the idealistic jackaroo Michael Deegan (Kevin Cotter) is about to leave for the Boer War, arguing with Estelle (Rosie Tonkin) about his motives and trying to convince her to leave her "sugar daddy" Dr Baumgarten (Cliff Ellen) and come with him.

'Living Rooms' - by Paul Davies is presented by Theatre Works and is playing at Linden, 26 Acland Street, St. Kilda, Monday to Friday at 8.15pm, and Saturdays at 5pm and 8.15pm, until August 23. Phone 534 4879.

The Herald

Melbourne, Thursday, July 24, 1986

Old St Kilda home a new kind of play-house

PLAY: Living Rooms, by Paul Davies
THEATRE: Linden, 26 Acland St, St Kilda. 8.15-10.30 p.m.

THEATRE

CLARK FORBES

Linden was until recently a mouldering Victorian pile serving as a boarding house to the down-on-their-lucks of St Kilda.

Then the National Trust fell upon the only house left in Acland St. and began to restore something of its former grandeur.

Now it has been taken over by Theatreworks to stage the Paul Davies play *Living Rooms*.

Sitting next to me last night was a descendant of the family who once lived in its splendid surroundings.

Davies makes something of a feature of environmental plays — *Storming Mont Albert By Tram* was played, naturally enough, on a tram.

This time his play has been written round the old house. The audience is shown into the gallery, then ushered into a seedy early 70s flatette where a draft dodger is preparing for the imminent coming of Gough.

Behind a boarded-up fireplace he discovers a letter written by a Boer War soldier to the woman he left behind.

Inspired, he concocts a story for the house. The audience then moves to the drawing room where the soldier is about to take his leave for the war.

The final scene returns to the gallery, 1988, where a couple wait with increasing irritation for the scene to begin.

The play touches of a number of concerns about duty, war and what "they've" done to St Kilda. Nothing that really leaves you gasping with admiration at its insight, but enough to tickle the imagination.

What could so easily end in mayhem works surprisingly smoothly. The result is a hugely enjoyable ramble round an inventive mind and a delightful extension of the normal theatrical boundaries.

MESSENGER

Award winning newspaper for Community Service.

No. 812   TUESDAY, AUGUST 5, 1986   Publishing Data — Page 2   Classifi

Living rooms is powerful drama

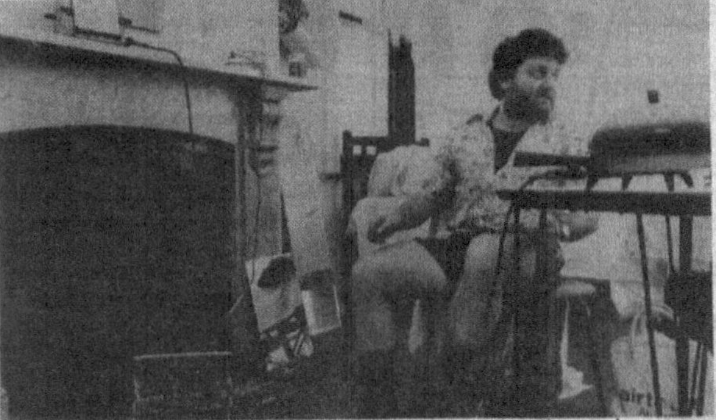

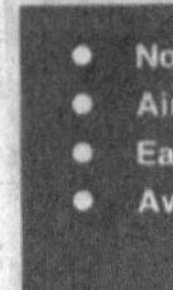

IT'S not so much the place you are in as the time when you are in it, utters Paul, a would be draft dodger wallowing in a seedy flatette on the eve of Whitlam's election.

LIVING ROOMS, an interesting play on words about different times in one place, is set in a renovated St Kilda mansion, and consists of three scenes in three separate rooms during three different times.

This is "location theatre," and therefore powerfully atmospheric, as the audience move in no sequential order to a dark candle lit Victorian drawing room, complete with roaring log fire and dueling lovers torn apart by the Boer war and romantic idealism.

Cut to the flatette in the early 70's, and this time it's Vietnam and socialist idealism, where the itinerant Paul chances upon a letter, sealed in the best dramatic tradition behind the original fireplace, from the Boer war soldier Deegan to his lover Estelle, mistress of Linden.

Suddenly inspired, Paul, who to blur the lines of reality further is played by the play's writer Paul Davis, begins to write a play beginning at the end of that Victorian love affair.

Suddenly it is 1988, we are in the mansions white walled gallery watching a yuppy couple fight over love, art and the future of St Kilda.

Constant cross references to other times and places ties the play together, with Cuthbert, Estelle's older lover who built Linden for her, declaring that in the march of time, Linden would become a boarding house to survive.

Later in the flattette, Paul wonders how the seedy dump could have ever been a grand mansion, until he discover a marble fireplace under the peeling paint and lino.

The sparing lovers' conversation in the near future gallery is all very topical, given the plans afoot to run St Kilda into another Surfers Paradise, although this dialogue, like that of the historically laden talk in the Victorian drawing room, seems too clever, too self-conscious and too ideologically sound.

Certainly the strongest writing was Paul's flatette scene, which was alive and yet very depressing.

Anyone with relationship problems will cringe at the cuttingly real arguments between the lovers in the gallery, where actor Peter Sommerfeld as the uptight townplanner Leon, gets most of the play's laughs.

Eventually, all the characters meet in the hallway for the last scene, which should have been eerie and surreal, but was marred by the high camp inclusion of a talking house.

Despite this totally unnecessary ending, and some labored dialogue, LIVING ROOMS rates amongst some of the most exciting theatre I have seen this year.

Location theatre offers something videos cannot, and that's being inside the action, well worth turning off the telly and heading down to St Kilda for, even in the snow.

• Would be draft dodger Paul, played by the play's writer Paul Davis, contemplates life under Whitlam, just before the election.

THE AGE

22 July 1986   250 Spencer St., Melbourne, 60 0421 (Classified 604 1144)   60 Pages (Incl. 8 pages Cwlth Games Feature, 6 pages Home & 6 pages Epicure)   132r

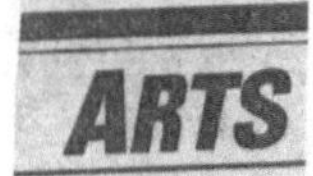

14   THE AGE, Tuesday 22 July 1986

Once-grand house makes room for a novel location drama

THEATRE

LEONARD RADIC

THEATRE Works has made something of a speciality of environmental or location theatre. First it devised a play which was acted out on the city-Mont Albert tram route. Then it staged a companion play on board a Yarra pleasure boat. Now in 'Living Rooms' it has taken for its setting a once-grand mansion in St Kilda.

The mansion in question is Linden at 26 Acland Street. Back in the Victorian period it was an elegant private home with a Guilfoyle garden and a view of the sea. Then it fell on bad times and became a boarding house. Today it operates as a community centre and an art gallery.

Paul Davies's play explores three stages in the house's history. For audiences, the novelty of the night is that the three historical episodes are enacted in different rooms in the building, though not necessarily in strict chronological order.

In the elegant drawing room, for example, with its Victorian settee and log fire and portraits on the wall, we are introduced to Estelle, Michael and Dr Baumgarten. The doctor is the owner of the house and Estelle is his mistress, while Michael, a commissioned army officer about to set off for the Boer War, is her would-be lover. The year is 1901.

Next door it is the night before the 1972 elections, and in a tiny flatette remarkable chiefly only for its scunginess a would-be writer and draft dodger (Paul Davies) dreams of better days ahead under a Labor government.

In the grate he finds a letter from South Africa, addressed to Estelle. And it is that that inspires him to write the mansion's history.

In the third scene, enacted in the gallery, it is 1988 and a modern couple are engaged in a lively argument over art, town planning, nuclear fallout shelters and the future of St Kilda.

This interchange, enacted between a social worker (Carolyn Howard) and a town planner with a bulldozer mentality (Peter Sommerfeld), is the best part of the evening. Their arguments are given pertinence by the fact that Theatre Works, a community theatre company previously based in the eastern suburbs, has found a new permanent home in St Kilda and will be launching its first season there in October.

Paul Davies does nicely as the down-and-out boarder. The writing in this scene, and in the gallery scene as well, has the ring of truth about it. But the 1901 scene is labored, both in its acting and its writing. It is the one weak link in the chain.

Like the earlier two location theatre works, this is a piece which consciously sets out to extend the boundaries of theatre and to give audiences a new and interesting experience. At that level it succeeds admirably. Who knows? It might even inspire one or two theatregoers to think about the environmental issues which the play raises.

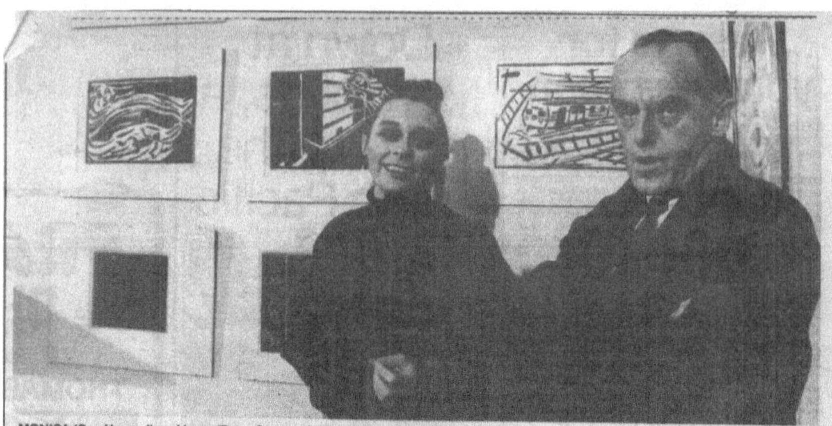

MONICA (Caz Howard) and Leon (Peter Sommerfeld) argue about art, life, relationships, redeveloping St. Kilda, and nuclear fallout shelters in Theatre Works' *Living Rooms* at Linden.

Linden relives its past in Theatre Works show

By GREG BURCHALL

LINDEN is one of the last of the great mansions that dominated the once-fashionable St. Kilda beachfront this time last century.

But times changed; the families who built houses like Linden moved east and the mansions with their landscaped gardens and esplanade-views were either torn down or divided up into a dozen seedy flatettes.

Now times are changing again and the "yuppies" are moving back into St. Kilda, doing up those little terrace houses that are left, and Linden has been bought by the St Kilda Council, to spend her old age as a community arts centre.

But right now Linden has come alive as an animated museum thanks to Theatre Works' *Living Rooms — If Walls Could Speak . . .* by Paul Davies.

Theatre Works and Davies has earned a reputation for "location theatre", performing *Storming Mont Albert by Tram* on a moving 42 and *Breaking Up in Balwyn* on board a Yarra River ferry. *Living Rooms* is another excellent use of "alternative theatre space".

Davies has taken Linden's three major periods — as a turn-of-the-century family mansion, an early-'70s boarding house, and a late-'80s art gallery — and fashioned three separate stores which are played out in three separate rooms.

The audience, divided into three, sees the three self-contained, but interrelated stories in a different chronological order as the groups move from room to room and activate the museum "display cases" in each well-dressed setting.

While not a documented history of Linden itself, the three stories present an expressionist version of the history of houses like Linden in the St. Kilda area, and of the suburb itself.

They also reflect some of Davies' concern for the area — the fear that, now the area is popular again, developers will tear down the Lindens and create another Surfers paradise with a Miami marina — and Theatre Works' own reasons for abandoning the eastern suburbs, where it was based for so long, in favor of St. Kilda.

The first period is 1901 — in the elegant drawing room, the idealistic jackaroo Michael Deegan (Kevin Cotter) is about to leave for the Boer War, arguing with Estelle (Rosie Tonkin) about his motives and trying to convince her to leave her "sugar daddy" Dr Baumgarten (Cliff Ellen) and come with him.

Next it is 1972 — on the eve of the federal election, a down-and-out Queensland migrant, would-be writer and draft dodger (Paul Davies) prepares to go to the St. Kilda town hall for free food and drink and to listen to Gough Whitlam's promises. He finds an old letter from Michael to Estelle.

Finally it is 1988 — in the art gallery, de factos Monika (Caz Howard) and Leon (Peter Sommerfeld) argue about redeveloping their house, their relationship, their lives and St. Kilda.

Leonie Hurry, as a maid in the first, a domestic in the second and an actress in the third, helps link all the characters together.

The rest of the cast is very good, especially Howard and Sommerfeld in the 1988 piece, which has the best script. They work well off each other and the audience. Davies is good delivering an almost-monologue, aided by some wonderful sight gags to do with his "kitchen".

Cotter, Tonkin and Ellen in the 1901 piece are hindered, by an overly soapie script which makes the piece the weakest of the three.

But the idea is good, and the direction — by Davies, Howard and Sommerfeld — is economic and clever. It is enjoyable, accessible theatre with something to say and a novel way of saying it.

The payoff for the nomadic audience comes in the fourth and final scene — which they all see together in the hall — when all the characters from the three eras come together . . . as well as another important "character", Linden herself, who finally gets to speak her piece.

Living Rooms by Paul Davies is presented by Theatre Works and is playing at Linden, 26 Acland Street, St. Kilda, Monday to Friday at 8.15 pm, and Saturdays at 5 pm and 8.15 pm, until August 23. Phone 534 4879.

Space and history

Living Rooms, by Paul Davies presented by Theatre Works at Linden, 26 Acland St, St Kilda. See What's On for details. Reviewed by Sheril Berkovitch.

The TheatreWorks company was formed six years ago and among other things, aimed to produce original works and to involve the community in drama activities. They are also committed to the use of "non-traditional theatre space".

Taking both the history of Linden, the house where the performance takes place, and the history of St Kilda itself, *Living Rooms* covers a whole range of different issues, including contemporary local politics and personal relationships.

The first scene takes place in a run-down "flatette", part of one of the rooming houses which flourished in St Kilda during the 1970s.

Its resident, Paul,is musing on the probable success of Whitlam, who goes to the polls the following day. He stumbles upon an old letter, hidden in the fireplace, from a young man off to the Boer war to his lover left behind, the mistress of the house.

From the content of the letter Paul creates his own history of the house, which strangely parallels Linden's actual history.

Contemporary change

Moving from the flatette (literally) to the drawing room, the audience witnesses the past - the breaking up of the lovers as the young man leaves for the war. The owner of the house is already contemplating its change into a boarding house, juxtaposing the style and beauty of the original home to the seedy, down graded boarding house of 1975.

Later, moving into the Gallery, it is 1988 and a couple are contemplating a contemporary sculpture - a breakfast table strewn with mess. Leon (Peter Somerfeld) is a St Kilda city planner and not in the least "arty"; Monika (Carolyn Howard) is a social worker and quite pretentious about the meaning of art.

Both Leon and Monika are indicative of the yuppies moving into St Kilda. Leon doesn't care about what's happening to the area - which is understandable as he's part of the move to change it. Monika, on the other hand, is too concerned.

While they argue over life and art and town planning, becoming more and more irritated because the scene hasn't started, it becomes clear that they are, in fact, the actors.

Disintegrate

As their life together disintegrates before the audience, characters from the past begin to merge with those of the future, consolidating the three stories into one history. Moving again into the hallway, the characters from the past and future mingle.

Theatre Works have certainly succeeded in utilising a non-traditional space while still maintaining continuity.

Linden is now used as an arts centre and in some ways it is ironic that while the St Kilda city council, through planners like Leon, have little interest in maintaining housing for the existing community, they are quite prepared to fund arts centres to bring people in from outside.

This isn't a bad thing. I think they should do both. But the irony lies in the history of Linden itself - from upper class home, to boarding house, to arts centre - and in the subject matter of the play.

Living Rooms is never boring, well crafted, well acted and excitingly different in its use of time and space. It makes a poignant point about the direction that St Kilda will take and maintains its integrity without becoming cliched or crass. It is, in my opinion, a performance not to be missed. ∎

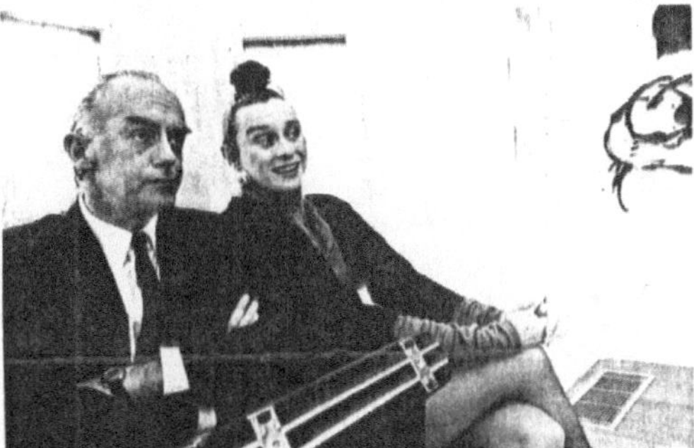

•Town planner Leon (Peter Somerfeld) with "arty" Monika (Carolyn Howard) in *Living Rooms*

Not my style

She Came Too Late, by Mary Wings. The Women's Press, 1986. Reviewed by Lyndell Fairleigh.

The title of Mary Wings' *She Came Too Late* gives a lot away about the style, if not the content, of this lesbian thriller.

The fly jacket tells us that it is "a fast-moving and contentious whodunnit in the Chandler tradition, and an urbane study of lesbian sexuality and the games people play".

Well, maybe so. ButI've got a few questions. What political mileage is to be gained from this tradition? And how does Mary Wings use it?

It may be worthwhile to look briefly at *Murder In the Collective*, Barbara Wilson's lesbian feminist. Much feminist, as well as traditional, women's writing is in the first person because it's subjective and personal. It's a way of airing feelings, thoughts, desires and doubts. A form of self-examination.

Following this tradition, *Murder in the Collective* is the heroine's personal chronicle. She's not alone, however. There's her twin sister who helps and advises her.

Multiple identities

Twins are a common motif in women's writing because they simultaneously suggest a woman's multiple identities and the hazy border between one woman's identity and another's.

The heroine is also a member of a collective, a political structure which questions the primacy of individual identity. When one of the collective is murdered, possibly by someone more, she may even be partly responsible for the "crime".

In this feminist thriller then, there's no sure line between personal and public truth, or any simple resolutions.

Emma Victor, the heroine of *She Came Too Late*, is very much Philip Marlowe's "daughter". She is tough, cynical, individualistic and, at times, misogynistic. I particularly disliked her attitude to other female lover's "innocence" could have come straight out of any Raymond Chandler novel.

Kissed

Following an episode in which she's kissed by a woman who she's "ninety-nine percent sure was straight", Emma glibly generalises: "I don't like it if straight women suddenly come on to me. I think it's

Just like having walls that speak

Theatre

Jacinta Le Plastrier

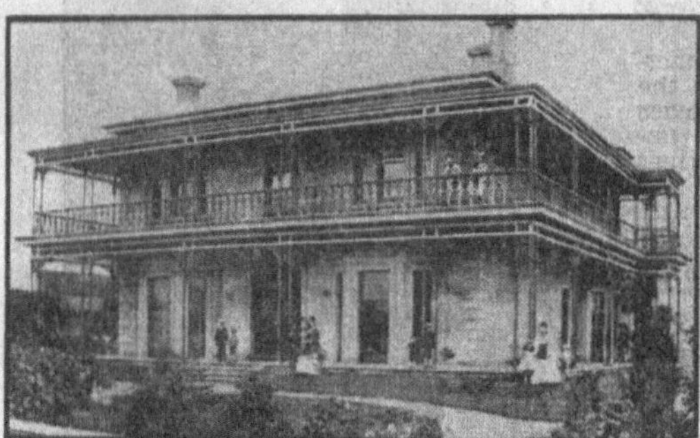

Linden in St. Kilda, as it was in its early days.

PAUL Davies, pioneer extraordinaire of Melbourne location theatre, has jumped both boat and tram in his time.

And while his feet are back on dry ground for his latest project with TheatreWorks, *Living Rooms*, as can only be expected, they won't be skirting the boards of conventional theatre.

"If only walls could speak . . . three scenes in a grand mansion." That's the wrap-up for the new child of Davies.

Living Rooms follows on the applauded *Storming Mont Albert by Tram* and *Breaking Up in Balwyn*.

The first was set on the No. 42 tram, the second on the Princess riverboat.

Talking to Davies, you feel part of a scenario itself, running around the busy circuits of the bearded creator/director/actor's head.

THE effect is magnified by the sparse parish hall that houses TheatreWorks in Acland St., St. Kilda, a low stage at the front crowded with props.

Sitting over a table, Davies rarely stops talking or watching, making coffee, pointing to notes and photographs, saying "hi" to actors trooping in over late morning.

Living Rooms will be performed just down the street from TheatreWorks at the magnificent old Victorian mansion Linden.

It's no mere coincidence.

"We're all St. Kilda residents here," says Davies fiercely.

Concerned citizens would be as sharp a term. For Davies' *Living Rooms* isn't just the plot of a house re-living its history, its peopling.

More relevant is its life as a gauge of the life of St. Kilda, originally a haunt of the aristocracy, later a seedy, sleazy but still lively downside of Melbourne and now, a slightly confused mixture of both as the council begins a re-gentrification of the suburb.

It is this conflict *Living Rooms* seeks to explore and confront, if not completely resolve.

Living Rooms consists of three scenes in three separate rooms.

The audience is given the original splendor of a drawing room in 1900 to witness the end of an illicit love affair between a jackaroo bound for the Boer War and the sophisticated "mistress" of the house. This scene is in fact the imagining of the inhabitant of the seedy flatette next door.

Time jumps to Gough Whitlam's election to Government.

The house is now boarding quarters and a conscientious objector resident, played by Davies, stumbles over an old letter telling of the affair and concocts a past for Linden.

As he writes, he is distracted by the noisy arguments next door of his own creations.

The next scene, all played simultaneously, is the public gallery which Linden has now become, restored to its original state.

It's 1988 and an exhibition of St. Kilda's history as objets d' Art is on show. A modern couple are deliberating over a "frozen living performance art piece" which leads to a study of their own problems.

The barriers between the rooms and time periods begin to break down and characters from all scenes join.

As the argument between past, present and future rises, St. Kilda's own spirit intervenes with the house having its say and grievance on its future.

The audience will move around the house for each scene.

IT'S an attempt to talk about progress and what represents real progress," says Davies. "You need change, getting rid of certain things. But you also require the people's desire for change.

"*Living Rooms* gets people involved in that future and the extraordinary things that have happened and are still happening here."

● *Living Rooms* begins on July 17 for a limited season at Linden, 26 Acland St., St. Kilda. Bookings through TheatreWorks on 534-4879 and Bass.

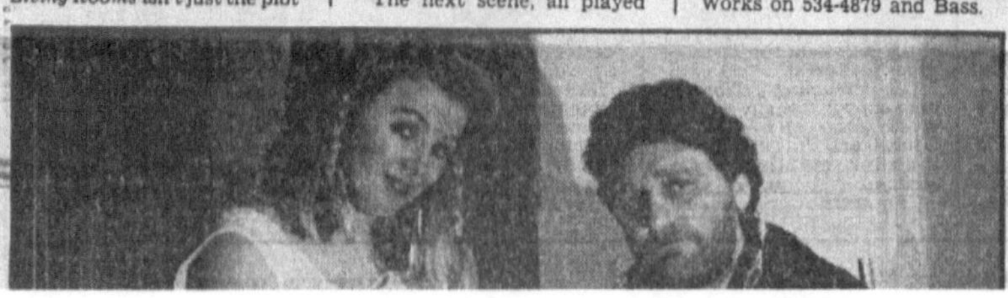

IN THE LIVING ROOMS OF ST. KILDA

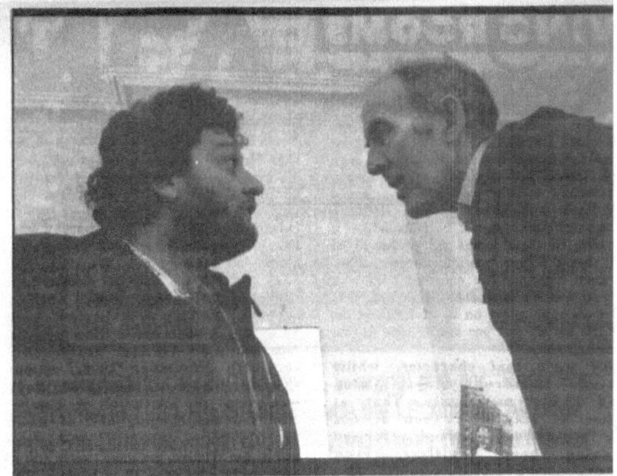

Theatreworks was established as a full-time professional theatre company in 1981 by five graduates of the Victorian College of The Arts. The company has recently moved from its original location in the Hawthorn Camberwell area to St.Kilda. Since arriving they have produced two plays, The Pub Show (written by Paul Somerfeld, and performed in a bar at the Esplanade Hotel), and Living Rooms (written by Paul Davies, and performed at Linden House). The latter has just completed its season, and the company are preparing their next production CAKE - An Acland Street Comedy.

WAVES spoke to Carolyn Howard and Paul Davies, both actors in Living Rooms in addition to being full-time members of the company.

Despite the fact that play has completed its run, many of issues (and Theatreworks) are relevant. As Paul Davies refers dialogue between the actions government, and the contribution of community, and the relevance Theatreworks as a community based group, WAVES continues presentation in a like manner.

LIVING ROOMS was conducte three different rooms of a fictional h *in* St.Kilda. Each room was designe represent different periods (1900, 1 and 1988) of St.Kilda's past, and the different styles of theatre were prese (e.g. the melodramatic scene set in was a legitimate style of that era), t were common themes of both a socia political nature present to link the pl

How did THEATREWORKS change from the eastern suburbs come about? And is there any particular reason why it came to St. Kilda?

CH: At that stage four out of the five core members of the artistic directorate of THEATREWORKS lived in St. Kilda. We'd been there for five years and we felt that artistically we needed more input;and also I think we got to the stage where we needed a performance venue of our own or to develop a low cost venue that was accessible to other groups as well.

Is there any other reason other than it's the location of this play?

PD: For me St. Kilda is a very exciting place to be, as a writer, at the moment because it is going through tremendous changes. I suppose the whole idea for LIVING ROOMS grew out of the fact that I discovered a suburb that had very aristocratic beginnings, became somewhat downwardly mobile this century, and is now trying to pull itself back up by the bootstraps.

I was fascinated by how those changes came about and what produced that huge socio-economic upheaval in the place; and when we found that the St. Kilda Council had bought Linden the two things came together. The idea for a play about the history of the suburb and being able to do it in a house which enshrined a

With this 'cultural renaissance' to which you seem to infer, have the St. Kilda Council been encouraging in this more by Theatreworks into St. Kilda apart from allowing you the use of Linden?

CH: Also they provided a lot of the artwork that has been used in the show. The paintings are mostly drawn from the St Kilda collection which is quite a substantial body of art for any local council to have, and that was freely provided for the show. They also provided us with carpenters and electricians to get the place up and running for us. We've had quite a good working relationship with the council and the staff,and they were keen to see the building used in this way. The play addresses some of the issues that the council is fighting, and that local residents are concerned about. All our work as a theatre company has been involved with expressing local issues and the concerns of local people with whom we work and live.

The two characters of the contemporary scene in the play are at times diametrically opposite- a rather callous town planner and a naive romantic with an artistic bent. Which do you see as having most effect on the future of St Kilda?

PD: We're not saying that all change is bad, or

the scene is to suggest that real progr really occurs when people feel involve change. The whole point of the suppose, is to alert people to the col energy and dynamism of St Kilda's because until people understand their don't think they havce any incentive to preserve what is good about the past... you do in a piece of drama is exaggerat things in the hope that audiences can there's a balance to be struck betw extremes,and you play off comedy and get a certain effect.

Do you in any way feel that from that socio-economic brack going to make those changes don't appear to beleive tha changes are going to come fro ground level or street level.

PD: Essentially that scene is a dialogue somebody who represents vaguely h values and somebody who seems to r total redneck Australian awful horrific at all cost Queensland style town plann sense the character in the flatette in t scene, even though it is set some 15 ye embodies some of the kind of ideal romanticism of people who are down

New stage of life for old home

IF the people won't come to the stuffy old theatre, then the theatre will have to come to them in the form of a grand old Victorian mansion.

That's the idea behind the local theatre company, Theatre Works, staging a comedy show, *Living Rooms*, inside Linden, a house in St Kilda.

One of the directors, the script writer and one of the actors, Paul Davies, 37, said recently the show highlights the transition of St Kilda through the characters living in the house from the turn of the century to the present.

The story traces the suburb's fascinating history from the elegance and wealth of a seaside suburb to a tacky red light district and now its transition to a renovated and trendy suburb.

The show is set in three rooms in the house and three audience groups rotate from room to room.

In the first scene the house is a mansion owned by a wealthy doctor and the story is set in a 1900 drawing room.

The story is based on a famous divorce case, the Sterling Divorce Case, a triangular love affair including the doctor, his wife and the man who lived with them.

"Then we jump 72 years to a couple of nights before Gough Whitlam is elected," Davies said.

"By then it (Linden) is a run down boarding house."

He said the plot in the second room is about a draft dodger, who is being evicted from the boarding house by an unsympathetic landlord.

Davies said the landlord, Cliff Ellen, is a "laconic, down-to-earth" character not dissimilar to John Cleese in the television show, *Fawlty Towers*.

In the final scene the house is a gallery owned by an architect and his family therapist wife, whose marriage is on the verge of collapsing after 10 years.

"It's like looking at history.

"It was an attempt to capture those kinds of changes by approaching it through the human element."

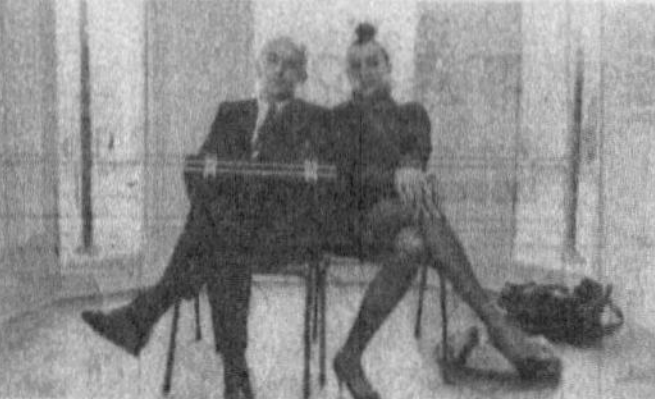

●Architect Leon (Peter Sommerfield) and his family therapist wife Monika (Carolyn Howard) in *Living Rooms*.

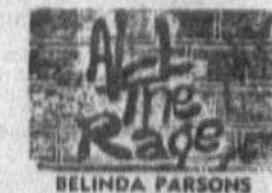

BELINDA PARSONS

Davies said the connection between the characters is that the draft dodger finds a letter in his room about the relationship between the doctor's wife and their tenant.

"People actually meet and confront each other about what's gone on in the house."

Davies said he got the idea for the play while living in St Kilda for the last two years.

He said Linden was the perfect vehicle to show the changes that St Kilda has gone through.

Davies said Theatre Works has a history of taking theatre out of its traditional place to explore new actor-audience relationships.

The show features music including Eric Satie's waltz, *I Want You*, for the 1900 scene, the Rolling Stones' *You Can't Always Get What You Want* for election eve in 1972 and for the gallery scene, Paul Kelly's *From St Kilda to King's Cross*.

Living Rooms started last night and runs for a limited season.

FANS who have enjoyed Venetta Fields' gospel show or the Slaughtermen will be interested in a new double album, *Straight Street*.

The album, subtitled *An Introduction to Black Gospel Music*, includes spiritually uplifting tracks by Sam Cooke and the Soul Stirrers, Mahalia Jackson, Sister Rosetta Tharpe and many more.

A NICE touch from a Melbourne band!

The singer of the Crumby Cowboys, Rick O'Shea, rang All the Rage concerned about disappointed fans who turned up at the Parkview Hotel in Fitzroy to see them last Friday.

O'Shea said the Crumby Cowboys regret the inconvenience caused through circumstances beyond its control.

THE Painters and Dockers will be at the Seaview Ballroom, Fitzroy St, St Kilda, tonight and tomorrow night with special guests X.

AN under 18 show will be held tomorrow night at Albert Park High School featuring heavy rockers Axatak, Knight and Mercury.

Doors open at 7.30 pm.

LINDEN is one of the last of the great mansions that dominated the once-fashionable St. Kilda beachfront this time last century.

But times changed; the families who built houses like Linden moved east and the mansions with their landscaped gardens and esplanade-views were either torn down or divided up into a dozen seedy flatettes.

Now times are changing again and the "yuppies" are moving back into St. Kilda, doing up those little terrace houses that are left, and Linden has been bought by the St Kilda Council, to spend her old age as a community arts centre.

But right now Linden has come alive as an animated museum thanks to Theatre Works' *Living Rooms — If Wall Could Speak*... by Paul Davies.

Theatre Works and Davies has earned a reputation for "location theatre", performing *Storming Mont Albert by Tram* on a moving 42 and *Breaking Up in Balwyn* on board a yarra River ferry. *Living Rooms* is another excellent use of "alternative theatre space".

Davies has taken Linden's three major periods — as a turn-of-the-century family mansion, an early-'70s boarding house, and a late-'80s art gallery — and fashioned three separate stores which are played out in three separate rooms.

The audience, divided into three, sees the three self-contained, but interrelated stories in a different chronological order as the groups move from room to room and activate the museum "display cases" in each well-dressed setting.

While not a documented history of Linden itself, the three stories present an expressionist version of the history of houses like Linden in the St. Kilda area, and of the suburb itself.

They also reflect some of Davies' concern for the area — the fear that, now the area is popular again, developers will tear down the Lindens and create another Surfers paradise with a Miami marina — and Theatre Works' own reasons for abandoning the eastern suburbs, where it was based for so long, in favor of St. Kilda.

The first period is 1901 — in the elegant drawing room, the idealistic jackaroo Michael Deegan (Kevin Cotter) is about to leave for the Boer War, arguing with Estelle (Rosie Tonkin) about his motives and trying to convince her to leave her "sugar daddy" Dr Baumgarten (Cliff Ellen) and come with him.

Next it is 1972 — on the eve of the federal election, a down-and-out Queensland migrant, would-be writer and draft dodger (Paul Davies) prepares to go to the St. Kilda town hall for free food and drink and to listen to Gough Whitlam's promises. He finds an old letter from Michael to Estelle.

Finally it is 1988 — in the art gallery, de factos Monika (Caz Howard) and Leon (Peter Sommerfeld) argue about redeveloping their house, their relationship, their lives and St. Kilda.

Leonie Hurry, as a maid in the first, a domestic in the second and an actress in the third, helps link all the characters together.

The rest of the cast is very good, especially Howard and Sommerfeld in the 1988 piece, which has the best script. They work well off each other and the audience. Davies is good delivering an almost-monologue, aided by some wonderful sight gags to do with his "kitchen".

Cotter, Tonkin and Ellen in the 1901 piece are hindered by an overly soapie script which makes the piece the weakest of the three.

But the idea is good, and the direction — by Davies, Howard and Sommerfeld — is economic and clever. It is enjoyable, accessible theatre with something to say and a novel way of saying it.

The payoff for the nomadic audience comes in the fourth and final scene — which they all see together in the hall — when all the characters from the three eras come together... as well as another important "character", Linden herself, who finally gets to speak her piece.

Living Rooms by Paul Davies is presented by Theatre Works and is playing at Linden, 26 Acland Street, St. Kilda, Monday to Friday at 8.15 pm, and Saturdays at 5 pm and 8.15 pm, until August 23. Phone 534 4879.

GREG BURCHALL

"COBURG COURIER"
Vic.
-6 Aug 1986

. . Pete Smith's Show Scene

THEATRE-WORKS TOP HIT!

Writer, director, actor, Paul Davies and the talented Theatre-Works company have a hit on their hands with their latest venture, "Living Rooms" now playing at "Linden", the grand old mansion situated at 26 Acland Street, St. Kilda (just up from the Village Bell).

"Living Rooms" is definately the most inventive piece of Australian theatre your correspondent has ever seen, consisting as it does of three seperate acts in three seperate rooms, with the action taking place in the present day and around the turn of the century.

TEN OUT OF TEN

The audience sits in the original splendour of a drawing room in 1900 to witness the end of a love affair between an idealistic jackaroo bound for the Boer War and the sophisticated mistress of the house.

Moving from the drawing room into a seedy flatette next door, it's the eve of Gough Whitlam's election to government as a boarder stumbles on an old letter tucked behind the fire-place. Inspired by the letter he concocts an elaborate past for the house and as he writes, he is distracted by noisy arguments in the next room, which are in fact, going on between the very characters he has created.

IF WALLS COULD SPEAK

The third scene, played simultaneously with the other two, but with a different audience, is the public art gallery which "Linden" has become, with a fascinating exhibition of objects d'Art from St. Kilda's rather chequered past. The time is 1988 and a couple are deliberating over a "frozen living performance art piece". They very soon come to realise that they are themselves the performers in this trilogy.

TIME INTO TIME

Eventually the characters from all three periods meet the audience in the large hallway and the arguments between past and present reach a climax with, of all things, the grand mansion itself intervening to bring the evening to a close.

The performers in Theatre-Works are amongst the most talented I have seen anywhere on any legit stage and Paul Davies and company are to be heartily congratulated for this unique "location theatre" production.

TOP TALENT

Paul Davies, the creator of "Living Rooms" came to melbourne in 1974 and worked as script editor on the last episodes of "Homicide"; he also worked as editor on the initial "Sullivans" episodes and has written for "The Box", "Skyways" and "Against The Wind" just to name a few.

With the Theatre Works group he conceived the comedy "Storming Mont Albert By Tram" which actually took place on board a tram going to and coming from Mont Albert. Paul also wrote "Breaking Up In Balwyn", another success which gained him top recognition, but

"Living Rooms" is by far his best work.

It's playing for a limited season Monday to Saturday at 8.15 p.m. and Saturdays at 5 p.m. Phone Kate Shaw for bookings on 534 4879 or 534 8689.

I promise you one of the most unique experiences in theatre.

At Linden the walls do speak

By ANNE WOODMAN

IF walls could speak ... what a tale they would tell — so Paul Davies would say.

Finally, they are having their say in *Living Rooms*, the latest work of the resident actor and playwright of St Kilda's theatre company, Theatreworks.

And the tale they tell captures the essence of the city while exploring the realms of contemporary theatre.

The walls are talking at Linden, a magnificent 1880s Victorian mansion, once home to aristocracy and hardluck boarders and now National Trust Art Gallery cum community theatre.

The audience, divided into three groups, observe moments in the past (and future) of a drawing room, flatette and gallery in the house.

Living Rooms comes in the wake of similar "location" productions such as *Storming Mont Albert By Tram* and *Breaking Up In Balwyn*.

The works, by Davies, were performed on Princess Riverboat and a No. 42 tram.

"The basic idea is to do shows that reflect the life of the community in which we work," said Paul last week.

"They are original Australian plays and usually have contemporary themes — it's cheaper and more relevant. We do try to push the boundaries in our perception of theatre using the location factor and sometimes involving the community directly as performers."

The 1983 work *Her Story*, a celebration of the lives of Australian women since 1900, was the result of a series of community workshops.

"We're mainly about giving a voice to the people. So much culture is imported or brought from above so it's important we're able to do that," he said.

"There's that sense of identifying with events and issues with which you are familiar."

Formed by a group of VCA drama students, Theatreworks started turning the ordinary into the extraordinary in 1980. Only two original members, Pete Sommerfeld and Cas Howard, remain.

The company found homes in Burwood State College and Canterbury Garden Centre before laying down its feathered cap in affable Acland Street, last December.

Its quaint Parish Hall base is a stone's throw from Melbourne's cake lovers' haven and the stretch of esplanade that is a Sunday wanderers' paradise.

"I'd always been interested in doing a play about St Kilda — a suburb which has had very aristocratic beginnings," Paul said.

"In the 1860s and 70s when it was built as a seaside resort it was the Toorak of its day."

Paul said there is a move to resist the predominant criminal element and remove the tarnished image of a once well-respected city.

"I was interested in how a suburb could become so downwardly mobile. Only now is it pulling itself up by the bootstaps," he said.

"The word everyone uses is gentrification — to literally clean up the city.

"You get the impression that a lot of people are passing through but there's a sense of community.

"A lot of people have been here a long time — St Kilda has inner resilience.

"And it isn't unique. We're talking about suburbs around the country like Bondi and Newtown.

"What is happening here is a dramatic part of changes in people. The implication of the characters' lives reflect the life of the larger community.

And Theatreworks is playing its part, adding credence to his belief the best change occurs when people are involved in that change.

"This is how we see our role as an active theatre company. We do it by blurring the borders of who are audience and who are actors," he said.

Originally from Queensland, Paul has a lot of love for Melbourne's continental coast describing the city as "a really desirable area which fell on hard times."

"There are almost different types of St Kilda and that is part of the attraction. The diversity makes it interesting," he said referring to the yuppy/redecorators' invasion, the poverty and lost glory of buildings gone to rack and ruin.

"The play attempts to raise all these issues.

"You see, people have no incentive to preserve their past unless they understand it. *Living Rooms* is a glimpse of that past."

Paul is concerned St Kilda may become Victoria's answer to the Gold Coast, becoming a site for "a lot of bad development."

"Progress must be borne out with human development," he said.

"A line in the play says 'all change involves compromise' — change must be required.

"It becomes a political issue, I guess — who you vote for in council.

"To give the council its due it is sensitive to the community and the restoration of old buildings is great. But council will always change so you have to vigilant about what is worth preserving.

The topicality of the play is bringing people back together, according to Paul.

A woman employed as a maid at Linden in the 1920s came on opening night and former boarders have also returned to experience the history absorbed by its walls.

"The thing is self-perpetuating there are a thousand stories which can be told," he said.

Living Rooms is seen as a special production at the time of the company's coming of age. It seemed the company was destined to take root "on location" as it were in the hall, a few blocks along from Linden in Acland St.

To bring Theatreworks to the masses the company used several "one off" publicity devices. Milk carton panels, drink coasters and inner city billboards are now singing the praises of this innovative company.

Part of a community promotion endorsed by the Building Workers' Industrial Union, Operative Painters and Decorators' Union and Melbourne Moomba Festival Ltd, the billboards are displayed on about 53 sites for a month.

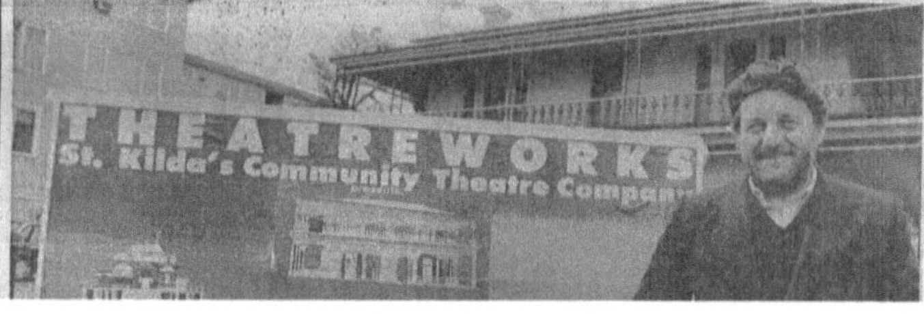

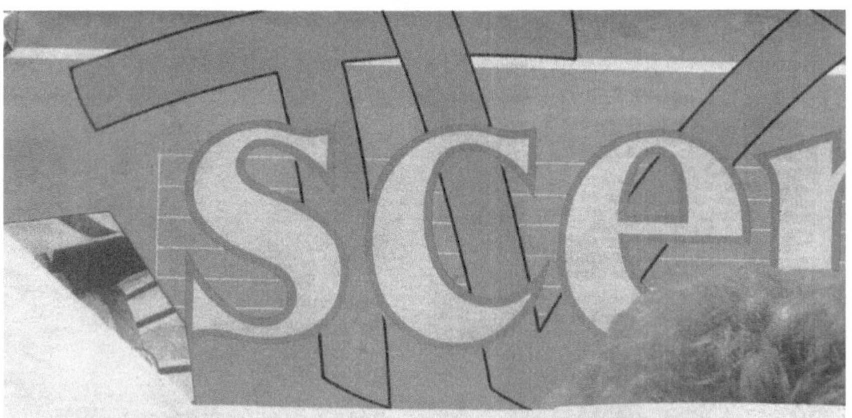

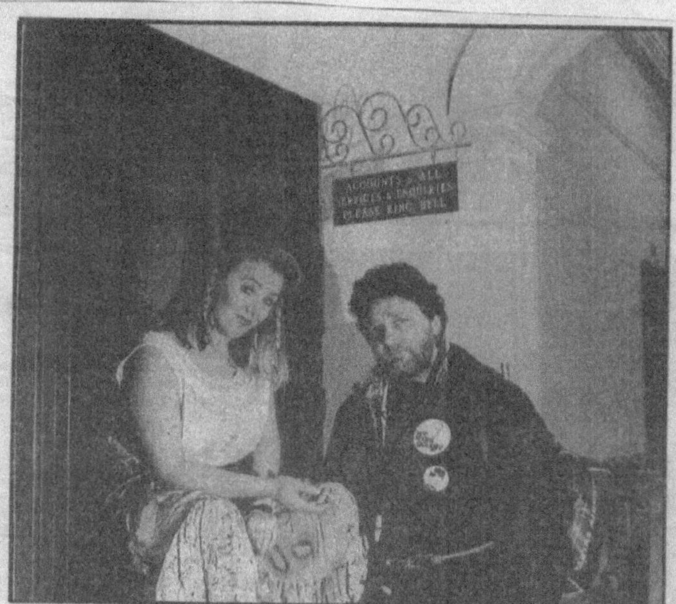

PAUL Davies and Leonie Hurry at Linden ... haunting.

If walls could speak

IT sounds like a most haunting production — Living Rooms, If Walls Could Speak.

That's part of the title of the latest effort from Theatreworks, a professional troupe of performers, writers and directors creating original Australian drama.

The rest of the title is Three Scenes In A Grand Mansion, an apt description of this highly inventive show.

It comprises three scenes in separate rooms and historical periods and will be staged in a large mansion in St. Kilda.

"The play deals with characters set in authentic settings during periods of 1900, 1972 and 1988," says writer Paul Davies.

"The three rooms and their respective history reflect the changes St. Kilda has gone through from the elegant aristocratic suburb to the seedy red light district."

The first scene takes place on the eve of the Boer War in South Africa. It examines the issues people faced in Melbourne during that time.

As we move from the Edwardian splendor of the drawing room into a downtrodden flatette next door, the year is 1972, the eve of Gough Whitlam's election to government.

In the third room, a middle-class residence, a couple are waiting to be shown into a gallery containing an exhibition of St. Kilda's past.

"This incident provides us with the opportunity to argue whether the change has been good or bad," Paul said.

Living Rooms stars Rosie Tonkin, Kevin Cotter and Cliff Ellen.

The three directors involved are Carolyne Howard, Peter Sommerfeld and Paul Davies.

Living Rooms will be performed at Linden, 26 Acland St., St. Kilda, from July 17.

In stately homes the yuppies grow

LOUISE BELLAMY

THEATREWORKS, who have already "stormed Mont Albert by tram" and "broken up in Balwyn" are about to transform an old mansion in the heart of St Kilda's creamy-cake precinct into a venue for more satirical social comment.

Linden, a magnificent 1860s Victorian residence, restored by the St Kilda Council as an *objet d'art*, has a history as chequered as that of St Kilda itself. First, it was the home of aristocrats when St Kilda was an elegant seaside resort; then, after the First World War, it became a boarding house; now it is a gallery and theatre.

It was with this past in mind that Theatreworks' playwright Paul Davies created the three scenes of his latest play, 'Living Rooms'. "St Kilda is enjoying a mini-renaissance," says Davies. "It is also in a state of upheaval. On the one hand, there are the Esplanade, cafe societies and street life, but there are also a lot of yuppies around who could destroy it." Davies stresses that residents must remain vigilant if they are to retain the character of St Kilda's rich past.

His play opens in 1900 in a splendid drawingroom in which the audience witnesses the end of a love affair between an idealistic jackaroo, Deegan, and Estelle, the mistress of the house.

The affair is based on the real-life Stirling divorce case which made headlines in 'The Argus' in 1900. The jackaroo is telling Estelle that he must leave to fight in the Boer War. He wins his point but, explains Davies, he "thought he'd be fighting for freedom but the British won and nothing changed". Davies is intent on questioning "progress" by examining the past 80 years. He sadly reflects: "You only have to look at South Africa now." But most of all, Davies is about sending up "the whole damned catastrophe".

After the parting between Deegan and the aristocratic Estelle, the audience moves from the drawing room into a seedy flatlet in an adjoining room. The time is 30 November 1972, the eve of Gough Whitlam's election to government. An artistic down-and-out boarder finds an old letter under the lino and is inspired to recreate the mansion's past. As he writes he hears noisy arguments in the next room: they are the voices of the very characters he is creating.

In the third scene it is 1986 and a modern couple are involved in an intellectual discourse about a "frozen, living performance-art piece". Soon, however, as egocentricity asserts itself, the couple resort to days-of-our-lives semantics.

Finally, the characters from all three periods meet in the hallway to argue about who is responsible for the past and "what on earth" is to come.

Davies's play is a humorous, hard-hitting attempt to embrace all the colors of St Kilda. He personally fears that the re-gentrification of the suburb could destroy its intrinsic historic nature. He says people tend to change the very characteristics that attracted them to an area. He is keeping his fingers crossed that it does not end up "like a version of the Gold Coast — like Carlton now is without the sea". Davies knows a lot about St Kilda, having spent the past two-and-a-half years there concocting "living rooms".

Since December 1985, Theatreworks have had their home base in Acland Street, where they rent the Christ Church on a two-year lease. Like many inner suburbs, St Kilda now has as many roundabouts as lamp posts and, "if you don't live here, you won't find us".

WHERE AND WHEN: 'Living Rooms' begins tonight at Linden, 26 Acland Street, St Kilda, and will run Monday to Saturday at 8.15pm for a limited season. Special $5 matinees will be performed on Saturdays at 5pm. For bookings, phone 534 4879.

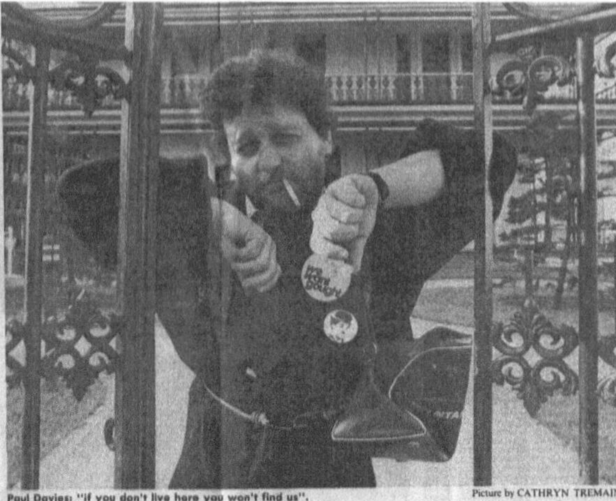

Paul Davies: "if you don't live here you won't find us". Picture by CATHRYN TREMAIN

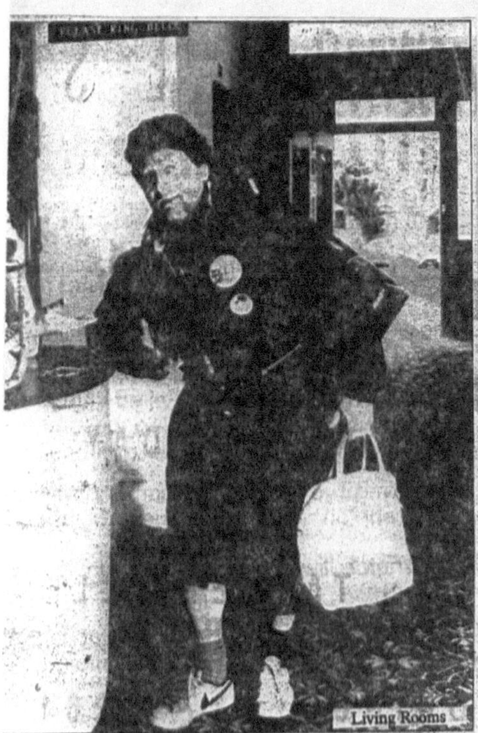

Theatreworks, that wonderfully innovative company that brought us the memorable *Storming Mont Albert By Tram* and *Breaking Up In Balwyn*, performed in a tram and on a Yarra River ferry repectively, now brings us *Living Rooms*.

The rooms of the title are those of Linden, a historic St Kilda mansion. The playwright, Paul Davies, told me how he has used the recent opening of Linden as a Community Cultural Centre as an opportunity to explore the history of St Kilda through what he calls "locational theatre". The different rooms are used as settings for scenes from three eras of the rich and varied history of the district. From a gracious drawing room of 1900 to a seedy flat of the early seventies and a trendy art gallery of today, the action traces the decline, fall and present revival in St Kilda's fortunes. As the house can only accommodate an audience of 90, you would be well advised to book early for this one.

SUN *leisure*

Whitlam years spark the Living Room fire

By SUSAN PEAK

GOUGH Whitlam, the man who combined a controversial flair with a talent for the dramatic, has provided inspiration for playwright Paul Davies.

In the dramatic vernacular, Davies sees Whitlam as a combination of Hamlet and Richard III, a Shakespearian king.

"He has that Shakespearian potential, you either love him or you hate him," Davies said.

That is one reason Whitlam and the fascinating people who surrounded him in those years often appear in Davies plays, including the successful *Storming Mont Albert by Tram* and its sequel, *Breaking Up in Balwyn*.

The other reason is Davies's belief that Whitlam was the only Australian politician to contribute something meaningful to the arts.

"To me Whitlam had a connection with the arts, a concern for our cultural life. He was one of the few prime ministers who recognised how important our view of ourselves was shaped by our culture," Davies said.

"**I** think we have to constantly remember the idealism we had then, the feeling of independence we had then. He sowed the seeds for Australians to recognise their identity. It was a crucial point in our history."

One of the scenes in Davies latest play, *Living Rooms*, performed by community theatre group Theatre Works in an old St Kilda house called Linden, is set in a boarding house on the eve of Whitlam's election.

There are another two scenes — one is a dining-room in the 1900s, the middle of the Boer War, and the other is a gallery on Australia Day in 1988.

"They are three key moments in Australia's history," Paul said. "Idealism surrounded federation, a belief Australia was about to become independent and we would control our destiny.

"That feeling resurfaced in 1972 — a feeling of genuine Australian independence. In 1988 we are going to have to assess what 200 years tenure of Australia has meant.

"They are three serious attempts to show through a relationship in each room. They

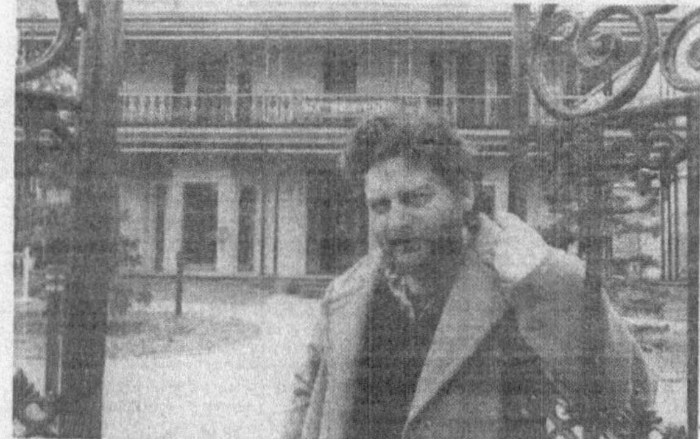

● Playwright Paul Davies outside Linden. Picture: RON WELLS

illustrate the broader social and historical changes going on."

But the audience is not in for a serious socio-political analysis. Rather the play provides a good belly laugh accompanied by a few subtle messages.

The audience of 90 is divided into three groups. Each group sees a different scene at a different time.

"This play is actually in a house, an old St Kilda mansion which had its heyday, became a grotty boarding house and moved on to become a council-owned art gallery," he said.

"In that tradition of location theatre we're sort of attempting to take theatre away from traditional theatrical places and put it in the community.

"As with the train and boat shows we like to create a special relationship with an audience. Again we are playing with three different types of audience/actor relationship.

"In the dining room we are treating the audience like flies on the wall. They are watching a private relationship unfold.

"In the boarding house the audience is behind a gauze screen. It's like a zoo — the audience is standing back looking at its own behavior.

"In the gallery the actors are part of an audience. They are not declaring themselves as actors.

"The purpose is not only to give the audience a trip through a house. It's a different way of relating — three different types of theatre in microcosm.

"It's a three-dimensional ex-

perience. As you are getting a scene in one room you might be hearing voices from the next room. Bits of the story add up as you go along."

Davies said he thought of performing in the house when he found the council had bought it to turn into an art gallery.

"I'd been thinking of doing something on the history of St Kilda. The house has actually physically embodied the changes the suburb has gone through.

"It has been a family mansion. It became a boarding house in the '60s. St Kilda has gone from being an elegant seaside resort to a somewhat rundown inner city rather seedy red light district.

"I was fascinated as to why those changes would happen.

"**T**here is a third change now — regentrification by council with rising property values. There is a new type of resident moving in to restore the suburb to its former glory out of recognition of the tourist potential. The house is reflecting this by becoming an art gallery."

Living Rooms has a good dose of the Davies formula — sex, politics and comedy. It's a formula which has always worked.

Davies also performs in *Living Rooms*, partly because Theatre Works is one of the struggling companies governments hate to hear about. So it can't afford to pay too many actors.

● *Living Rooms* starts tonight for a limited season.

From
"BRUNSWICK SENTINEL"
Vic.
-5 AUG 1986

Theatre

By GREG BURCHALL

LINDEN is one of the last of the great mansions that dominated the once-fashionable St. Kilda beachfront this time last century.

But times changed; the families who built houses like Linden moved east and the mansions with their landscaped gardens and esplanade-views were either torn down or divided up into a dozen seedy flatettes.

Now times are changing again and the "yuppies" are moving back into St. Kilda, doing up those little terrace houses that are left, and Linden has been bought by the St Kilda Council, to spend her old age as a community arts centre.

But right now Linden has come alive as an animated museum thanks to Theatre Works' *Living Rooms — If Wall Could Speak . . .* by Paul Davies.

Theatre Works and Davies has earned a reputation for "location theatre", performing *Storming Mont Albert by Tram* on a moving 42 and *Breaking Up in Balwyn* on board a yarra River ferry. *Living Rooms* is another excellent use of "alternative theatre space".

Davies has taken Linden's three major periods — as a turn-of-the-century family mansion, an early-'70s boarding house, and a late-'80s art gallery — and fashioned three separate stores which are played out in three separate rooms.

The audience, divided into three, sees the three self-contained, but inter-related stories in a different chronological order as the groups move from room to room and activate the museum "display cases" in each well-dressed setting.

While not a documented history of Linden itself, the three stories present an expressionist version of the history of houses like Linden in the St. Kilda area, and of the suburb itself.

They also reflect some of Davies' concern for the area — the fear that, now the area is popular again, developers will tear down the Lindens and create another Surfers paradise with a Miami marina — and Theatre Works' own reasons for abandoning the eastern suburbs, where it was based for so long, in favor of St. Kilda.

The first period is 1901 — in the elegant drawing room, the idealistic jackaroo Michael Deegan (Kevin Cotter) is about to leave for the Boer War, arguing with Estelle (Rosie Tonkin) about his motives and trying to convince her to leave her "sugar daddy" Dr Baumgarten (Cliff Ellen) and come with him.

Next it is 1972 — on the eve of the federal election, a down-and-out Queensland migrant, would-be writer and draft dodger (Paul Davies) prepares to go to the St. Kilda town hall for free food and drink and to listen to Gough Whitlam's promises. He finds an old letter from Michael to Estelle.

Finally it is 1988 — in the art gallery, de factos Monika (Caz Howard) and Leon (Peter Sommerfeld) argue about redeveloping their house, their relationship, their lives and St. Kilda.

Leonie Hurry, as a maid in the first, a domestic in the second and an actress in the third, helps link all the characters together.

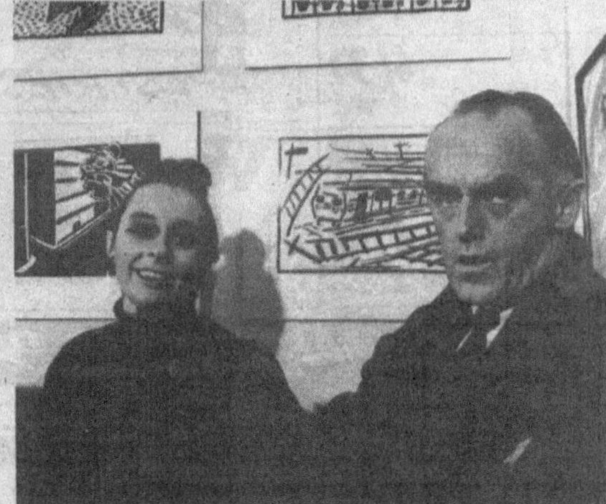

MONICA (Caz Howard) and Leon (Peter Sommerfeld) argue about art, lif[e], relationships, redeveloping St. Kilda, and nuclear fallout shelters in Theat[re] Works' *Living Rooms* at Linden.

The rest of the cast is very good, especially Howard and Sommerfeld in the 1988 piece, which has the best script. They work well off each other and the audience. Davies is good delivering an almost-monologue, aided by some wonderful sight gags to do with his "kitchen".

Cotter, Tonkin and Ellen in the 1901 piece are hindered by an overly soapie script which makes the piece the weakest of the three.

But the idea is good, and the direction — by Davies, Howard and Sommerfeld — is economic and clever. It is enjoyable, accessible theatre with something to say and a novel way of saying it.

The payoff for the nomadic audience comes in the fourth and final scene — which they all see together in the hall — when all the characters from the three eras come together . . . as well as another important "character", Linden herself, who finally gets to speak her piece.

Living Rooms by Paul Davies is presented by Theatre Works and is playing at Linden, Acland Street, St. Kil[da], Monday to Friday 8.15 pm, and Saturd[ay] at 5 pm and 8.15 pm, [un]til August 23. P[h] 534 4879.

JULY 1986

St. Kilda Today

OFFICIAL JOURNAL OF THE COUNCIL OF THE CITY OF ST. KILDA

Arts News

TheatreWorks

TheatreWorks is a company of actors, writers and directors committed to the creation of original Australian drama. The company has been working together on a full-time basis for the past six years. Early this year TheatreWorks relocated its base of operations from the Eastern Suburbs to St. Kilda, making it the city's own professional theatre company.

Amanda Smith, our current administrator, is leaving the company to take up an appointment with the Next Wave Festival as assistant director.

She is being replaced by Wolfgang Wittwer, who comes to us from the Last Laugh Theatre Restaurant. Wolfgang worked for the company for a short period last year, while Amanda was attending the Edinburgh Festival.

Our new full time publicist is Kate Shaw. The position has been created under the Community Employment Program. Kate is currently working with board member, Graeme Stephen, who is training her in publicity and promotion.

Another new full time position for TheatreWorks. Peter Aland is working with us as production assistant, and is at present co-ordinating the production and design for our forthcoming play, "Living Rooms". Peter has also worked with the company on a number of occasions in the past, most recently as stage manager for "The Pub Show".

The setting for TheatreWorks next production, *Living Rooms*, is a recently restored Victorian mansion. "Linden" was built in 1870 as a family home. By the 1960's it had been subdivided into a 26 room boarding house. The building is now owned by the St. Kilda City Council and operates as a cultural centre for the local community.

The play has been written by company member Paul Davies, who also provided the scripts for TheatreWorks' legendary shows, "Storming Mont Albert By Tram" and "Breaking Up In Balwyn". "Living Rooms" continues the company's exploration of theatre in unusual places.

The play concerns an itinerant writer (and conscientious objector) who arrives in St. Kilda on the eve of Gough Whitlam's election to government in 1972. Down on his luck and at the end of his emotional tether, he checks into an old St. Kilda boarding house. In his room he discovers a letter left over from a period when the place was obviously an elegant family mansion.

Inspired by his discovery he imagines a story in which a principled chap from the bush enlists for the Boer War out of a belief that racial freedom and justice are at issue. The soldier's naivety is challenged by the mistress of this elegant "bachelor hall" – a woman to whom the soldier is deeply attached. Their relationship is explored against a background of war in South Africa and the federation of the new Australian Commonwealth.

Meanwhile, in a scene set slightly in the future, a couple of upwardly mobile St. Kilda residents arrive at the house which has by now become a publicly owned gallery. They expect to see a play but instead become bogged down in their own drama – a collapsing relationship and continuing argument about what constitutes real progress.

Throughout all this weird leakages occur from scenes set in other rooms and other peri-

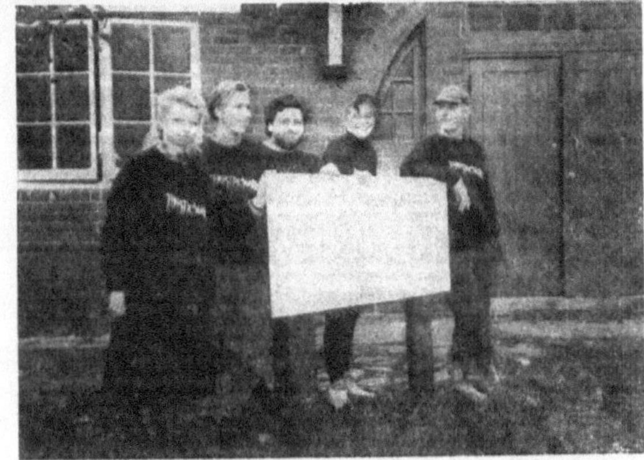

● *Some TheatreWorks people*

at 'Linden' – 26 Acland St. St. Kilda. It will play Mondays to Saturdays at 8.15pm, plus Saturdays at 5pm. Tickets are $14.90 ($10.90 concession price). Group concessions are available and there is a $5 special rate for concession card holders on Monday evening and Saturday afternoon sessions. Book through all Bass agencies or for credit card bookings phone 11 500. For enquiries phone TheatreWorks on 534 4879 or 534 8986.

Page 4 — The Herald, Tues., July 22, 1986

New billboards a site better than BLF graffiti

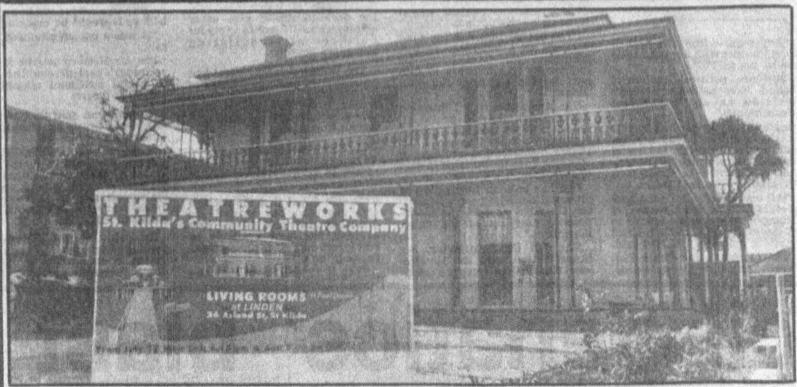

By NICK PLACE

BLF posters complaining of persecution or more recently of obliteration have traditionally decorated building sites, but now that has all changed.

Instead, Melbourne's inner-city building sites will be adorned by colored billboards promoting community groups and arts.

The Minister for the Arts, Mr Mathews, and the industrial officer of the Victorian Trades Hall Council, Mr Nick Moore, unveiled the billboards today.

The campaign is a Moomba initiative and has been achieved in conjunction with the Operative Painters and Decorators Union and the Building Workers Industrial Union.

For $3000 a community group can have the unions design and produce a three-colored billboard and emblazon 50 copies across inner city building sites.

As the project becomes more established the billboards will spread into the suburbs, says promoter Chris Minko.

The first group to make use of the idea is Theatre Works, a St. Kilda performing arts group, which has been granted the inaugural billboards to advertise *Living Rooms* a new play from Paul Davies, of *Storming Mont Albert By Tram* fame.

The billboards measure 3.1 x 1.8 m and will be available to groups concerned with environmental issues, education, health and welfare, performing arts, special celebrations, social action and other causes, says Mr Minko.

Phone: 67 5133

Cuttings Agency

bourne, Victoria

"SCENE"

Melbourne, Vic.

1986

History through a house

FOLLOWING its policy of taking theatre away from the stage, Theatreworks has come up with a brilliant concept in its latest show, Living Rooms, at Linden.

It's worth going just for a good look at the gracious St. Kilda mansion, Linden, in which it takes place.

But what goes on in the play is worth looking at, too. The house, at 26 Acland St., is an integral part of the performance.

The play is based on its history, first as a house built by a wealthy Victorian businessman for his mistress, then as a tawdry boarding house and finally as a cultural centre for St. Kilda.

Living Rooms explores the idea that houses have lives of their own, activated by the occupants.

The audience almost becomes part of the play, sitting in often surprising intimacy with its characters in different rooms.

The audience is divided into three groups, and each section sees the three scenes in a different order.

We assembled firstly in the gallery, moving for the first scene to the flatette.

Paul, a would-be activist and writer, rents a room in a boarding house, which at this time, on the eve of Gough Whitlam's accession to power in 1972, is less than salubrious.

His anger with the house, his landlord and the other tenants dissipates when he discovers a letter from Linden's past, sent to the woman who lived there from her lover away fighting in South Africa in the Boer War.

Inspired, he starts writing his own novel, which bears an uncanny resemblance to the next scene in the drawing room between a young woman, Estelle, her soldier-lover Deegan and Cuthbert, the man who has set her up as his mistress in Linden.

Unfortunately, here the script heads straight into a thicket of improbables.

I found it impossible to imagine an elegant Victorian mistress arguing with her lover about the rights of blacks and fighting racial prejudice — even the vocabulary was much more radical 1980s than Victorian 1900s.

However, the slackness of this scene was redeemed by the third scene in the gallery, which switched to 1986 and canvassed many issues peculiar to St Kilda — urban development, homelessness and its traditional role as a home to artists.

This section was totally entertaining, surprising and pertinent — the highlight of the evening. — A.C.

From

"SOUTHERN CROSS"

Brighton, Vic.

13 AUG 1986

A clever location

THEATREWORKS is presenting yet another clever 'location theatre' piece. After 'Storming Mont Albert by Tram' and 'Breaking Up in Balwyn', set on a boat on the Yarra, Paul Davies has devised 'Living Rooms', playing at the magnificent Victorian mansion, 'Linden', in St Kilda.

The play consists of three scenes in three separate rooms. From the full original splendor of a drawing room in 1900, the audience moves to a seedy flatette next door, where it is the eve of Gough Whitlam's election to government. Finally we are thrust into 1988, in the public gallery which 'Linden' has now become.

Gradually, the barriers between the rooms and time begin to break down as characters from all three periods meet and things become faintly surreal. The argument between past present and future rises in pitch as each accuses the other for the bewildering state of things, until finally, the house itself intervenes.

'Living Rooms' is playing now at 'Linden', 26 Acland Street, St Kilda. For futher details call 534 4879 or 534 8689. Tickets are available from all Bass agencies on 11500.

From
"SOUTHERN CROSS" **Brighton, Vic.**
3 SEP 1986

Demand extends show's season

IT'S HARDLY surprising that the season for Living Rooms has been extended by popular demand.

The talented TheatreWorks crew have hit again upon a novel idea for a play.

Though not as travel bound as 'Storming Mont Albert by Tram' and 'Breaking Up in Balwyn', the latest offering takes the audience on an engaging tour of the old mansion, Linden, in Acland Street, St Kilda.

This highly entertaining play by Paul Davies moves from room to room, through the time tunnel, into the lives of former and future inhabitants.

By a mixture of satire, melodrama and comedy, it makes some interesting comments on the politics of class, war, conservation, art and last but not least, love.

Performances from all are first rate and chances are, after seeing this, you may never view your own abode in the same light.

Living Rooms runs until September 14. Further information is available by telephoning 534 4879 or 534 8689.

— *Barbara O'Sullivan*

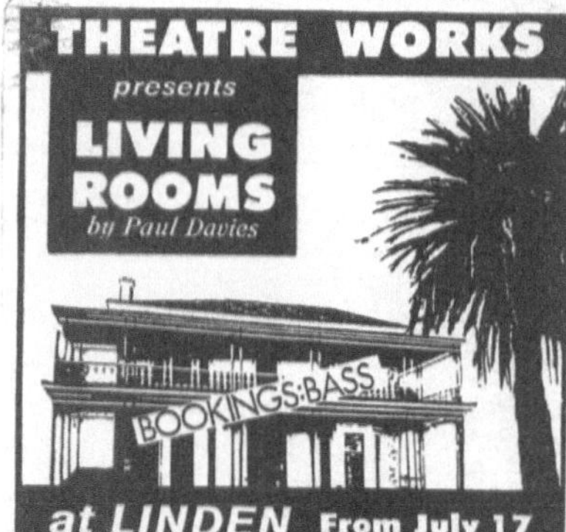

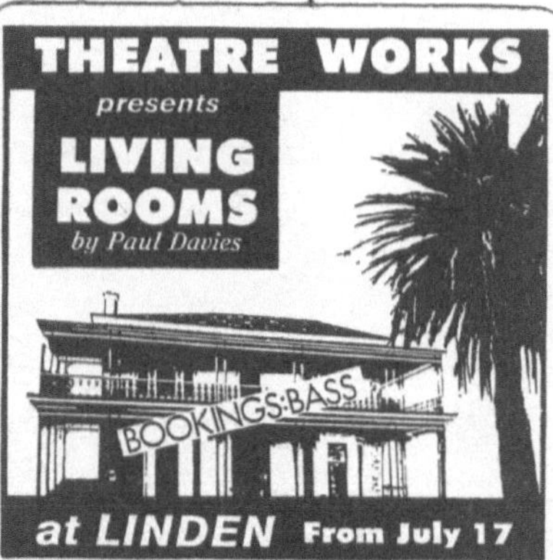

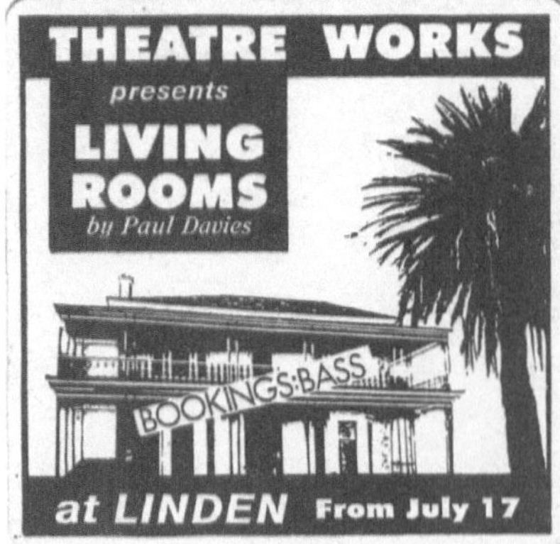

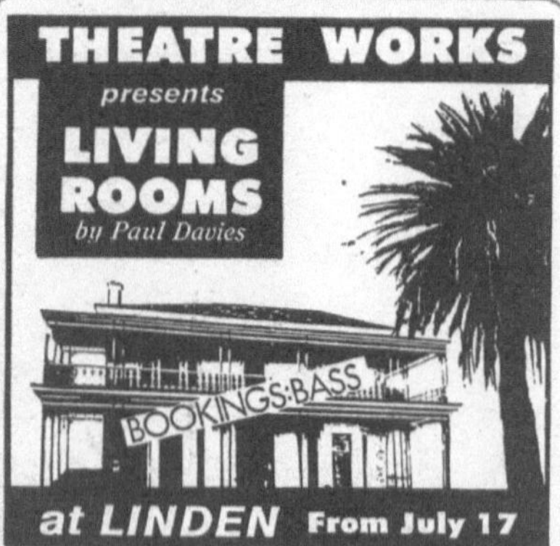

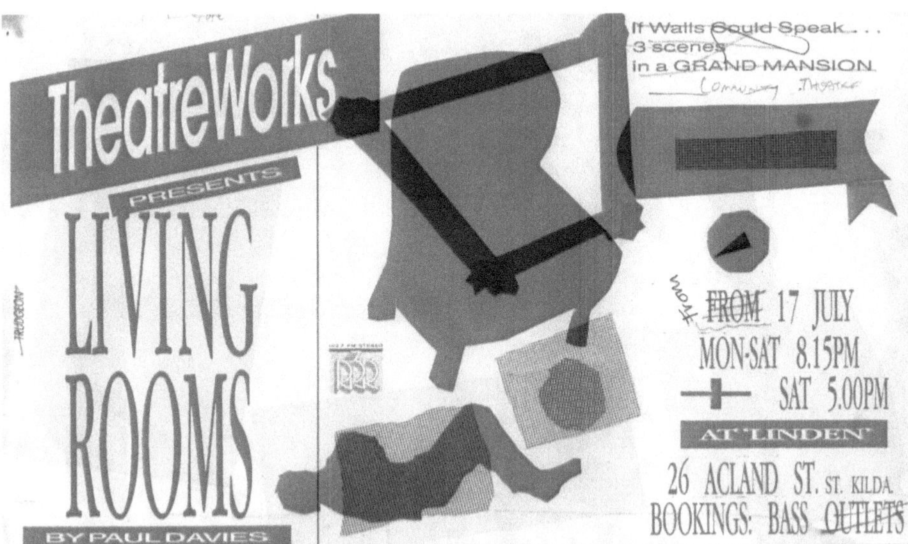
TheatreWorks
PRESENTS
LIVING ROOMS
BY PAUL DAVIES
If Walls Could Speak . . .
3 scenes
in a GRAND MANSION
FROM 17 JULY
MON-SAT 8.15PM
SAT 5.00PM
AT 'LINDEN'
26 ACLAND ST. ST. KILDA.
BOOKINGS: BASS OUTLETS

US BY
TO OPEN
877506004
323
Blanks made
under licence from
Ex-Cell-O Corporation by
J. GADSDEN PTY. LTD.
FLEXIBLE PACKAGING DIVISION.
A member of the
GADSDEN Group of Companies
MILK
ONE LITRE
THEATRE
WORKS
St. Kilda's Theatre Company
presents
"LIVING
ROOMS"
by Paul Davies

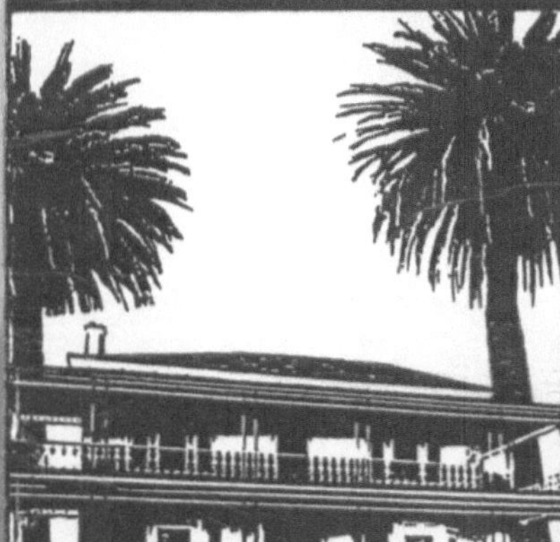

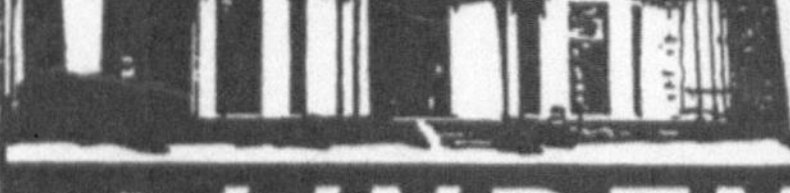

at LINDEN
26 Acland St, St Kilda
From July 17
BOOKINGS
BASS 11 500

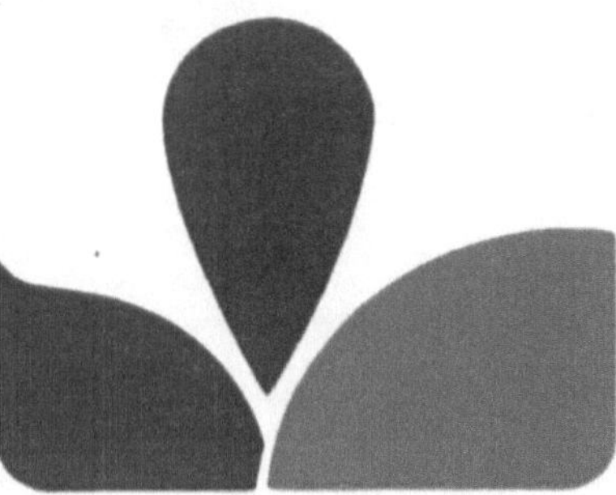

Woodruff Farms Pty. Ltd.
HOMOGENISED
PASTEURISED
MILK

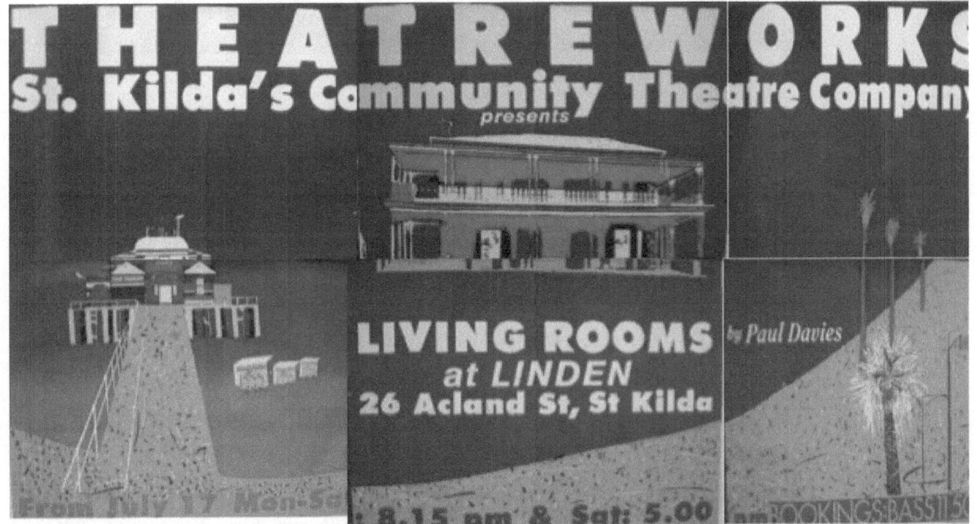
THEATREWORKS
St. Kilda's Community Theatre Company
presents
LIVING ROOMS
at LINDEN
26 Acland St, St Kilda
by Paul Davies
From July 17 Mon-Sa
: 8.15 pm & Sat: 5.00 pm BOOKINGS BASS 11

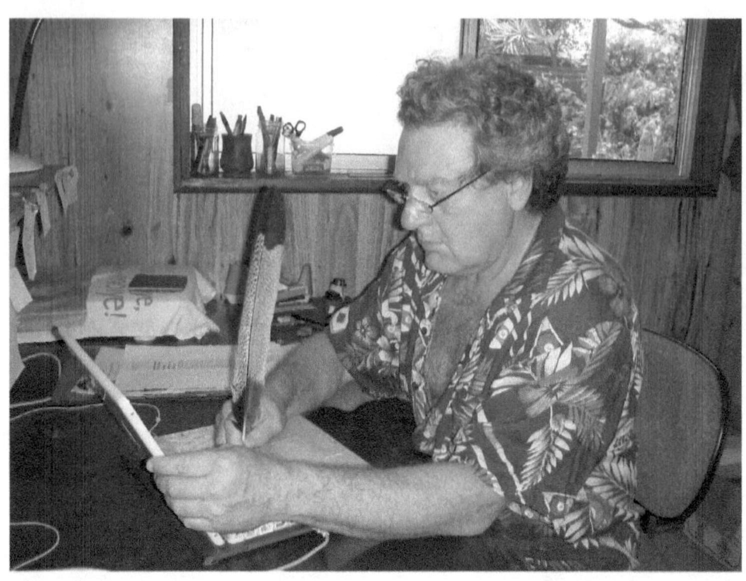

Paul Davies is an award winning screenwriter, editor and playwright who sharpened his quill on over a hundred episodes of Teledrama from classic Crawford series such as *Homicide* (1974-5), *The Box* (1975-76) *The Sullivans* (1976-78) and *Skyways* (1979), to *Rafferty's Rules* (1985), *Blue Heelers* (1997), *Pacific Drive* (1996), *Stingers* (1998-2003), *Something in the Air* (1999-2001) and *Headland* (2005). He also helped spark the site-specific performance revolution in Melbourne in the 1980s with TheatreWorks' production of his first play *Storming Mont Albert By Tram* (1982). What became known as *The Tram Show* played across a dozen years to packed trams in both Melbourne and Adelaide, travelling a total distance that would have taken the show halfway round the world. Its success lead to an outbreak of 'location theatre' in Melbourne throughout the 1980s including three other plays in real places: *Breaking Up In Balwyn* (1983, on a riverboat), *Living Rooms* (1986, in an historic mansion) and *Full House/No Vacancies* (1989, in a boarding house). These works became the subject of his book *Really Moving Drama.* Both *The Tram Show*

and *On Shifting Sandshoes* (1988) were awarded AWGIES, along with *Return of The Prodigal* (2000) an episode of *Something In The Air* (ABC). Paul co-wrote the feature *Neil Lynn* with David Baker in 1984, and the docu-fiction *Exits* (1980) with Pat Laughren and Carolyn Howard. He also worked on a number of "speculative" documentaries with director John Hughes. These include *Traps, All That Is Solid and One Way Street, Fragments for Walter Benjamin.* His novel, *33 Postcards From Heaven* was published by Gondwana Press in 2005. Numerous articles, reviews, stories and interviews have been published in *Metro, Cinema Papers, Cantrill's Filmnotes, Popular Entertainment Studies* and *Australasian Drama.*

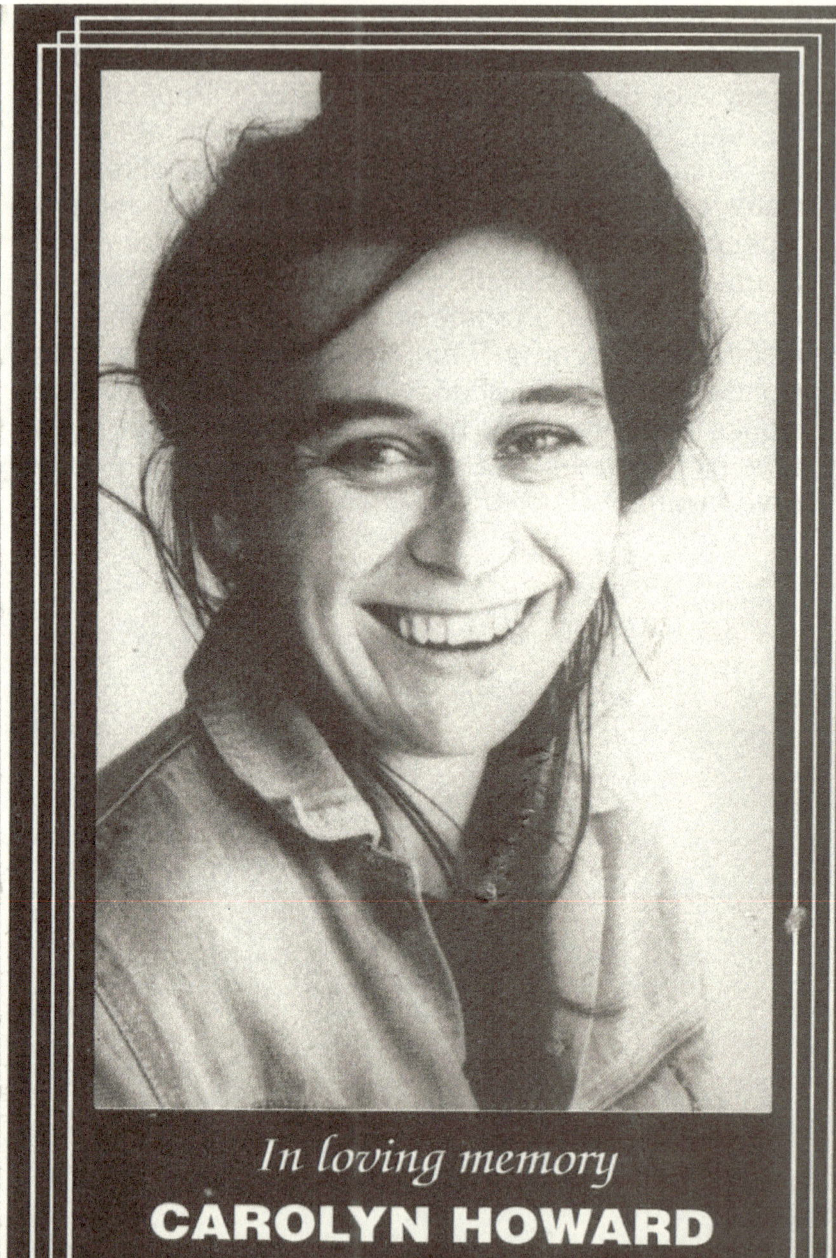
In loving memory
CAROLYN HOWARD
1952 - 1990

www.ingramcontent.com/pod-product-compliance
Lightning Source LLC
Chambersburg PA
CBHW022203050726
47590CB00002B/625